# Queer Media Images

# Queer Media Images

## *LGBT Perspectives*

Edited by Jane Campbell
and Theresa Carilli

LEXINGTON BOOKS
Lanham • Boulder • New York • Toronto • Plymouth, UK

Northwest State Community College

Published by Lexington Books
A wholly owned subsidiary of The Rowman & Littlefield Publishing Group, Inc.
4501 Forbes Boulevard, Suite 200, Lanham, Maryland 20706
www.rowman.com

10 Thornbury Road, Plymouth PL6 7PP, United Kingdom

Copyright © 2013 by Lexington Books

British Library Cataloguing in Publication Information Available

**Library of Congress Cataloging-in-Publication Data Available**

978-0-7391-8028-0 (cloth : alk. paper)

♾™ The paper used in this publication meets the minimum requirements of American National Standard for Information Sciences Permanence of Paper for Printed Library Materials, ANSI/NISO Z39.48-1992.

Printed in the United States of America

We dedicate this book to the brave and dangerous act
of being, and/or loving someone, queer.

# Contents

## Part III: Living in the Margins

## Part IV: Queer Issues

# Acknowledgments

We extend a special thanks to our department heads, Dr. Daniel Punday, head of the Department of English and Philosophy, and Dr. Yahya Kamalipour, head of Department of Communication and Creative Arts, for their support on this project. Thanks to Ronald Corthell, Dean of the School of Liberal Arts and Social Sciences, for release time to continue work on this project. Also, we are very grateful to Mark Buckner for his careful work on this manuscript.

# Introduction

## Jane Campbell and Theresa Carilli,
## Purdue University Calumet

During the summer of 1979, I was in New York when the gay community actively protested the making of the film *Cruising*, a psychological thriller about a serial killer who targets gay men. At that time, I watched several hundred angry protesters sit down on Fifth Avenue, blocking the flow of traffic. This was an important event for me because it taught me about the power of the media to create and perpetuate discriminatory images of an already marginalized group of people.
—Theresa Carilli

Coming out in a culture of silence has never been an easy task. For most members of the LGBT (lesbian, gay, bisexual, transgendered) community, coming out has been fraught with painful self-reflection and agonizing discussions about identity. The process of coming out has been complicated by media invisibility and fear of rejection resulting from such invisibility. For those of us who came out in the 1970s, we quickly learned that our double lives should be kept secret and contained in bars with unmarked marquees, in spite of the 1973 American Psychiatric Association ruling that being "homosexual" was not a mental illness. Members of the gay and lesbian community quickly learned to be masters at coded language in interpersonal encounters where we tried to manage our way to understand others' perceptions of us.

Now that we are ushering in a new era which promises acceptance and even marriage equality, is the LGBT community being represented fairly in the media? According to GLAAD's 2011 report "Where We Are on T.V.," nineteen LGBT series regulars appear on the five major networks (CBS, NBC, ABC, The CW, and Fox). Out of 647 series regulars on 91 scripted programs, these nineteen LGBT regulars comprise 2.9 percent of all series regulars. While this indicates progress for the LGBT community, the community continues to struggle for acceptance and authentic media representation.

In *Queer Media Images: LGBT Perspectives*, we present chapters that address how gay, lesbian, bisexual, and transgendered people are depicted in the media. This collection focuses on how the LGBT community has been silenced or given voice through the media. Through these chapters, the media is scrutinized for its representations. In his 2007 book *Media Queered*, Kevin Barnhurst explores the issue of queer visibility in the media. Barnhurst advocates a movement for the LGBT community which demonstrates difference. Caught between being exoticized, where the gay individual is an anomaly, and normalized, where the gay individual is perceived like every heterosexual, the LGBT community, according to Barnhurst, must locate itself in the media as a visible, viable force—something different, something unique, yet something that has the ability to transform and change the landscape of homophobic perception. We believe that the LGBT community is in the formative process of constructing a media identity—one that breaks away from being either a tragic oddity or a predator. This identity will shape future media depictions of the LGBT community, eventually ensuring visibility and authenticity.

The book is divided into four sections: Queer Images, Performances of Sexuality and Gender, Living in the Margins, and Queer Issues. The chapters in the first section, Queer Images, introduce particular media images presented to a mainstream public and the public's reaction or relationship to these images. Jason Zingsheim's chapter, "Focus on the SpongeBob: The Representational Politics of James Dobson," examines how Dobson, conservative head of the organization Focus on the Family, creates a controversy by declaring SpongeBob, a favorite television icon of both children and adults, a homosexual. Zingsheim shows how Dobson uses SpongeBob to further his conservative agenda. In "The Complex Relationship Between (and Within) the Oppressed and the Empowered: Contradiction and LGBT Portrayals on *The L Word*," Jennifer Guthrie, Adrianne Kunkel, and K. Nicole Hladky conduct focus group research to determine audience views on the show *The L Word*. Backed by the belief that *The L Word* problematizes LGBT portrayals, the authors prove their hypothesis yet underscore just how important viewers perceive the show to be. Showing the parallels between gay and Jewish sensibility, Rachel E. Silverman examines the role of the family on the shows *Will & Grace* and *Queer as Folk* in her chapter, "Family Perfection: The Queer Family as Perspective by Incongruity on *Will & Grace* and *Queer As Folk*." Both shows, one considered to be more popular than the other, demonstrate an integrated gay Jewish identity. In "Re-visiting Vito Russo's *The Celluloid Closet*," Jane Campbell and Theresa Carilli take a look back at Russo's study of film, which showed archetypal and problematic depictions of the LGBT community. Campbell and Carilli study four current films to determine whether or not they follow the same archetypal pattern. In her chapter, "To *Glee* or Not to *Glee*: Exploring the Empowering Voice of the *Glee* Movement," Lori Montalbano captures the power and charm of *Glee*, demonstrating how the show has been a transformational point for LGBT television depictions.

The second section, *Performances of Sexuality and Gender*, explores the impact that media performances might have on audiences, beginning with Kristen Norwood's "A Pregnant Pause, a Transgender Look: Thomas Beatie in the Maternity Pose." By challenging the classic image of the pregnant nude, Norwood argues that Beatie achieves a "transgender gaze" with his photograph in a 2008 issue of *The Advocate*. In "The Rhetoric of Sexual Experimentation: A Critical Examination of Katy Perry's 'I Kissed A Girl,'" Brittani Hidahl and Richard D. Besel uncover how the bi-curious experimentation advocated by Perry undermines and trivializes lesbian identity. With "Queer Male TV Commentators: *Kinjo-no-Obasan* in Advanced Capitalism," Kimiko Akita analyzes the history of Japanese queer male TV commentators and how they negotiated a presence in the Japanese television market. Akita explores how they have influenced the culture and become more of a commodity than a reality.

In the section *Living in the Margins*, we showcase chapters that present marginalized images or views, beginning with K. Nicole Hladky's "The Construction of Queer and the Conferring of Voice: Empowering and Disempowering Portrayals of Transgenderism on *TransGeneration*." By employing a grounded theory approach, Hladky studies the documentary miniseries *TransGeneration*, concluding that while the series shows transgenderism as a complex phenomenon, it problematizes viewers' perceptions of transgendered individuals. In "Born This Way: Biology and Sexuality in Lady Gaga's Pro-LGBT Media," Shannon Weber explores the issues surrounding a pro-biological determinism stance taken by the well-intentioned pro-gay celebrity, Lady Gaga. The section ends with Bruce Drushel's examination of why Kathy Kozachenko was not credited as being the first openly-gay elected official in the United States in his article, "First But (Nearly) Forgotten: Why You Know Milk But Not Kozachenko."

The final section of the book, *Queer Issues*, examines issues that affect the LGBT community and the possible ramifications from these issues. Rick Kenney and Kimiko Akita's "'Is She a Man? Is She a Transvestite?': Critiquing the Coverage of Intersex Athletes" examines the media's role in the controversy surrounding the gender of sprinter Caster Semenya in the XXX Olympic Games and Santhi Soundarajan in the 2006 Asian Games. In "The Commercial Closet: How Gay-Specific Media and the Imagery of 'the Closet' Erases the LGBT Community from the Mainstream Gaze," Kristin Comeforo argues that advertising aimed at the LGBT community has failed mostly due to embedded advertising of "the closet." Through images intended to appeal to the gay community, Comeforo explains how certain images reinforce secrecy for the LGBT community. In "Should We Stop Believin'?: *Glee* and the Cultivation of Essentialist Identity Discourse," John Wolf and Valarie Schweisberger build the case that *Glee* reinforces essentialist identity, thus making "sweeping statements about social identity." And finally, Zoe Kenney, in her chapter

"The Play's the Thing: Representations of Heteronormative Sexuality in a Popular Children's TV Sitcom" explores mediated sexual socialization through her analysis of the show *The Suite Life on Deck*, introduced by The Disney Channel.

With this critique of queer media images, we present chapters that examine the LGBT community and the media as well as exploring what it means to study or research images through a queer lens. Our primary goal is to advance a dialogue about the media and the LGBT community through a snapshot of the current research in this area. Our hope is that this book will contribute to a growing body of research which validates queerness.

## REFERENCES

Weintraub, J. (Producer), and Friedkin, W. (Director). 1979. *Cruising* [Motion Picture]. USA: Focus Features.

"Where We Are on TV." 2012. *GLAAD.* Retrieved January 5, 2013. http://www.glaad.org/publications/whereweareontv12

*Part I*

# Queer Images

# ONE

## Focus on the SpongeBob

### *The Representational Politics of James Dobson*

### Jason Zingsheim

*Beware of sponges that live in pineapples under the sea. These insidious crea-tures will corrupt your children and destroy the institution of family, disinte-grating the moral fabric of our country.* These were the warnings dispatched to parents in 2005. This simplistic reduction makes the cautionary tales seem absurd, yet mainstream media also encouraged the public to scoff at the allegations of the religious right with headlines such as "Conserva-tives Take Aim at Soft Target" (Kirkpatrick 2005) and "Are SpongeBob's Pants Really Square?" (McElroy 2005). These news reports originated at an inaugural dinner (for George W. Bush's second term) where Dr. James Dobson, founder of Focus on the Family, was (mistakenly) reported to have called SpongeBob SquarePants a homosexual, setting off a firestorm of media coverage.

In the ensuing years, similar confrontations have erupted over issues of marriage equality, adoption by same-sex couples, hate crimes legisla-tion, the military's "Don't Ask, Don't Tell" policy, and workplace dis-crimination. Given the abundance of disputes, why might it be useful to pause and look at the issue between Dobson and SpongeBob? Each of these examples can be seen as a nexus of religious, political, and media interests. While most of these debates foreground political issues, SpongeBob's predicament privileges the religious perspective, based on Dobson's position of religious authority, within a mass mediated context. In this respect, his influence is well established and infused with divine motives. Furthermore, his tenure and influence goes beyond that of most elected political officials. As Dobson's own organization, Focus on the Family, claims to reach over 220 million people around the globe, his constructions of LGBTQ individuals have far-reaching influences.

This chapter interrogates the representation of the LGBTQ community in Dobson's response to the release of the We Are Family Foundation's children's video featuring SpongeBob SquarePants (and approximately one hundred other children's characters). I begin by offering additional context, both historical and contemporary, for the dispute over Sponge-Bob. This is followed by a summary of Dobson's February 2005 newsletter, in which he explicitly addresses the situation and clarifies his position on the matter. The analysis then excavates the implicit power structures of the ideology grounding his newsletter and highlights implications for his representational politics.

## HISTORICAL AND CONTEMPORARY CONTEXTS

To fully understand the skirmish surrounding SpongeBob, we need to locate it within the historical context and within the contemporary rhetorical and political environment. Throughout the history of the entertainment industry, there have been battles between competing ideological factions who want their perspectives demonstrated and embodied in popular culture. Some of these clashes have been widely publicized while others have occurred behind the scenes. Some ruptures result in legislation or boycotts while others result in a good laugh, depending on which ideological side you find yourself. A recurring location of dispute is that of children's media, perhaps most famously instigated in the 1950s by Fredric Wertham's attacks on comic book characters such as Wonder Woman for misleading girls about the place of women in society, and Batman and Robin for leading boys to become homosexual. His campaign against comics led to congressional hearings, the Comics Code Authority, and self-censorship (Hendershot 1998; Heins 2001).

Despite this history of sexual surveillance, clashes between social conservatives and the media industry continue. Bert and Ernie of *Sesame Street* are repeatedly accused of being gay. In 1999, the Reverend Jerry Falwell argued that Tinky Winky, of the children's show *Teletubbies*, was homosexual, and consequently the show "undermines the moral fabric of America by surreptitiously condoning gay values" (Dalrymple 1999, B10). Similar to the attempted outing of SpongeBob, this charge was not new; however, because a religious leader made the claim, there was enormous media coverage (Buckingham 2002).

In 2002, Nickelodeon came under fire for what was read as the gay subtext of *SpongeBob SquarePants*. SpongeBob had become a camp icon for gays in the United States, fueling rumors that the animated sponge, who held hands with his male friend Patrick, a pink starfish, was indeed homosexual. Stephen Hillenburg, the show's creator, claimed that there was "no intent to portray SpongeBob or his pals as homosexuals" (Beatty 2002, A1). For our current purposes, whether or not there was intent is not the point. What is interesting is that these rumors, while passing in the media, did not garner the attention in October 2002 that they did in January 2005, when a reporter mistakenly claimed that James Dobson, an evangelical leader, said that SpongeBob was gay.

On the evening of Tuesday, January 18, 2005, at a black tie dinner leading up to the second inauguration of President George W. Bush, Dobson expressed concern that SpongeBob SquarePants was being used to promote a homosexual agenda (Kirkpatrick 2005). After *The New York Times* reported the events of the evening, a media flurry ensued, declaring that Dobson had come out against SpongeBob because SpongeBob was gay. Many news outlets did clarify that Dobson did not call Sponge-Bob gay, but that he was concerned about a music video featuring SpongeBob from the We Are Family Foundation (WAFF) that was going to be released to 58,000 elementary schools. More than the video itself, he was concerned about the homosexual agenda he saw in the materials on the foundation's website. The founder of the WAFF suggested that Dobson had confused his website with that of the similarly named We Are Family Organization, which works with gay youth. By the beginning of February, the issue fell off the mainstream media's radar, just as Dobson fully articulated his position in relation to SpongeBob SquarePants and the We Are Family Foundation video in his monthly online newsletter.

The fact that this entire situation began at a dinner celebrating the presidential inauguration warrants special consideration. The rupture occurred in an explicitly political context shortly after a close and divisive presidential election. Many credit the success of the Bush campaign to its focus on moral issues and the ability to mobilize evangelical moderate and conservative Christians (McCarthy 2005). National public debate on marriage equality, school prayer, displays of the Ten Commandments in public, and even the teaching of creationism presents a fertile ground in which to raise concerns over the education and moral well-being of the nation's children. In this context, Dobson was a host and speaker at a banquet celebrating the recent electoral victory and attended by members of Congress. This was not his first time in the nation's capital. Dobson has served on a variety of panels and commissions since 1980, at the request of former presidents and legislators. Amid all the coverage and opinions surrounding the situation from the media, the WAFF, politically conservative organizations such as the American Family Association, and pro-gay groups like Tolerance.org, Dobson's articulation carries special weight. Not only does he have a significant following and global support in evangelical Christian circles through Focus on the Family, but he also has an influential political audience in Washington, DC. I now turn to analysis of the ideological underpinnings and representational politics of Dobson's February 2005 newsletter.

## "SETTING THE RECORD STRAIGHT"

Dobson begins his newsletter, entitled "Setting the Record Straight," by clarifying the object of the debate. He states that he has nothing against SpongeBob, assuring readers that the issue does not involve this loveable animated sea sponge. Rather, at issue is the agenda behind the video in which SpongeBob appears. His next task is to establish that an agenda does exist and to delineate what that agenda entails. He does this by referring to materials on the WAFF's website that he characterizes as "pro-homosexual," which he claims have since been removed. Dobson asserts in his newsletter and interviews that Focus on the Family has "clear documentation that these materials were being promoted on the Web site" (Dobson 2005, paragraph 10). At this time, none of the lesson plans or handouts he references are available on either site. Still, how Dobson presents these materials, regardless of their origins or current whereabouts, functions to represent LGBTQ folks in particular ways. Dobson's representational politics (re)construct a particular ideology supporting specific power structures and enabling certain realities.

After claiming that a pro-homosexual agenda exists, Dobson (2005) explains that we must protect our children from this agenda. These children, "wide-eyed five-year-olds," will believe anything that their teachers tell them; for example, that reindeer can fly and that large bunnies can lay candy eggs (paragraph 19). Thus we must beware what our children are taught under the guise of "tolerance and diversity" (paragraph 11). This becomes even more important in today's climate where Christianity is being forced out of the public schools. Given these pressures, he calls on parents to monitor what goes into the minds of their children and to keep a close eye on their children's textbooks and teachers. He closes by reminding parents of programs available through Focus on the Family and thanking parents for "helping us continue to nourish and defend the institution of the family" (Dobson 2005, paragraph 27).

## INTERSECTIONS OF POWER

An ideological critique directs our attention to the implicit power structures evident in Dobson's representational politics (Wander 1983/2000, 1984; Griffin 1995). These power structures, predominantly concerning sexuality, religion, and gender, are not discrete and mutually exclusive. They overlap, contradict, and support one another in myriad ways. It is important to keep in mind how each power structure relates to other discursive systems.

Because Dobson's newsletter, and "SpongeGate" as a whole, centers on the issue of a homosexual agenda, it is appropriate to begin with his representation of sexuality. Dobson sets up a clear dichotomy between heterosexuality and homosexuality, eliminating other possibilities (such as bisexual, asexual, and so on). Those who do not self-identify as either gay or straight are excluded from existence or conflated with homosexuals. This rhetorically constructs both sides as uniformly homogeneous, denying the radical differences that exist among heterosexuals, as well as between those under the umbrella term of "homosexuality." Furthermore, this dichotomy is clearly hierarchical for Dobson. Heteronormativity is established because heterosexuality is constructed as the unmarked norm against which all else is judged (Butler 1990; Yep 2003). As studies in whiteness demonstrate, there is much power in the ability to elude demarcation and be perceived as normal (Dyer 1997). In Dobson's own words, he uses the term "heterosexuality" only once, when he states, "But kids should not be taught that homosexuality is just another 'lifestyle,' or that it is morally equivalent to heterosexuality" (Dobson 2005, paragraph 16). In this manner, the single time Dobson marks heterosexuality in his own words, he does so in direct opposition to homosexuality and in a manner that explicitly frames heterosexuality as morally superior. Heterosexuality and Christianity (also mentioned only once), are the assumed identifications for all people, unless noted otherwise, within Dobson's writing. Heterosexual people and pro-heterosexual organizations or agendas are never marked as such. They are simply (straight, Christian) people working (a heteronormative agenda) to protect (straight, Christian) children.

This superiority is further supported in his references to homosexuality. He represents homosexuality as a homogeneous collective of people who possess an "agenda." Homosexual people and their agenda are described as "sinister," "vile," and as having "hijacked" childhood symbols (such as SpongeBob) to promote homosexual "propaganda" (paragraphs 4, 25). Thus, because of the negative connotations of the words used to describe homosexuals as a group, heterosexual people and heterosexuality are silently presented as positive, good, and normal by comparison. Given the religious nature of Dobson's position, in addition to being represented as "normal," heterosexuals are also silently blessed, while homosexuals are cursed.

Furthermore, heterosexuality is presented as inherent in childhood symbols. Thus there is no need to "hijack" them for heterosexual purposes; children's television characters such as SpongeBob are innately or naturally aligned with heterosexuality. When homosexual advocacy groups are purportedly attempting to "brainwash" children, said children must inherently all be heterosexual (paragraph 29). Homosexuality is also limited to adults when it is described as "adult perverse sexuality" (paragraph 19). As a perversion, homosexuality is something that can be controlled and changed. It is not one of the "immutable characteristics, such as race or gender" over which people have no control (paragraph 11). Based on Dobson's construction of sexuality, LGBTQ individuals are represented as unnatural by choice/coercion and actively working together to brainwash helpless (straight) kids.

The power structure of gender plays an important, though often silent, role in supporting Dobson's representation of LGBTQ communities. Dobson describes gender as "immutable," meaning that it is an unchanging and permanent part of a person's life. Elsewhere in the newsletter he describes gender as a "loaded term" when it is defined by the WAFF materials as "a cultural notion of what it is to be a woman or a man; a construct based on the social shaping of femininity and masculinity. . . . Gender includes subjective concepts about character traits and expected behaviors that vary from place to place and person to person" (paragraph 8). While this definition is consistent with research in Women's and Gender Studies, Dobson asks if "this is the kind of nonsense you want taught to your kids" (paragraph 8). He offers an absolute rejection of this academically sound perspective, framing gender roles as universal across cultures and time. For Dobson, what it means to be masculine and feminine is objective, universal, and biologically innate, not culturally or socially based (despite extensive interdisciplinary research to the contrary). This indicates an essentialist view of gender resulting in the belief that there is a right and wrong way to enact one's gender. Part of the right way to enact one's gender is to be sexually attracted to the opposite gender. An essentialist view of gender is then used to support the "natural" superiority of heterosexuality.

Dobson actively resists the notion of compulsory heterosexuality or heteronormativity as being oppressive. From this point, with heterosexuality represented as normal, natural, and inherent and homosexuality constructed negatively as an adult perversion, it cannot be possible for heterosexuality to be oppressive in any way. Anything that conflicts with heterosexuality must be unnatural or abnormal and is not worthy of serious consideration. Terms such as homophobia, heterosexism, and compulsory heterosexuality, which call into question the preeminence of heterosexuality, are written off as "nonsense" (paragraph 9), merely propaganda under the guise of "'tolerance and diversity,' which are almost always buzzwords for homosexual advocacy" (paragraph 11).

This view of gender is buttressed by Dobson's reliance on the ideologically pervasive power structure of Christianity within U.S. society. As an evangelical Christian, Dobson's personal reliance on a Christian worldview is expected. His newsletter, though, is not only about himself or his beliefs. He extends Christian ideology as an authorizing mechanism beyond his own life, and beyond the lives of his assumed Christian audience, to encompass the entire nation. He explains that, "Scripture teaches that all overt sexual activity outside the bonds of marriage is sinful and harmful" (paragraph 16). In terms of power structures, a hierarchy is established by characterizing all those who are not within the bonds of marriage, whether by choice or the denial of marriage as an option, as being sinful and harmful. In this manner, those who are married, and can properly engage in overt sexual activity, are not sinful, not harmful, and thus are superior to the others.

Again, essentialized gender roles are intimately tied to this positioning of marriage, especially when coupled with the central focus of the text on protecting children. Because rightfully enacting one's gender involves being attracted to the opposite gender, getting married, and then engaging in procreative sex, the resulting implicit assumption is that all children live in households with two parents who are heterosexual and whose relationship is officially sanctioned by the church and state through marriage. While we know that this is not always the case, these are the children who are deemed worthy of protection by Dobson. Dobson makes no attempt to protect children whose parents engage in "overt sexual activity outside the bonds of marriage" despite his insistence that all such behavior is "sinful and harmful" (paragraph 16). This includes children with single parents and cohabitating parents of any sexual orientation. If his object was to protect children from believing that sexual behavior outside of marriage was acceptable, then in addition to denouncing homosexuality, he also should be railing against unmarried heterosexuals (cohabitating and/or single) who engage in sexual activity. He ignores the threat from these "sinister" or "vile" heterosexuals. His silence on this issue can be explained by the legitimating function of gender. While sexually active, non-married heterosexuals may be violating some tenets of the Christian faith, they do not threaten to disrupt essentialist notions of gender and heteronormative desire. Furthermore, by limiting the discussion of those who practice "overt sexual activity" to homosexuals, Dobson rhetorically equates the two and reduces homosexuality to taboo sex acts. This rhetorical strategy effectively renders LGBTQ people as abstract and menacing, obscene and vulgar, void of humanity and familiarity.

The centrality and power of Christian ideology is further established through the construction of Christianity as a benevolent and homogeneous group. Dobson implies the teachings of Christian scriptures should be applied to every person's life, even if they do not believe in the faith, and he suggests all Christians interpret the scriptures in the same way. The sheer number of divisions between and within Catholic, Orthodox, and Protestant traditions indicates that not all Christians see things the same way; yet there is no room for differentiation in Dobson's newsletter. Those who do fall into the apparently uniform Christian worldview are those benevolent people who "care about defending children" (paragraph 2). Throughout the newsletter, children are described as needing protection from the media, their teachers, and the homosexual agenda.

Those who follow Dobson's teachings are constructed as looking out for the good of innocent, naive, defenseless (straight) children who will believe anything they are told. This rhetorical framing implies that those who do not ascribe to Christian ideology, or who disagree with Dobson's interpretation, must not care about children or, worse, are attempting to harm children. Christian ideology is constructed as unified, pervasive, good, and noble. Perspectives based on different faith traditions, on skepticism toward faith, or on a rejection of organized faith, are by comparison framed as inferior and invalid.

The ideological perspective established by Dobson's (2005) newsletter is based on essentialist notions of gender, which are used to legitimate hierarchical power structures that privilege heterosexuality and Christianity. This perspective simultaneously vilifies all LGBTQ people and erases non-Christians. False dualisms are established between heterosexuality and homosexuality, male and female, as well as between Christians and secular others. These dualisms create the appearance of homogeneous groups setting up clear (yet fictitious) boundaries between us and them in a battle over the children. These power structures paint a simplistic version of the world and society at large. This ideological oversimplification is part of a social system that enables and constrains the material realities of living people.

## MATERIAL & SYMBOLIC REALITIES

As these interdependent power structures animate one another, they simultaneously enable and foreclose certain material and symbolic realities (Griffin 1995). Dobson's representational politics enable and affirm certain realities, such as the lived experiences of those who identify as heterosexual and middle-class, who desire marriage and children, and who believe in traditional gender roles as defined in the United States. However, there are many people who do not fit this narrow description, and the realities of their lived experiences are denied.

From Dobson's perspective, there cannot be Christians who accept homosexuality, much less an LGBTQ Christian. People who identify as both homosexual and Christian are not permitted in this space; their existence is unimaginable within the parameters of the discussion. As an "adult sexual perversion" homosexuality must be corrected, not tolerated, not accepted, but converted to the correct sexual orientation of heterosexuality. There is no rhetorical space for an LGBTQ (or LGBTQ-friendly) Christian to enter the conversation. It becomes difficult to debate and impossible to dialogue when the material reality of one's life is precluded.

Based on Dobson's constructions of sexual, gendered, and religious hierarchies, he urges parents to monitor teachers to enforce similarly narrow curricula. This limits the subjects, knowledge, and experiences taught in schools and written about in textbooks. It is already difficult for LGBTQ youth, and particularly LGBTQ youth of color, to see themselves or their reality reflected in popular culture (Goltz 2010). Children who know LGBTQ people, either as parents, relatives, or friends, also do not see their world represented.

In Dobson's representations, the economic reality is also limiting. Gays are those who can afford to influence the media and have access to the Internet to spread "propaganda." There are no working-class LGBTQ people, no homeless gay teens who are focused on survival first with scarce time to devote to an agenda of any kind. The physical, or rather virtual, location of this ideological construction limits Dobson's audience to those with access to a computer and the Internet. His unilateral concern for middle-class children is foundational to his position. After admitting that the video is harmless, he claims that of "particular significance" is the Tolerance Pledge which asks readers "to have respect for people whose abilities, beliefs, culture, race, sexual identity, or other characteristics are different from my own" (Dobson 2005, paragraph 12). Dobson claims that he seeks to protect the children from the homosexual agenda within this pledge, which is posted online. Consequently, the only children he is worried about are those with Internet access. His fear is that economically and technologically advantaged kids can go to the WAFF website and be subjected to the "propaganda" of the Tolerance Pledge. The economic realities implied in Dobson's text also erase working-class people who are not included in his use of "the children," "parents," or "family."

The ideological positioning in Dobson's (2005) newsletter also has political ramifications for material realities, especially given the current policy debates over who is and who is not entitled to marriage, employment protection, military service, and so on. Dobson's ideological mandates, which transcend the specificity of the WAFF video, are directed toward a particular audience, encouraging political consequences. This ideology engenders a sense of duty to act in order to protect children, motivating parents to take action for fear of what may happen to their children. The audience for the newsletter is rhetorically limited to middle class parents who have the economic resources and employment flexibility that allow easy voting. Because homosexuality is framed as a homogeneous sinister force, anything related to homosexuality, such as marriage equality, gay employees, or gay soldiers, is seen as part of a dangerous agenda ultimately targeting kids. This call to action has material consequences in terms of limiting whose relationships receive the recognition of the state. The denial of economic, legal, and medical rights, along with the denial of social legitimacy, accompanies the denial of this official sanctioning. Thus, material realities are limited for LGBTQ people who desire marriage, and for their children. This material inequity is authorized by Dobson's simplistic representations of Christianity and his essentialist views of gender.

## CONCLUSION

In addition to limiting those who are invited to engage with the mediated text, the newsletter and the ideological system at large rhetorically frustrate dissent. Because of the language employed, those who speak out against Dobson's position face significant rhetorical obstacles. Who wants to claim that protecting children is not important or that we should not defend the family? Despite these obstacles, a critical rhetorical analysis teases out the implicit power structures within Dobson's newsletter. More than simply a call to protect children, the newsletter constructs a heteronormative structure where heterosexuality is privileged as normal, and homosexuality is presented as the perverted alternative. This structure is buttressed by universalizing Christianity and Christian values and supported by essentialized notions of gender. These power structures work together to legitimate certain realities and deny the existence of other realities. People who do not fit within this simplistic dichotomy of sexuality and/or who do not possess at least middle-class economic status are reduced to non-subjects and rhetorically denied existence.

This ideological critique of Dobson's newsletter reveals that SpongeBob is indeed being used to further one agenda. Capitalizing on SpongeBob's popularity, Dobson articulates an agenda that privileges a specific portion of the population and simultaneously marginalizes multiple other sections of the citizenry. This agenda seeks to maintain dominant notions of the status quo and oppresses those who do not conform to its essentialist ideological views. Between the inauguration and his online newsletter, Dobson was provided a political/religious/mediated platform to clarify his views and crystallize his representation of LGBTQ individuals. There is no equivalent discursive location from which such individuals may (re)present themselves or respond to Dobson's characterizations or framing. While the media may question the legitimacy of his claims concerning SpongeBob, they did not interrogate his claims concerning LGBTQ individuals or the concepts of gender and sexuality at large. SpongeBob was created to teach children how to respect those who are different. It seems Dobson offers us a sinister cautionary tale about those who fail to learn this lesson.

## REFERENCES

Beatty, S. 2002. "There is something about *SpongeBob* that whispers 'gay'—Nickelodeon cartoon series, a big hit with kids, has an adult camp following." *Wall Street Journal*, October 8, A1.

Buckingham, D. 2002. "Child-centered television? *Teletubbies* and the educational imperative." In *Small screens: Television for children*, edited by D. Buckingham, 38–60. London, UK: Leicester University Press.

Butler, J. 1990. *Gender trouble: Feminism and the subversion of identity*. New York: Routledge.

Dahinten, J. 2005. "SpongeBob SquarePants has no gay agenda." *The Washington Post*, January 28. http://www.washingtonpost.com/wp-dyn/articles/A43479-2005Jan28.html

Dalrymple, S. 1999. "The strange, sad truth about *Teletubbies*." *Chronicle of Higher Education* 45 (June 25): B10.

Dobson, J. C. 2005. "Setting the record straight." Originally retrieved January 29 from http://www.family.org/docstudy/newsletters/a0035339.cfm Also available as of February 26, 2013 at http://www.degreeinfo.com/political-discussions/17879-truth-lies-james-dobson-spongebob-controversy.html.

Dyer, R. 1997. *White*. London, UK: Routledge.

Goltz, D. B. 2010. *Queer temporalities in gay male representation: Tragedy, normativity, and futurity*. New York: Routledge.

Griffin, C. L. 1995. "Teaching rhetorical criticism with 'Thelma and Louise.'" *Communication Education* 44: 165–76.

Heins, M. 2001. *Not in front of the children*. New York: Hill and Wang.

Hendershot, H. 1998. *Saturday morning censors*. Durham, NC: Duke University Press.

Kirkpatrick, D. 2005. "Conservatives taking aim at soft target." *The New York Times*, January 20, A16.

McCarthy, S. 2005. "The court is next for SpongeBob foes." *Newsday.com*, January 27. http://www.newsday.com/news/columnists/ny-vpmcc274126310jan27,0,4039119.column?coll=ny-news-columnists

McElroy, W. 2005. "Are SpongeBob's pants really square?" February 1. http://www.foxnews.com//story/0,2933,146085,00.html

Wander, P. 1983/2000. "The ideological turn in modern criticism." In *Readings in rhetorical criticism*, edited by C. R. Burgchardt, second ed., 107–25. State College, PA: Strata.

Yep, G. A. 2003. "The violence of heteronormativity in communication studies: Notes on injury healing, and queer world-making." *Journal of Homosexuality* 45 (2/3/4): 11–59. doi:10.1300/J082v45n02_02

# TWO

# The Complex Relationship Between (and Within) the Oppressed and the Empowered

*Contradiction and LGBT Portrayals on* The L Word

Jennifer A. Guthrie, Adrianne Kunkel, and K. Nicole Hladky

Since its debut in 2004, *The L Word* has become a television phenomenon. Despite its popularity, however, little research has examined individuals' responses to the show and its portrayal of the LGBT population. Lavigne (2009) argues that the popularity of primetime television shows provides an impetus for the critical analysis of these texts. In 2004, Showtime's president of programming, Bob Greenblatt, reported that the critically acclaimed and Emmy-nominated series *The L Word* had about three times the viewers of other Showtime original series (Anderson-Minshall 2006). A 2006 anthology edited by Akass and McCabe presented articles reifying the cultural and scholarly impact of *The L Word*. Although the show aired six seasons and was the first to "attempt to make lesbians, and to a lesser extent, bisexual women, the centre of attention," it was met with mixed reviews (ranging from excitement to skepticism) from scholars, critics, and the media (Warn 2006, 3). Critical analysis of this text has important implications because of its ground-breaking nature and popularity. Thus, this chapter aims to extend the analysis by examining the audience's perspectives in accordance with Dhaenens, Van Bauwel, and Biltereyst's (2008) call for current media studies addressing queer representations to focus on the "real" audience's perceptions of these texts.

In response to the attention given to this television show and the need for greater understanding of the audience's perspective, this chapter combines voices from a focus group and responses to an open-ended survey to examine the ways in which the show empowers or silences lesbian voices. Despite *The L Word*'s opportunity to represent and give voice to members of the LGBT community, our analysis leads us to believe that *The L Word* nonetheless problematizes LGBT portrayals by the apparent stereotyping, sensationalizing, and polarizing of its characters' issues and relationships. Social identity theory is utilized as a lens to help us explain how viewers with various identities identify with and gain pleasure from viewing media.

Tajfel (1978) defined social identity as "that part of an individual's self-concept which derives from his knowledge of his membership in social group (or groups) together with the value and emotional significance attached to that membership" (63). Thus, social identity is part of the self-concept, but it is separate from personal identity; it is how we relate to and identify with groups we belong to, and this group membership in turn influences our self-concept. According to Harwood (1999), social identity theory suggests that "positive social identity is derived from positively comparing one's ingroups with relevant outgroups" (125). In addition, research suggests that "we receive self-esteem from favorably comparing our ingroups with relevant outgroups" (125). For example, according to Hajek and Giles (2002), younger gay men may discriminate against or make efforts to separate themselves from older gay men in order to increase their own self-esteem through the comparison. Social identity theory inherently relates to media representations of groups because we can possibly identify with characters if we believe we share a group membership, such as sexual preference, with them.

Before *The L Word*, there were few television shows that featured LGBT characters, and there was not a single one in the United States that featured a mostly lesbian (and, arguably, entirely queer) main cast. This lack of representation resulted in the LGBT community's reliance on queering mainstream media in order to "see" representations of themselves. Thus, *The L Word* increased the media representation of lesbians, and for some, this meant having characters to identify with. As one lesbian viewer mentioned in the season finale DVD special features, "With *The L Word*, for an hour, you are not an outsider. You relax. Everyone you see is very similar to you." This opinion is reflected in research; Harwood (1999) found that people prefer to watch television shows that feature their own ingroup members—whether those group memberships are based on class, age, ethnicity, gender, or sexual identification, and so forth.

Moreover, Harwood and Roy (2005) explained that representation in the media is needed for positive group vitality. Groups and communities can possibly find strength, energy, and cohesion from simply seeing representation of themselves in the media. As Evans and Gamman (1995) note, "Representation is a basis for political struggle and cultural intervention because representation is not free of social ideologies" (17). Representation connotes strong messages regarding what is considered "right" or "wrong," "natural" or "unnatural" in the mainstream, and this can have extreme negative effects on minority group members' self-esteem or sense of group vitality. As Warn (2006) states,

> To those who are straight or white (or both), and used to seeing reflections of themselves every time they turn around . . . it's difficult to adequately describe what it feels like to not see reflections of yourself anywhere. It's even more difficult to convey what it feels like when you do—the rush and jumble of emotion that is often all out of proportion to the actual event itself. (1–2)

Representation and the ability for groups to "see reflections" of themselves is obviously an important component of self-esteem, identity, and group vitality.

However, Harwood and Roy (2005) remind us that not only the quantity, but the *quality* of representation in the media also is important because of how "cognitive representations of those groups might be perpetuated" (193). Because social identity is a way people receive identity support, it may possibly be important for representations to be of accurate quality in order for identification to take place and self-esteem to be supported. The quality of representations of the LGBT community on *The L Word* has been hotly debated. For example, the main lesbian characters on the show are "power" or "lipstick" lesbians in Los Angeles—they have prestigious jobs, are wealthy, and generally live "fabulous," sexually fulfilled lives (Akass and McCabe 2006). Accordingly, while *The L Word* gave voice to some lesbians, it simultaneously silenced others who may not "fit" with the portrayal. Based on these ideas and the exploratory nature of the study, we asked the following research question:

RQ1: How do lesbians perceive the television show *The L Word*?

## METHOD

To address our research question, we accessed two complementary data sources. Specifically, we combined voices from a participant focus group, in conjunction with responses to open-ended survey questions (we asked the same questions with each methodology; a list is available upon request). Both methodologies were approved by the University Human Subjects Research Board, and participants were required to be at least eighteen years of age and informed of the confidential and voluntary nature of the study. We asked general demographic questions, as well as questions about *The L Word* viewing habits. In general, our content questions asked why people watched *The L Word*, what they liked and disliked about it, and whether they perceived the representation of lesbians on the show to be accurate and/or empowering. We also asked whether certain story lines or characters resonated with their experiences.

## FOCUS GROUP DATA

The focus group participants were seven women who identified as lesbian. The average age of participants was fifty years old. One participant indicated that she was Hispanic, while the other six indicated that they were Caucasian. Occupations included student/self-employed, geologist, drafter/artist, legal assistant, and two psychologists. All seven focus group participants were college educated, with five out of seven (71 percent) completing graduate school. All seven focus group participants indicated that they had viewed all episodes (that is, all seasons) of *The L Word*. The focus group was led by one of the researchers for this project and lasted approximately 39 minutes. The "conversation" was audio-recorded and transcribed. To preserve confidentiality, we did not use any participant names in our analysis.

## OPEN-ENDED SURVEY DATA

Forty-nine participants completed our online open-ended survey. While one of the requirements for taking the survey was self-identification as lesbian, only thirty-three actually did so. Five participants identified as bisexual, one as queer, one as same-sex orientation, and one as gay. The other eight participants did not specify their sexual orientation. Thirty-nine of the forty-nine survey participants were specific in identifying their actual age. The average age of these participants was approximately thirty-six years old. Thirty participants indicated that they were Caucasian, while ten did not specify their ethnicity. We also had two participants who indicated that they were Hispanic, and one each in the following categories: Black, Mexican American, Latin, Asian, Jewish, Spanish, and other. Like our focus group participants, the survey participants' occupations ranged from student to librarian to professor to dancer. Eighty-four percent of the survey participants indicated that they had some college experience (while nine participants did not provide information about their education). About thirty-five percent of survey participants indicated that they had viewed all episodes/seasons of *The L Word* (while others indicated that they viewed less, and some did not specify their viewing habits).

## ANALYSIS

Thematic analysis, as proposed and utilized by Owen (1984), was used to analyze the focus group conversation, as well as the open-ended survey responses. Owen defines a theme as "the patterned semantic issue or locus of concern around which a couple's interaction centers" (275). Owen specifies three criteria that must be met in order for data to constitute a theme: (1) recurrence, (2) repetition, and (3) forcefulness. Recurrence occurs when ideas are repeated. Repetition occurs when key words, phrases, or sentences occur numerous times. Forcefulness occurs when vocal cues or pauses stress certain pieces of discourse.

## RESULTS

We coded the data and found three major or overarching themes that met Owen's (1984) criteria for thematic analysis: Representation, Awareness, and Entertainment.

### *Representation*

Data that fit the Representation theme mentioned portrayals of lesbians, class, gender, appearance, and issues within the lesbian community on *The L Word*. While some participants viewed the representation of lesbians as accurate, others expressed discontent with the ways in which *The L Word* constructed its lesbian characters. For example, a survey respondent expressed that, "due to the realistic experiences and accurate personalities portrayed, the show provided a sense of identity and involvement. In a lot of ways you often felt like you were part of the girls." Similarly, one said, "I felt, generally speaking, most of the characters and their story lines were believable . . . That I could definitely see their lives being played out realistically." Another survey participant, however, wrote that, "it was shallow, exclusive, not part of my reality." Another concluded that the show "was wildly unrealistic for the most part, though it did have its moments. I feel like anyone who might look to this show for validation of homophobia might well find much to support their arguments." Many participants described more specific ways that the show did or did not represent their lives as lesbians. Numerous participants mentioned a discrepancy between the portrayed socioeconomic class of the characters and themselves. A focus group participant, for example, pointed out that "for the most part, the show represents a very, very small amount of lesbian culture—that of the economically privileged." Both data sets featured respondents who noted that *The L Word*'s locale and lifestyle were not indicative of the entire lesbian community. For instance, one woman surveyed said, "I think it portrays the affluent lesbian community in L.A., but I do not think this community represents most of the LGBT population or the issues that affect them."

Another flaw detected by respondents was the overrepresentation of a certain type of lesbian, the attractive femme. In the words of a survey respondent, "few of them looked like lesbians, which made me crazy. No one was fat, or dressed in a dyke-y fashion." Another pointed out that *"The L Word* does not represent the real diversity of the dyke communities I know." Then again, a dissenting voice among those surveyed opined, "I liked the fact that some of the women on the series were feminine. I don't like the fact that lesbians are always portrayed as fat, bland, and ugly."

There was widespread praise for *The L Word's* representation of issues relevant to the lesbian community. In her survey response, one participant wrote, "I think they accurately portrayed a wide range of LGBT issues (especially bisexual issues). They hit on everything from: coming out of the closet to having a child with your partner to infidelity." Another agreed, "It dealt with the issues that I face. It deals with sexual orientation and how same-sex groups (lesbian/gay/bisexual/transgender) interact day-to-day, not just in porn."

*Awareness*

The Awareness theme included any data that addressed *The L Word's* role in normalizing lesbianism, its potential to educate others about lesbian issues, its ability to provide empowerment, and its role in sensationalizing lesbians. Participants varied in their views of the quality of awareness created by *The L Word*. Many expressed positive reactions to the series' ability to normalize lesbian life. A focus group participant emphasized that "the whole series is normalizing, and the whole series is about lesbians. I mean you know it's not treated like something freakish on the show; it's just who they are and how their lives are chosen." Some even viewed the show as an educational tool. A survey participant wrote, "I think that it is a generally solid show that could at least get some points and understanding across to those who want to learn more about the lesbian and LGBT community as a whole."

Participants were divided in their beliefs about *The L Word's* ability to empower the lesbian community. Most echoed the sentiments of a survey participant who said, "I find the show very empowering. It is inspiring to see beautiful, confident, strong, smart lesbian women owning their sexuality and not letting it hinder their success. It is also empowering to see the importance of supportive relationships." Likewise, another surveyed wrote, "I think the show sends a message that every lesbian is unique and beautiful and should not be afraid to be who they are, which can be very empowering." Others saw the show as disempowering and sensationalizing. One wrote "I . . . didn't think the characters treated each other with respect, didn't uplift each other, and therefore didn't empower themselves or our community."

*Entertainment*

The Entertainment theme addressed participants' comments relating to *The L Word*'s functions as a television show, including the constraints of media expectations, the characteristics of drama, and the qualities that attracted viewers. A large number of participants expressed not expecting the show to provide anything but entertainment for viewers. Many agreed with a focus group participant who expressed that "It is entertainment. It takes you outside yourself. It takes you outside of your normal life." In fact, several participants even compared the show to a soap opera. A survey participant wrote, "just as any other drama, it is overdone because everyday life is not 'interesting' enough." Other participants mentioned that they watched the show because of its "beautiful women" and for the "good sex scenes."

Several participants also noted that the accurate representation of an entire community need not be the responsibility of fictional television programming. When the focus group discussion turned to the veracity of the series, one participant exclaimed, "It's a TV show! It's not supposed to be like reality," and another concurred, "why would you expect it to [be realistic]? It's a TV show." Survey participants largely felt the same way. For instance, one survey included the statement, "I think it is impossible for any one show to 'accurately' portray any community—that's a lot of pressure for a TV show," while another asked, "Who wants to see their own struggles on TV reminding us of our reality? Was the Brady Bunch real? No, but millions watched it and for at least 30 minutes, their life was better."

## DISCUSSION AND IMPLICATIONS

Our project examined lesbians' perceptions of Showtime's television series *The L Word*. Results indicated that lesbians viewed the show in terms of its representation of the lesbian community, its potential to affect awareness, and its role as entertainment. Participants revealed generally positive evaluations of the show, particularly its attempts at capturing experiences relevant to the underrepresented lesbian community. However, participants' responses also illustrated the complexities of portraying a group of individuals in popular media.

The theme of Representation illustrated several areas of lesbian life that our participants perceived in *The L Word*. Harwood and Roy (2005) acknowledge the importance of media representation for group vitality. The fact that participants also recognized inaccurate portrayals of lesbian identity on the show, however, problematizes the issue of representation. While many participants acknowledged that seeing their social group on the television screen led to positive feelings about the show, others criticized the quality of those representations and questioned their potential effects on viewers' perceptions of the LGBT community as a whole. Research on media portrayals of underrepresented groups reflects this tension. While some researchers (such as Evans and Gamman 1995) maintain that simple representation can be beneficial for group members' identity support and self-esteem, others argue that stereotypical and/or negative representations of group members can harm the group by reinforcing outgroup members' assumptions about ingroup members (Harwood and Roy 2005; see also Burns and Davies 2009).

Responses coded within the Awareness theme revealed mixed feelings regarding the portrayal of lesbians on *The L Word*. Though there seemed to be a general sense of appreciation regarding the creation of a television series focused entirely on a lesbian cast, as well as in the introduction of a transgender character, Max/Moira (also consistent with research by Reed 2009), some participants hesitated to praise *The L Word*'s contributions to advocacy efforts in the LGBT community. While some expressed feeling empowered by the inclusion of lesbian issues in popular media, others thought the show took away the voice of "real" lesbians by stereotyping and sensationalizing lesbian life (Burns and Davies, 2009). Disagreements about *The L Word*'s effectiveness in raising awareness about the LGBT community were nuanced by varying opinions about the show's role as a source of education versus entertainment.

Our third theme, Entertainment, reflected another set of participants' perceptions of *The L Word*, on its role as a source of fun and entertainment. Some participants reported they felt there was too much responsibility placed on the show; as reported in our results, some viewers did not believe the show should serve as an educational tool. Rather, these participants believed the main purpose of the show was to entertain. These differing beliefs about the aims of the television show reflect the constraints of many television shows in their attempts to represent social groups. While such television shows may aim to positively and accurately portray group members, they nonetheless must cater to the demands of a diverse audience seeking entertainment and pressures from advertisers, executives, and other stakeholders. Our participants clearly recognized this tension in their responses, expressing disappointment with certain inaccuracies in the television show's portrayals but recognizing its primary purpose as a cable television show.

This dilemma has previously found relevance in the literature regarding accuracy and representativeness of another important television drama realm with huge social implications: the medical profession. Though Brodie et al. (2001) conceded that "viewers may not consciously watch fictional programs to learn about health information," some evidence along with "cultivation theory suggests that health information present-ed in entertainment media could affect their ideas about health-related issues" (192). Their telephone survey of more than 3,500 regular viewers of the program *ER* showed that information about emergency contracep-tion and about the human papilloma virus was both acquired and re-tained from *ER* plotlines. Buttressed by Brown and Singhal's (1990) con-tention that viewers model prosocial functions seen in television epi-sodes, Sharf and Freimuth (1993) examined the season-long portrayal of one character's struggles with ovarian cancer on the primetime drama *thirtysomething*. They found seven distinct "take-home messages" (157) that may be applied to actual coping with cancer.

Turow and Coe (1985) found that primetime television programming during the critical "sweeps week" period of ratings tended to glorify doctors, hospitals, and the traditional medical establishment while down-playing the changing face of health care and its controversies regarding access, appropriateness, and effectiveness. Crucially, Turow and Coe argue that accurate portrayal is not just a matter of educating viewers as they are entertained but is also one of setting "a shared national agenda that politicians most strongly feel a need to respond to publicly when formulating health care policy" (36). As cities, states, and the federal government continue to shape laws concerning gay rights, marriage, and service in the military, the import of the entertainment as prosocial infor-mation issue is evermore underscored.

The implications of our participants' responses also should be exam-ined in light of previous research about media portrayals of underrepre-sented groups. Researchers employ the parasocial contact hypothesis as a lens from which to examine how and why individuals relate to television characters and the ways in which they generalize perceptions of these characters to the groups they represent. In studies of the LGBT commu-nity, parasocial contact researchers have examined television shows like *Six Feet Under, Will and Grace*, and *Queer Eye for the Straight Guy* (Calzo and Ward 2009; Schiappa, Gregg, and Hewes 2006). These studies pro-vide support for the idea that exposure to positive portrayals of a group in media can decrease prejudice against members of that group as a whole. This is particularly important to our study, as participants indicat-ed that many portrayals of lesbians on *The L Word* were inaccurate and/or stereotypical. Though many claimed that the sheer representation of their group on *The L Word* provided a step in the right direction, the assump-tions of the parasocial contact hypothesis point to the importance of the *quality* of the representations in influencing perceptions of lesbians in general.

The potential influence that mediated portrayals of social groups can have on audience members is complex. On the one hand, they seek to provide entertainment for viewers, maintain marketability and viewer-ship, and ultimately make money. On the other hand, even dramatic, nonfictional shows may nonetheless affect perceptions of the groups they represent (see Burns and Davies 2009 for a similar critique and argument). This poses a challenge for writers of television shows who must simultaneously consider the interests of the group they hope to portray and the constraints of their positions.

Overall, this project provides a preliminary discussion of lesbian viewers' perceptions of *The L Word*. The survey data provided a diverse sample of women across the United States. The focus group data, however, represented a small sample of individuals from a similar geographical location in the Midwest. Future research should attempt to seek the perceptions of even larger and more diverse samples. For example, heterosexual viewers could provide additional information about the role of mediated portrayals of underrepresented groups.

## REFERENCES

Akass, K., and J. McCabe. (Eds). 2006. *Reading the L Word: Outing contemporary television*. New York: St. Martin's Press.

Anderson-Minshall, D. 2006. "Sex and the clittie." In K. Akass and J. McCabe (Eds.), *Reading the L Word: Outing contemporary television* (11–14). New York: St. Martin's Press.

Brodie, M., U. Foehr, V. Rideout, N. Bare, C. Miller, R. Flournoy, and D. Altman. 2001. "Communicating health information through the entertainment media." *Health Affairs* 20: 192–99.

Brown, W. J., and A. Singhal. 1990. "Ethical dilemmas of prosocial television." *Communication Quarterly* 38: 268–80.

Burns, K., and C. Davies. 2009. "Producing cosmopolitan sexual citizens on *The L Word*." *Journal of Lesbian Studies* 13: 174–88.

Calzo, J., and L. Ward. 2009. "Media exposure and viewers' attitudes toward homosexuality: Evidence for mainstreaming or resonance?" *Journal of Broadcasting and Electronic Media* 53: 280–99.

Dhaenens, F., S. Van Bauwel, and D. Biltereyst. 2008. "Slashing the fiction of queer theory: Slash fiction, queer reading, and transgressing the boundaries of screen studies, representations, and audiences." *Journal of Communication Inquiry* 1: 335–47.

Evans, C., and L. Gamman. 1995. "The gaze revisited, or reviewing queer viewing." In *A queer romance: Lesbians, gay men and popular culture*, edited by P. Burston and C. Richardson, 13–56. London: Routledge.

Hajek, C., and H. Giles. 2002. "The old man out: An intergroup analysis of intergenerational communication among gay men." *Journal of Communication* 52: 698–714.

Harwood, J. 1999. "Age identification, social identity gratifications, and television viewing." *Journal of Broadcasting and Electronic Media* 43: 123–36.

Harwood, J., and A. Roy. 2005. "Social identity theory and mass communication research." In *Intergroup communication: Multiple perspectives*, edited by J. Harwood and H. Giles, 189–212. New York: Peter Lang.

Lavigne, C. 2009. "Death wore black chiffon: Sex and gender in *CSI*." *Canadian Review of American Studies* 39: 383–98.

Owen, W. F. 1984. "Interpretive themes in relational communication." *Quarterly Journal of Speech* 70: 274–87.

Reed, J. 2009. "The Moira/Max transitions." *Journal of Popular Film and Television* 37: 169–78.

Schiappa, E., P. Gregg, and D. Hewes. 2006. "Can one TV show make a difference? Will and Grace and the parasocial contact hypothesis." *Journal of Homosexuality* 51: 15–37.

Sharf, B. F. and V. S. Freimuth. 1993. "The construction of illness on entertainment television: Coping with cancer on *thirtysomething*." *Health Communication* 5: 141–60.

Tajfel, H. 1978. "Social categorization, social identity, and social comparison." In *Differentiation between social groups: Studies in the social psychology of intergroup relations*, edited by H. Tajfel, 61–76. London: Academic Press.

Turow, J. and L. Coe. 1985. "Curing television's ills: The portrayal of health care." *Journal of Communication* 35: 36–51.

Warn, S. 2006. "Introduction." In *Reading the L Word: Outing contemporary television*, edited by K. Akass and J. McCabe, 1–10. New York: St. Martin's Press.

# THREE

## Family Perfection

### *The Queer Family as Perspective by Incongruity on* Will & Grace *and* Queer as Folk

### Rachel E. Silverman

"Being different is what makes us all the same; it's what makes us family." —Michael Novotny, *Queer as Folk*

In September of 1998, the National Broadcasting Channel (NBC) premiered a show unlike anything seen before on television. The show, set in New York City, was the highest rated sitcom for adults age eighteen to forty-nine, from 2001 to 2005, and is currently syndicated in sixty countries. *Will & Grace* is by all accounts a groundbreaking program; as the first network show to center on the lives of gay men, it paved the way for more gay and lesbian television characters—characters such as those on Showtime's *Queer as Folk*, which premiered two years later. Similar to *Will & Grace* (*W&G*), *Queer as Folk* (*Folk*) attends to the daily experiences of thirty-something professionals as they navigate friendships and family while living in metropolitan areas. While the construction of the characters' identities and resultant plot lines vary dramatically between the two shows—due in large part to audience and network affiliation—both shows exemplify a restructuring of family. Indeed, the characters on *W& G* and *Folk* did more than transform the television landscape by inviting audiences into the homes of gay and lesbian adults; they gave Americans access to a transgressive space of difference, the queer family.

Over the course of eight seasons for *W&G* and five seasons for *Folk*, audiences came to know and love the characters on each program. Critics of the shows have, however, commented on the disparity of identity construction on each. Whereas *W&G* is highly praised by the popular press and awards committees, [1] media scholars criticize the show for adhering to heteronormative values by continuing to present gay men as asexual sidekicks (Battles and Hilton-Morrow 2002) who care only for fashion and home decor (Provencher 2005) while at the same time exerting male privilege (Shugart 2003). *Folk* never won an award and received minimal attention from the popular press, yet is praised by media scholars for providing diversity and authenticity to representations of gay and lesbian identity on television (Noble 2007; Porfido 2007).

The disparate nature of the shows' reception, production, and network affiliation sets them apart; *W&G* is a show about gay men created for a national audience, whereas *Folk* is a show about gays and lesbians for a niche audience. Contained in *Folk* and *W&G* are important clues about the ways in which mediated representations influence and affect viewers' understandings of identity and "Otherness." In terms of "Otherness," this chapter examines not only gay and lesbian identity but also the role Jewish identity plays within both shows.

Jewish identity is, and has been, constructed as having parallel qualities to gay and lesbian identity; both identities are ostensibly invisible (Stratton 2000), both identities privilege from their ability to "pass" as non-Jewish or non-gay/lesbian (Jakobsen 2003), both identities exhibit non-normative gender practices (Pellegrini 1997), and both identities have been attributed with social sensibilities leading to creativity (Sontag 1966). Due to their similarities, it is no surprise that Will, the first openly gay man on mainstream television, is partnered with a Jewish woman, and comparisons between and jokes about the similarities of the two groups are regularly made. For example, in season seven, Will tells Grace, "I figure, since you're practically a gay man, I should become a little Jewish"; in season six, Karen returns from the theater and tells Will and Grace, "Between the Jews on stage and the homos in the audience, it was like paying a hundred bucks to hang out here."

Likewise, Melanie, the glue that holds the *Folk* family together, is Jewish and regularly uses her Jewish identity and the history of the Jewish people to support claims for gay and lesbian rights. This can be seen in season three, when a court rules against gay adoption and Melanie states, "it's not any different than what the fucking Nazis did to the Jews. Or what happened to Cicely Tyson when she tried to take a sip out of that drinking fountain," and again in season five when, discussing a new law limiting gay and lesbian rights, Melanie exclaims, "Sorry to sound like such an alarmist, but these days I feel like I am living in Nazi Germany, like we're [gays and lesbians] the new Jews."

References to Jewishness are made repeatedly throughout both series, and outside each show's premise of illustrating life as a lesbian or gay person in today's world, each show spends a considerable amount of time showcasing Jewish identity as well. The different ways *W&G* and

*Folk* negotiate lesbian, gay, and Jewish identity speak to the audiences of the shows and explain why one is a popularly acclaimed sitcom while the other is a rarely heard-of dramatic serial. By putting two Othered identities together, *W&G* fits safely within the confines of normative television standards and allows audiences to act as distant observers, safely shifting their attention between Will and Grace without any pressure to align themselves with either character. Conversely, Melanie, an out-and-proud butch lesbian, exemplifies a co-constructed Jewish lesbian identity and repeatedly uses Jewishness and the history of the Jewish people as a source from which to argue for lesbian and gay rights. Her in-your-face tactics combined with her civil rights convictions make her impossible to ignore. That one show is successful because of its mass appeal and the other a niche program due to its radical content makes a strong case for using both texts to articulate the importance of the queer family.

## THE SHOWS

Unlike most television programs in which gays and lesbians exist as peripheral identities, *W&G* and *Folk* situate gay men and lesbians as lead characters. The principal characters on *W&G* are Grace Adler (Debra Messing), a loud-mouthed, Jewish interior designer; and her best friend Will Truman (Eric McCormack), a cleanliness-obsessed, gay lawyer. Karen Walker (Megan Mullally) is an outlandishly wealthy, bisexual socialite who supports Jack McFarland (Sean Hayes), a flamboyant, unemployed actor. Other notable characters are Rosario (Shelley Morrison), Karen's El Salvadorian maid; and Leo Marcus (Harry Connick, Jr.), a Jewish doctor who is Grace's boyfriend, husband, ex-husband, and baby's dad, in that order. The show is largely staged in Will's apartment, although at times the characters traverse New York City and visit Grace's office, Karen's "mans"(ion), a coffee shop, and various venues for Jack's performances.

*Folk* is set in Pittsburgh, Pennsylvania, suggesting that the characters are everyday people living in a working-class town. *Folk* goes beyond making gay men and lesbians lead characters; it is the first show to provide gays and lesbians with individually nuanced identities and construct gays and lesbians "as regular people rather than exotic curiosities" (Pereen 2006, 64). The principal characters are a group of four close friends who each offer a different type of gay masculinity: Michael Novotny (Hal Sparks), a romantic "mama's boy"; Brian Kinney, the show's Lothario; Emmet Honeycutt (Peter Paige), a fashionista southern belle; and Ted Schmidt (Scott Lowell), a soft-spoken accountant. Other primary characters are Debbie Novotny (Sharon Gless), Michael's mother; Justin Taylor, an art student and Brian's intermittent love interest; and Ben Bruckner (Robert Gant), Michael's HIV-infected boyfriend. Melanie Marcus (Melanie Clunie), a butch Jewish attorney, and Lindsay Peterson

(Thea Gil), an artist, are the lone lesbians and only consistent couple. Throughout the series they have two children: Gus, borne by Lindsay with Brian as sperm donor, and Jenny Rebecca, borne by Melanie with Michael as sperm donor.

While the premises of both shows center on "out" gay and lesbian characters, none of the characters in either text are marked as "normal." Among the main characters of the two shows, not one exists within the ideology of normative U.S. citizen (that is, white, Christian, heterosexual, middle-class, and able-bodied/healthy). In fact, most characters embody multiple outsider characteristics, which work to construct them as "queer." As queer identities, they resist any single label (Meyer 1994). Apart from the gay and lesbian characters, Melanie, Grace, Leo, and Bobbi are not Christian. Rosario is not white. Karen, Michael, Debbie, and Rosario are not middle class. Jack and Emmet are not traditionally masculine. Melanie and Grace are not traditionally feminine. Ben is not healthy. Justin is not "legal." And Will and Ted can't find love. Importantly, each character is marked repeatedly by her or his non-normative identity, and none of the characters exist within society's orientation toward perfection.

## SOCIAL PERFECTION

According to Kenneth Burke (1954), social perfection—our upward movements toward social ideals—can be understood through the concept of orientation. Orientations determine how life is experienced and dictate what frames our reality. As one orientation is selected, others are necessarily rejected, inevitably creating limitations and hindering one's capacity to operate outside her or his selected orientation. Orientations become problematic when/as they fail to account for situations or people who do not fit into an accepted orientation, such as heterosexuality or Christianity in American culture. Ideals of normalcy are the "perfection" a society expects. Our current culture constructs heterosexuality and Christianity as the norm, thereby rendering gays, lesbians, and Jews "abnormal" or "imperfect" in Burkean terms (1959). Because heterosexuality and Christianity are the "invisible center," they work as the "quintessential force(s) creating, sustaining, and perpetuating the erasure, marginalization, disempowerment, and oppression of sexual [and religious] others" (Warner 2005, 18). Where heterosexuality is the norm, a trained incapacity to operate outside it "perpetuates self-inflicted, as well as externally inflicted, violence toward gays" and lesbians (Goltz 2007, paragraph 3), or renders them invisible. And for Jews, "The price of achieving political efficacy in a Christian centered culture turns out to be the abandonment of Jewish difference" (Freedman 1998, 92). In other words, within American ideals of perfection (which will hence be called heteronormativity and Christia-normativity), Jews, lesbians, and gay men are abnormal.

Goltz claims that heteronormativity, and the resulting trained inca-pacity for society to operate outside an orientation toward heterosexual-ity, casts gays and lesbians into the tragic frame of immoral or invisible. Furthermore, social hierarchies are reified by positioning the "normals" (heterosexuals/Christians) in contrast with the "abnormals" (gays, les-bians, and Jews). As a result, Goltz (2007) suggests, "culture is rooted in the limitations of binary thinking," and portions of society will necessari-ly be cast into "the role of evil, wrong, or villainous" (paragraph 5). Those who are or have been cast out are tragically framed; and, according to Burke, the only way to reframe their position is through the comic correc-tive of perspective by incongruity—which for *Folk* and *W&G* is the queer family structure.

## PERFORMING GAY AND LESBIAN WITHIN HETERONORMATIVITY

The orientation toward heteronormativity operates very differently on *W&G* than *Folk*, particularly in the ways in which the characters construct their identities. The characters on *W&G* must appease an audience orient-ed toward heteronormativity, and in doing so, rarely perform "gay" in the true sense of a sexual orientation—in other words, having boyfriends. The characters on *Folk* live in a world oriented toward heteronormativity, and their attempts to show the realities of life as an "out" gay man or lesbian are marred with the realities of being gay or lesbian—in other words, they are cast as immoral villains by society. Where Jewishness plays a role in heteronormativity is how gayness materializes for the viewers. By constructing *Folk*'s most outspoken activist for gay rights as Jewish, Melanie's voice within the show can be minimized because she is doubly Othered, and the tragic frame in which gays and lesbians find themselves can be ignored. Likewise, on *W&G*, constructing both main characters as Other, audience members are allowed to shift their atten-tion between Will and Grace without feeling pressure to relate to either character, because neither character is "normal."

On *W&G*, neither Jack nor Will offers the necessary performances of gay identity for their sexual orientation to be taken seriously. Jack's sexu-ality is more childlike than gay, and Will's sexuality is hardly more than a form of male privilege, which allows him unrestricted access to Grace's body (Shugart 2003). Whereas in one episode Will grabs Grace's breasts and jokes about their inability to fill out a dress, in another episode he pulls out the tissues she has stuffed in her bra.

The orientation toward heteronormativity on *W&G* limits gay identity to stereotypes and self-deprecating remarks. As such, gayness is ren-dered almost invisible, and neither Will nor Jack ever suffers from homophobia. Conversely, the characters on *Folk* regularly perform their gay and lesbian identities. Gay sex is the norm; a young boy's journey of coming out centers much of the melodrama, and each character's gay or lesbian identity is asserted repeatedly throughout the series. From Melanie identifying herself as a "career dyke" and riding with the "dykes on bikes" at Gay Pride, to each of the male characters engaging in a series of relationships with a variety of men, the continuous acts of lesbian and gay self-declaration on *Folk* offer the necessary performance for these identities to materialize.

However, because *Folk*'s gay and lesbian characters transcend stereotypes and push the boundaries of what it means to be gay and lesbian—in other words, because they refuse to acquiesce to heteronormativity—they suffer, as a result, from externally inflicted acts of violence. Living a gay and lesbian life for the characters on *Folk* is not easy; rather, the characters are an attempt at authenticity, which includes the real-life struggles that gays and lesbians face. In *Folk*'s premiere episode, young kids spray paint "FAGGOT" on Brian's car; midway through season three, Ted is fired from his job for being gay; and in the final season of the series, the club Babylon is bombed during an LGBT community fundraiser. These homophobic acts articulate the punishments lesbians and gay men suffer as a result of existing outside heteronormative culture.

## PERFORMING JEWISH WITHIN CHRISTIANORMATIVITY

The orientation toward Christianormativity operates similarly to heteronormativity on *W&G* and *Folk*, in similarly satiating and subversive ways. Whereas the entire first season of *W&G* goes by without any specific mention of Grace's Jewishness, by the third episode of *Folk* we meet Melanie's entire Jewish family and her rabbi, and glimpse a variety of Jewish delicacies—brisket, bagels, lox, and gefilte fish. When Grace's Jewish identity is mentioned, it, like gay identity, is a joke. In season five, Jack tells Grace, "You're so generous. I swear if you weren't Jewish, you'd definitely go to heaven," and in season six, Karen asks Grace "to keep the Jew talk down to a whisper." Conversely, on *Folk*, Jewishness repeatedly materializes and is repeatedly put down in more vicious ways. The parents of Melanie's partner Lindsay describe her as "The slick Jew lawyer, come to shake [them] down for a few *sheckels*." And when Brian prevents Gus's *bris* from occurring, he states, "Gus has been in this world less than a week, and already there are people who won't accept him for the way he is. Who would even mutilate him rather than let him be the way he is, the way he was born," conflating the ritual act with hate speech and gay-bashing.

Whether it is hate or invisibility, on *W&G* and *Folk* the characters are forced to negotiate their position outside heteronormative Christianormativity. Will's gayness and Grace's Jewishness are either invisible or sources of jokes; and the characters on *Folk* are victims to acts of violence, both physical and emotional, because in their world, social perfections exist (just as they do in real life) and abnormal people are punished for their differences.

## QUEER FAMILY

In order for dominant ideologies to change or for the abnormals to become normal, a society must be confronted with an incongruous perspective regarding its ideals of perfection. According to Goltz (2007), the term *queer* is "perspective by incongruity in one word" (paragraph 12). Meyer (1994) claims that *queer* "indicates an ontological challenge to dominant labeling philosophies" (1), and that the task of queer theory is to identify ways in which people on the margins can resist dominant culture. As such, *queer* is meant to denaturalize and problematize social norms. Within this homology of the term, the characters on *W&G* and *Folk* are queer by virtue of their multiple othered identities and the role they play within television culture.

Real-life queer families emerge from the close bonds gays and lesbians make with their friends as a result of the frequent loss of their biological family upon coming out (Weston 1991). Queer families recognize friend-based social systems as family in addition to normative conceptions of biological relations (Elias 2003). The televised queer families on *Folk* and *W&G* offer the necessary perspective by incongruity to queer the norms of perfection, which renders lesbians, gays, and Jews abnormal Others. Because both shows exemplify the ways that gay and lesbian identities are tragically othered within society's orientations toward perfection, an examination of their parallel family structures as a perspective by incongruity has the potential to unearth a transformative and queer version of "normal."

## THE FRIEND-MADE FAMILY OF *WILL & GRACE*

The queer family of Grace, Will, Jack, and Karen can be seen throughout the series; however, it is most clearly articulated in a special hour-long episode of *W&G* in which Grace marries Leo. Will is distraught about losing Grace and distracts himself by running around the synagogue handing out *yarmulkes*. In the dressing room, Karen is watching Grace ready herself when Grace's mother comes in to tell Grace that her father has hurt his back and cannot walk her down the aisle. Whereas Grace suggests putting "a pastrami sandwich and a TV guide under the *chuppa*" to motivate her father, Karen quells the idea and offers up Will to be the man by her side. She reiterates her idea by saying, "It'll be perfect—out with the 'mo and in with the Jew!" The episode cuts from the opening notes of the wedding march to Central Park. Will, Grace, Jack, Karen, and Leo stroll along the grass as one big happy queer family. Nowhere in sight are Grace's parents, anyone's siblings, or any blood-related member of her (or Leo's) family. The entire ceremony goes unseen, as does everyone's biological relations. Rather, Grace's close-knit group of friends has replaced biological connections.

In the final season, Grace discovers she is pregnant with her now ex-husband Leo's baby. After a disheartening conversation with him, Grace returns to the apartment she shares with Will, scared of being alone. As Will welcomes her into his arms, she admits, "I guess I was crazy to think that all of a sudden we could just have a happy family." To which Karen firmly responds, "Honey, you do have a family. And I don't mean those Jews in Schenectady. I mean us."

## QUEERING FAMILY ON *QUEER AS FOLK*

Not only do the characters on *Folk* regularly call each other "family" and understand the notion of queer families, but *Folk* also pushes the limits of queer family by queering the characters' families through biological ties. Melanie and Lindsay's son was borne by Lindsay with Brian as the sperm donor, and their daughter, carried by Melanie, is Michael's biological child. While these biological ties do create legal and personal issues, the radical shift in parenting and parental control queers both traditional kinship systems and the boundaries of the queer family.

During Melanie's pregnancy, she and Lindsay have marital problems, and after Jenny Rebecca is born, they briefly separate. While Melanie is still in the hospital, Michael and his partner Ben take care of her and Jenny Rebecca, as good fathers would do. Jenny Rebecca is a baby with two moms, two dads, a non-biological brother, and a stepbrother who used to be a male prostitute. She exists in a radical space of queer transformation as her family transcends any and all traditional notions of family—but is, undeniably, a family.

On both *W&G* and *Folk*, it is the non-normativity and queerness of each character's individual identity that make them part of each other's family. None of the characters are marked as normal, yet all have a loving and supportive queer family, showing how they avoid being tragically framed. The queer family is an incongruous perspective on normative assumptions about family and not only gives each character a community accepting of difference but reframes the characters as normal, loving people, rather than evil, villainous ones.

## CONCLUSION: MUTUAL RECIPROCITY

Social change takes many shapes and forms. From the yellow and blue Human Rights Campaign emblem on the bookshelf of Will's apartment to Melanie and Lindsay leaving their home in Pittsburgh for Canada at the end of the series, both *W&G* and *Folk* work to comically correct the tragic frames of homophobia and anti-Semitism through the queer family as perspective by incongruity. Although different in their approach and appeal, both shows changed the television landscape. The queer families of *Folk* and *W&G* encourage mutual support, reciprocal acts of kindness, and a space wherein each character has the chance to be who she or he is. Their communities and their families offer a space of mutual reciprocity to each of their members.

David Kohan, creator of *W&G*, named the characters Will and Grace after Martin Buber's thesis on human existence (Brooks 2003). For Buber, a person's foundational construction of Being exists only through genuine interactions with others. The necessarily inter-subjective relationship of *I-Thou* requires "the will to seek the 'I-Thou' and grace to realize this transcendent state" (Brooks 2003, 163). Being requires that one's "will and intentionality [are] passionately involved" (Kramer 2003, 22); however, will is not enough. Only through the grace of *Thou's* "reciprocal acts of compassion" can a genuine meeting of each individual's personal uniqueness occur (Kramer 2003, 22).

Reciprocity of self and other *is* the relationship between the characters on *W&G* and *Folk* and is what allows them to *be* gay, lesbian, and Jewish. Brooks (2003) suggests that *W&G* "appear(s) to be saying that Will and Grace, like gays and Jews, need each other more than they know. Each group must acknowledge the other in themselves and the self in the other" (163). In other words, each must approach the other with mutual reciprocity so that each can see the other's "unique wholeness." The characters on *W&G* and *Folk* exist in *I-Thou* relationships of mutual reciprocity with one another in regards to their Jewish, lesbian, and gay identities. Because gayness, lesbianism, and Jewishness often go unseen, the characters on *W&G* and *Folk* look beyond simple identity constructions to "acknowledge the other in themselves and the self in the other" (Brooks 2003, 163) and become family. And as such, both programs work to create change for Jewish, gay, and lesbian identity on television and in real life.

## REFERENCES

Battles, K., and W. Hilton-Morrow. 2002. "Gay characters in conventional spaces: Will and Grace and the situation comedy genre." *Critical Studies in Media Communication* 19 (1): 87–105.

Brooks, V. 2003. *Something ain't kosher here: The rise of the "Jewish" sitcom.* New Brunswick: Rutgers University Press.

Burke, K. 1959. *Attitudes toward history.* Los Altos, CA: Hermes.

———. 1954. *Permanence and Change: An anatomy of purpose.* Los Altos, CA: Hermes.

Elias, J. 2003. "Queering relationships." *Journal of Homosexuality* 45 (2): 61–86.

Freedman, J. 1998. "Angels, monsters, and Jews: Intersections of queer and Jewish identity in Kushner's angels in America." *PMLA* 113 (1): 90–102.

Goltz, D. B. 2007. "Perspective by incongruity." *Genders Online Journal.*

Jakobsen, J. R. 2003. "Queers are like Jews aren't they? Analogy and alliance politics." In *Queer theory and the Jewish question,* edited by D. Boyarin, D. Itzkovitz, and A. Pellegrini, 64–89. New York: Columbia University Press.

Kramer, K. 2003. *Martin Buber's I and thou: Practicing living dialogue.* Mahwah, NJ: Paulist Press.

Meyer, M. 1994. "Reclaiming the discourse of camp." In *The politics and poetics of camp,* edited by M. Meyer, 1–22. New York: Routledge.

Noble, B. 2007. "Queer as box: Boi spectators and boy culture on Showtime's *Queer as Folk.*" In *Third wave feminism and television: Jane puts it in a box,* edited by M. L. Johnson, 147–65. New York: I.B. Tauris.

Pellegrini, A. 1997. "Whiteface performances: 'Race,' gender, and Jewish bodies." In *Jews and other differences: The new Jewish cultural studies,* edited by D. Boyarin and J. Boyarin, 108–49. Minneapolis: University of Minnesota Press.

Pereen, E. 2006. "Queering the straight world: The politics of resignification on *Queer as Folk.*" In *Queer Popular Culture: Literature, media, film, and television,* edited by T. Peele. New York: Palgrave Macmillan.

Porfido, G. 2007. "*Queer as Folk* and the spectacularization of gay identity." In *Queer popular culture: Literature, media, film, and television,* edited by T. Peele. New York: Palgrave Macmillan.

Provencher, D. M. 2005. "Sealed with a kiss: Heteronormative strategies in NBC's *Will & Grace.*" In *The sitcom reader: America viewed and skewed,* edited by M. M. Dalton and L. R. Linder, 177–89. Albany: State University of New York Press.

Shugart, H. A. 2003. "Reinventing privilege: The new (gay) man in contemporary popular media." *Critical Studies in Media Communication* 20 (1): 67–91.

Sontag, S. 1966. *Against interpretation, and other essays.* New York: Farrar, Strauss and Giroux.

Stratton, J. 2000. *Coming out Jewish: Constructing ambivalent identities.* New York: Routledge.

Warner, M. 2005. *Publics and counterpublics.* New York: Zone Books.

Weston, K. 1991 *Families we choose: Lesbians, gays, kinship.* New York: Columbia University Press.

## NOTE

1. *W&G* earned eighty-three Emmy nominations and won sixteen. *W&G* also won a People's Choice Award, a Golden Globe, two GLAAD (Gay and Lesbian Alliance Against Defamation) Awards, and a Founders Award from the Viewers for Quality television and was ensconced in the Nielsen Top 20 for half its network run.

# FOUR

# Revisiting Vito Russo's *The Celluloid Closet*

## Jane Campbell and Theresa Carilli

"The history of the portrayal of lesbians and gay men in mainstream cinema is politically indefensible and aesthetically revolting." —Vito Russo, 1987

In the 2010 blockbuster film *Black Swan*, nominated for five Academy Awards, a young female dancer, Nina Sayers (Natalie Portman), is cast in a ballet where she must embody both white and black swans. This embodiment means that Nina must inhabit two worlds: one that is good and pure, and the other, dark and evil. While attempting to embody the black swan, Nina descends into a world of sexual confusion, engaging in a graphic lesbian sex scene marked by a creepy, incestuous subtext, as well as getting involved in a world of violence characterized by torture, dismemberment, and death. *Black Swan* reinforces fear, anxiety, and panic, equating lesbianism with madness, in spite of the landmark 1973 ruling by the American Psychiatric Association that there is no connection between gayness and mental illness.

This deeply sexist and homophobic film was positioned as a brilliant psychological thriller directed by Darren Aronofsky. When Portman received the Oscar for her performance in *Black Swan*, she followed two female predecessors receiving the award who portrayed troubled queers. In 2000, Hillary Swank took on the role of transsexual Teena Brandon/Brandon Teena in the film *Boys Don't Cry*, and Charlize Theron portrayed Aileen Wuornos, a lesbian serial killer in the 2003 film *Monster*. All three actresses—Portman, Swank, and Theron—received critical acclaim for their performances as sexually confused individuals, raising the issue of whether Hollywood primarily rewards women who are willing to perform queerness as a marginalized embodiment that disrupts the master narrative.

This chapter revisits Vito Russo's 1981 book and 1995 film *The Celluloid Closet*, exploring whether mainstream gay film depictions have changed over the last twenty to thirty years. We discuss four films that have been nominated for Academy Awards wherein a central part of the plot is driven by a main character's sexual confusion. These films include *Monster* (2003), *Brokeback Mountain* (2005), *The Kids Are All Right* (2010), and *Beginners* (2011). As mainstream films, these movies echo much that Vito Russo found objectionable in the history of gay and lesbian images. First, the films contain an underlying sexism/heterosexism and hegemony that exoticizes gay images. Second, some of the depictions have a caricature-like quality and speak to a primal fear of gay individuals. And finally, while these films might seem to increase queer visibility, they impede that visibility by presenting gay characters as victims or villains, even when the characters are somewhat dimensional. Nonetheless, these depictions give insight into queerness by demonstrating some of the issues facing the LGBT community through standout performances, strong scriptwriting, and sensitive direction.

## SEXISM/HETEROSEXISM AND HEGEMONY

Vito Russo begins his discussion of *The Celluloid Closet* by examining the role of the "sissy" in film. While the sissy might inspire laughter and poke fun at maleness, at its core the image of the sissy challenges what it means to be a man and just how ineffectual and unflattering it is to be a woman. After acknowledging sexism in the movies, asserting that all movie behavior is cast in male terms, Russo writes, "Homosexuality in the movies, whether overtly sexual or not, has always been seen in terms of what is or is not masculine . . . it is supposed to be an insult to call a man effeminate, for it means he is like a woman and therefore not as valuable as a 'real' man" (1981, 4). Russo launches us into the sexist reality that maleness, or the male gaze, the theory that Laura Mulvey created in her landmark article, *Visual Pleasure and Narrative Cinema*, teaches both men and women how to experience films. Heterosexual masculinity is the preferred convention in the film industry. The notion of the male hero or superhero who defeats the villain and wins the damsel has firmly implanted itself in the consciousness of film-goers. Thus, movies about masculinity and heterosexuality create a hegemony of film-viewing. Given this hegemony, current images of maleness and femaleness exaggerate masculinity and femininity. Both men and women are given the message that it is possible to transform their body parts via plastic surgery to be in line with these hyper-images of femininity and masculinity. Actors and actresses present sculpted bodies that belie their acting talents. With this extreme focus on masculinity and femininity, the story, which once was the focus of films, becomes inconsequential. The emphasis on extreme heteronormativity has accompanied an increase in science fiction and fantasy movies. Movies which glorify vampires, were-wolves, or characters with superhuman strength bring in the biggest box office numbers (for example, *The Twilight Saga, Transformers, The Hunger Games,* and *The Dark Night Rises*). In the last decade, while America has been in two wars, the news has abounded with stories of patriotism and heroism, reinforcing both patriarchy and the hegemony of masculinity. With this type of hyper-masculinity and -femininity, images and stories about real people's lives seem to have little appeal. While the film-sissy is not as overtly visible as before, his decline and erasure has accompanied an exaggerated machismo. Given hegemonic masculinity, depictions of gayness are sometimes exaggerated, or even horrifying.

## STEREOTYPING

In his book *Up from Invisibility: Lesbians, Gay Men, and the Media in Ameri-ca,* cultural studies theorist Larry Gross (2001) writes, "Our vulnerability to media stereotyping and political attack derives in large part from our isolation and pervasive invisibility" (15). In other words, stereotyping is fed by the silence that many gay people learn for their own safety and protection. Throughout a major portion of the twentieth century, gay bars, a primary social setting for community members, remained hidden from the straight community. Gay people learned about bars through word of mouth; police interference could mean shutting down the bars due to sodomy laws. When the LGBT community issued notification of a queer presence, as in the 1969 Stonewall Uprising, the 1979 protests against the film *Cruising,* or the annual LGBT parades, news cameras would focus on the flamboyant displays of gayness, particularly drag queens and transgendered individuals. There was an overall sense that gayness meant effeminate men, masculine women, and individuals clothed in outrageous costumes. Because members of the LGBT commu-nity broke conventional rules of what it meant to be male or female in hetero culture, hetero culture did not look favorably upon us.

Stereotyping, which pigeonholes all minority cultures, presents cari-catures of cultural members. Film audience members are taught to locate those traits which are identifiable markers of gayness. Viewers are not encouraged to seek an understanding of the day-to-day lives of LGBT individuals and what it might mean to live as a gay person in a hetero-sexist world. In his book *Gays and Film,* Richard Dyer explores what media stereotyping has meant to the gay community. Dyer (2001) elo-quently explains, "What we should be attacking in stereotypes is the attempt of heterosexual society to define us for ourselves, in terms that inevitably fall short of the 'ideal' of heterosexuality" (31).

As is the case with any minority, audiences who are not members of the LGBT community must struggle to look past the caricatured images to witness authentic depictions. As long as there are few films about gayness, whether told from a mainstream or independent perspective, stereotypical characters will continue to shape heterosexual audiences' perceptions about what it means to be queer.

## VISIBILITY

In the afterword to his book, Russo concludes, "Gay visibility has never really been an issue in the movies. Gays have always been visible. It's how they have been visible that has remained offensive for almost a century" (325). Russo explores images of the gay community ranging from victims to victimizers. The two classic examples for his research are *The Children's Hour* and *Cruising*.

The 1961 film *The Children's Hour*, based on the play of the same name by Lillian Hellman, is the story of two female teachers who run an up-scale boarding school for young girls. So as not to return to the school, one of the young girls informs her grandmother that the two schoolteachers are lovers. As parents of all the young girls remove their daughters from the school in response to this rumor, one of the teachers (played by Shirley MacLaine) realizes she has sexual feelings for her friend and co-worker. After revealing those feelings to her, she commits suicide, reinforcing a commonly-held belief of the time that individuals of "such persuasion" were unstable outcasts. *The Children's Hour* is the classic example of the lesbian as victim, one who views life without a future because of her dark and terrible secret.

While the victim image was perpetuated throughout the 1950s and 1960s, the 1970s and 1980s ushered in the gay villain. The 1980 film *Cruising* proclaims the evil of queerness through a story about a gay serial killer who engages in sexual encounters with his victims before stabbing them to death. *Cruising* created an eruption of protests from the gay community, outraged at such a negative depiction. Though the 1980s attempted to present a few positive stories, such as the 1982 film *Personal Best*, a film about two female athletes who become lovers, or the 1982 film *Making Love*, about a physician who comes out and leaves his marriage, the dominant images equate queerness with death—whether through suicide or homicide. The "dead queer" has become a film convention when an LGBT character takes a leading role.

Given the aforementioned discussion, we examine the films *Monster* (2003), *Brokeback Mountain* (2005), *The Kids are All Right* (2010), and *Beginners* (2011), by looking at how sexism and heterosexism, stereotyping, and visibility operate in these films. Our main focus is to explore whether images of the LGBT community are more substantive than they used to be, giving authentic insights into gay life that seemed to be absent in the past, or whether such images continue to reinforce the timeworn, negative images that have prevailed for so long. Of course, independent filmmakers continue to offer excellent, positive examinations of life in the LGBT community, but what these four films share is their mainstream prominence. Each received numerous nominations and awards. The acclaim was well-deserved, for each film is beautifully constructed and sensitively portrayed. But the fact is, because these films reached large audiences, they were lauded as landmark portrayals of LGBT life. Their impact was huge, offering audiences an opportunity to form antiquated assumptions about gay men, lesbians, and bisexuals.

## MONSTER

Written and directed by Patty Jenkins, *Monster* fictionalizes the 1989–1990 crime spree of Aileen Wuornos, the first documented female serial killer. Intrigued by Wuornos's story, Jenkins set out to evoke empathy for the Florida prostitute who murdered six men, claiming self-defense. Although Wuornos was in prison while Jenkins was making the film, Jenkins worked with her as closely as possible, and before her execution in 2002, Aileen offered the filmmaker the thousands of letters she wrote to her best friend while incarcerated.

Jenkins wanted to cast Charlize Theron from the beginning, believing she had the necessary strength, character, and talent. Born and raised in South Africa, Theron was fifteen years old when she watched her mother kill her alcoholic father in self-defense, after he threated to murder both of them. This experience shaped her sensitivity toward victims of domestic violence, and she has commented that Aileen's story pulled her in as soon as she read the script. In a review of the film, critic Roger Ebert wrote, "What Charlize Theron achieves . . . isn't a performance but an embodiment. . . . With courage, art, and charity, she empathizes with Aileen Wuornos, a damaged woman" (Ebert 2004). Theron not only won an Oscar for her performance; she also won a Golden Globe, an Independent Spirit Award, a Screen Actors Guild Award, and a Broadcast Film Critics Award, as well as awards from the Berlin, Chicago, New York, and San Francisco film societies for Best Actress. To be sure, the film captivates the viewer in its sensitive portrayal of Wuornos, a tragically abused woman. At the age of eight, Wuornos was raped by a friend of her father, and the rapes continued for years. When she told her father, he beat her. At her trial, Wuornos asserted that her brother fathered the child she gave up for adoption. Aileen's father, a pedophile and psychopath, killed himself while incarcerated, and her mother disappeared. At age thirteen, Aileen began a career in prostitution.

Much has been made of Theron's transformation from a stunning, model-thin actress to a somewhat larger, unattractive duplicate of Wuornos. Theron gained thirty pounds for the role and wore extensive make-up and a long, greasy-looking wig. Photographs of Theron's character bear a striking resemblance to the real Wuornos. To Theron's credit, however, her transformation went far beyond body size, hair, and makeup. She acquired a southern accent and an extremely butch manner and gait. On Theron's part, the gait and mannerisms represented a genuine effort to embody Wuornos; to the viewer, however, Wuornos's persona comes close to caricaturing the stereotypical butch lesbian. Paired with her homicidal actions in the film, Jenkins's Wuornos fuels homophobic beliefs about lesbians: that they hate all men and want to murder them. Though Wuornos is the first documented female serial killer, the uninformed viewer might find her to be his or her worst nightmare. Such a perspective not only dovetails with homophobia, it reinforces heterosexist fears that women often murder men, although statistics show that the opposite is the case.

To Jenkins's credit, she makes a genuine effort to humanize Wuornos and provide motivation for her crimes. At the beginning of the film, we are introduced to Wuornos as a pretty blond child who dreams of being famous and who slips into prostitution without knowing what she is doing. Later, we learn of her sexual abuse and homelessness as a child. When she meets Selby Wall (Wuornos's lover was actually named Tyria Moore), she considers herself straight but through with men. Selby and Aileen (called "Lee") meet in a gay bar, although Aileen only learns that the bar is gay by accident. A homeless prostitute who has just left an abusive relationship with a man, Aileen is beaten down both physically and mentally, possessing only five dollars and an old car to call home. After resisting Selby's advances initially and calling her a "dumb dyke," Aileen finally agrees to go home with Selby as long as no sex is involved. The loneliness of both Aileen and Selby (played beautifully by Christina Ricci) is palpable; both are starving for love and validation.

The film juxtaposes scenes of Aileen and Selby's relationship and their mutual love with Aileen's encounters with her customers, encounters that escalate into a series of murders. The first murder is in self-defense; a john abuses and tortures Aileen, and she kills him before he kills her. As the film progresses, Lee spins out of control, her rage growing with each encounter, until she begins killing out of desperation and fear, ultimately shooting a man who is genuinely trying to help her. With each murder, the viewer would find it more and more impossible to connect with Lee were it not for Jenkins's masterful handling of the material. Lee appears to love Selby deeply and seeks to protect and support her financially. In one heartbreaking episode, Lee attempts to leave prostitution and find a secretarial position, only to meet derision and humiliation in the work-place.

Unfortunately, heterosexism affects the mainstream audience's perspectives on *Monster*. Even though Selby is a young, immature character struggling with her sexual identity, her whiny selfishness makes her unsympathetic. For LGBT viewers used to the constraints of heteronormativity, Lee's murder spree arises from Lee's growing awareness of the disgust her clients feel for her and her relative powerlessness as a woman and as a lesbian. For a hetero audience without feminist and queer awareness, Aileen Wuornos probably deserves the title of "monster." Even with all the compassion and empathy one may feel for Lee, the fact remains that she is a deeply disturbed individual who finds justification for her actions and claims, "I'm not a bad person. I'm a real good person." Several innocent (though unsympathetic) men die violently, and the predominantly heterosexual audiences who watched this film arguably felt far less sympathy than did LGBT audiences. Jenkins strives to humanize Aileen Wuornos, but in the absence of countervailing images of lesbians, *Monster* ends up contributing to a stereotype: a man-hating, man-killing dyke who is executed for her villainous crimes.

## BROKEBACK MOUNTAIN

Ang Lee, Larry McMurtry, and Diana Ossana's screen adaptation of Annie Proulx's story "Brokeback Mountain" emerged in 2005, boasting a star-studded cast (Heath Ledger, Jake Gyllenhaal, Anne Hathaway, and Michelle Williams). As with *Monster*, those involved in the production approached the project with sensitivity and a commitment to humanize the characters. Proulx herself, a heterosexual writer who was not involved in the production, has expressed delight with the way the film succeeds in fleshing out the characters appearing in her 1999 short story. In interviews, Proulx has explained that observing a seemingly closeted gay cowboy in a bar in Wyoming and pondering what his life might have been like inspired her to create Ennis del Mar (Ledger) and Jack Twist (Gyllenhaal) (Proulx 2011). Two uneducated, destitute young men working as sheep-herders in the summer of 1963 on Brokeback Mountain in Wyoming, Ennis and Jack fall in love. Twenty years elapse while they both marry women, father children, and meet periodically for torrid sexual encounters disguised as fishing and hunting trips. Whereas Ennis's wife, Alma, sees them kiss passionately a few years after their first encounter, Jack's wife, Lureen, can only guess at her husband's infidelities. Ennis declares that he's "not queer," while Jack gradually realizes his sexual identity and tries to persuade Ennis to establish a life with him.

*Brokeback Mountain* deftly explores the agony of being closeted. Remembering the story of a gay man who was killed and dismembered by a mob, and his father warning Ennis that this was the fate of men who dared lead an openly gay life, Ennis refuses to consider Jack's hope of living together as a couple, even after Ennis and Alma divorce. With very little dialogue, Ennis and Jack transmit their passionate connection, a connection that punctuates the rage and despondency they feel because the rural communities they both inhabit prohibit same-sex relationships. Strapped to a life of hard work, Ennis barely makes ends meet, just managing to send child support to Alma after their divorce and seeming to live without love for anyone except his oldest daughter. He attempts a relationship with another woman, but his emotional paralysis and gayness scuttle any chance for a heterosexual relationship to work out. Jack's marriage provides financial security but clearly only the façade of family, and Jack begins seeking out male prostitutes to satisfy his sexual cravings. For both men, the memory of that first summer represents a peak experience, and their relationship with each other allows for the only intimacy they ever know.

Like *Monster*, *Brokeback Mountain* enjoyed enormous critical acclaim, boasting a list of awards too long to enumerate, including Oscars for Best Director, Best Screenplay, and Best Original Score, and Academy Award nominations for performances by Ledger, Gyllenhaal, and Williams. Given the film's prominence, it is important to note how well it succeeds in depicting certain gay relationships as tragic, reinforcing gay victimization. The heartbreaking ending, in which we learn of Jack's violent death, realistic as it may be, nevertheless fits a little too neatly into Vito Russo's characterization of gay films. Hauntingly reminiscent of the murder of Matthew Shepherd in Wyoming in 1998, the ending reminds us too starkly of the conclusion to far too many films about gay men and lesbians. Taken together with *Black Swan* and *Monster*, *Brokeback Mountain* shows that the tragic ending is still often the consequence of visibility in mainstream contemporary films about lesbians and gay men, reinscribing the "dead queer" motif of old.

## THE KIDS ARE ALL RIGHT

With Lisa Cholodenko's 2010 film *The Kids Are All Right*, hope emerged that mainstream LGBT film had moved beyond the tragic conclusion formula. *The Kids Are All Right* is the director's first mainstream success. Her earlier films, *High Art* (1998) and *Laurel Canyon* (2002) won critical acclaim, but *The Kids Are All Right*, a Sundance release, featured a high profile cast and won Golden Globes for Best Picture and Best Actress (Annette Bening). Bening was also nominated for Best Actress by the Academy (she lost to Natalie Portman for *Black Swan*). In addition, the Academy nominated Mark Ruffalo for Best Actor in a Leading Role. The film received two more Oscar nominations: Best Picture and Best Original Screenplay. With a small budget of four million dollars, Cholodenko's film represents a landmark in LGBT film-making, because the lesbian filmmaker set out to portray a contemporary lesbian couple in a comedic, realistic manner. Cholodenko remarks, "I think people have found *The Kids Are All Right* incredibly fresh because . . . finally, somebody doesn't have to die. I feel really cynical about the gay martyr movie" (Cooke 2010, 1). Her assertion is curious, given that her 1998 film "High Art" concludes when a central lesbian character, played by Ally Sheedy, dies of a drug overdose.

Inspired by Cholodenko's experiences of seeking an anonymous sperm donor so that she and her long-time partner Wendy Melvoin could have a baby, the film focuses on a lesbian couple, Nic (Bening) and Jules (Julianne Moore), and their two teenagers, both fathered by the same sperm donor. Cholodenko plays with the convention of the dark, handsome stranger who arrives to incite conflict. When the kids decide to track down their heterosexual donor father, Paul (Ruffalo), the idyllic gay family begins to unravel. The director asserts, "I had no political agenda. But there is a core value I wanted to illuminate: no matter what kind of family you have—straight, gay, married, single parent, separated, no kids, two kids, 20 kids . . . we all go through the human comedy. But if the bonds are strong enough, and the desire is there, you can get to the other side, still together and still a family" (Cholodenko 2010, 1). Unapologetic about the subject matter, eschewing tragedy, Cholodenko and Stuart Blumberg, her cowriter, definitely tried to change the rules for what goes into mainstream LGBT filmmaking. Devoid of obvious monsters, villains, or victims, the film offers fine acting and an upbeat story. Like all good comedies, *The Kids Are All Right* contains dimensional characterization and poignant scenes; one could argue that the depth and authenticity emerge from Cholodenko's sexual identity. Among the four recent filmmakers we discuss here, Cholodenko is the only one who is gay.

In *The Kids Are All Right*, Nic and Jules have been together a long time, and their marriage shows signs of strain. Their sexual relationship appears to have reached a point of infrequent and unsatisfying encounters and Nic, a physician, has grown rather tired of Jules's repeated efforts to find herself. Jules has run through at least two failed careers: architecture and a Balinese furniture business. Her latest venture to become a freelance landscaper meets with skepticism from Nic. More or less the sole breadwinner of the family, Nic seems tired, cranky, and frustrated, and her reliance on wine to de-stress creates tension for Jules, who believes Nic has a drinking problem. From Jules's point of view, Nic has become distant and unsupportive, and Jules feels neglected.

When the kids, Joni (Mia Wasikowska) and Laser (Josh Hutcherson), introduce Paul to Jules and Nic, Jules becomes instantly infatuated with him. They share a love for gardening, so of course she finds the support she lacks from Nic. Paul's charismatic, spontaneous personality, along with his biological link to her children, intensifies the chemistry. The attraction leads to an affair, setting off a series of events that culminate in a heartwrenching scene in which Nic realizes what is happening during a dinner party between Paul and the entire family. Bening's attempt at composure constitutes a brilliant piece of acting, a performance that becomes the centerpiece of the film's authentic rendering of betrayal in a lesbian relationship.

Certainly, Cholodenko and Blumberg deserve praise for their film, one that unapologetically embraces gay families and targets both straight and gay audiences. The film ends without death or punishment for the characters, and the family rebuffs Paul, the outsider, and stays together. Still, the film in many ways offers the same formulas that have bogged down cinematic representations of lesbians in the past. In an interview about her pioneering movie *Desert Hearts* (1986), Donna Deitsch commented that she wanted to make a lesbian movie that didn't end with "a suicide, a murder, or a bisexual triangle" (Silverstein 2013). With *The Kids Are All Right*, although the family remains intact at the end, the bisexual triangle undermines that very family and resounds with heterosexism. Sex between Nic and Jules is represented in a single comedic but unsettling scene in which they watch gay male porn to get aroused and then are interrupted and abruptly end the encounter. In contrast, the sex between Jules and Paul is wild and intense, suggesting that hetero sex is more valid and more exciting than lesbian sex. When Laser announces at the end that he does not think Nic and Jules should break up because they are "too old," one wonders whether co-writers Cholodenko and Blumberg are celebrating the gay family or reinforcing the idea that even gay families must resign themselves to staying together "because of the kids." Yes, Nic and Jules stay together, but their relationship has been shattered by betrayal. We might even argue that their relationship is irrevocably broken by a hurtful transgression into heterosexuality.

In discussing the sexual relationship between Jules and Paul, Cholodenko maintains that sexuality is fluid, and that we should be past blaming or judging Jules for having sex with a man. She eschews lesbian feminist ideology as limiting (Anderson 2010). In interrogating that point of view, we wondered whether the filmmakers might simply be seeking a wider audience, one whose heterosexuality might more closely identify with a heterosexual character and heterosexual coupling. Did Blumberg, a heterosexual, encourage such a plot twist? Could Cholodenko and Blumberg have introduced another woman to provide conflict rather than a heterosexual male? Ultimately, *The Kids Are All Right* broke new ground for gay filmmakers to succeed in a mainstream market, but at the cost of relying on pervasive heteronormativity.

## BEGINNERS

Heterosexual writer and director Mike Mills's 2011 film *Beginners* was not positioned as an LGBT film, but its inclusion of a gay theme makes it an appropriate subject for this chapter. *Beginners* also garnered much critical acclaim, with Christopher Plummer winning the Oscar for Best Supporting Actor in 2012. The film is an homage to Mills's father, a gay man who married a woman out of obligation. He and his wife both knew that he was gay, but hoped that he could change. At age seventy-five, he came out after his wife died and entered a long-term, happy relationship with a younger man, but died of cancer several years later. Flashing back and forth in time, *Beginners* beautifully captures the joyous coming out of Hal (Christopher Plummer), his long, unhappy marriage, and the sad, lonely childhood of Oliver (Ewen McGregor). Oliver's childhood, in which he knows his parents are miserably disconnected, leaves him unable to commit to a relationship with a woman. As he grieves his father's death, so too he grieves his father's closeted life, wondering whether Hal experienced numerous anonymous sexual encounters with men or none at all.

The title refers not only to Hal's nascent sexual openness but also to Oliver's beginning a relationship with a woman. As Oliver learns to accept his father's demise, he begins to allow himself to risk commitment to Anna (Melanie Laurent). Anna, whom Mills has said is not based on his own wife but on himself, also fears commitment, so their slowly growing relationship creates tremendous dramatic tension. A sensitively written and beautifully performed film, *Beginners* rightfully deserved the accolades it received, offering an honest, touching portrait of the agony of leading a closeted life, the buoyancy of coming out, the despair of grief, and the joy of falling in love. At the same time, we once again see a film that explores tragedy: forty-five years of repressed gay sexuality, followed by a too-brief period of acknowledging and acting on that sexuality. Hal's death at age seventy-nine, realistic as it is (and based on fact), nevertheless reinforces the all-too-prevalent notion that being gay leads to tragedy. Moreover, the heterosexual story line eclipses the gay one.

With the exception of *The Kids Are All Right*, each of these four films invites us to question whether Hollywood can ever fully embrace being gay as a cause for celebration without framing queer life within heterosexuality. In an era in which gay marriage may soon become legal throughout the United States, when films and television include more gay and lesbian characters, we find ourselves disappointed by portrayals in the first decade of the twenty-first century. Most mainstream films still promote a hegemonic, patriarchal, heterosexist sensibility. When films do allow queer visibility, we are still subjected to the same villains, monsters, and victims, or queers appear in supporting, tangential, often buffoonish roles. Granted, the four films analyzed here provide authentic and moving portrayals of gay men and lesbians, but the portrayals continue to suggest that it is sad to be gay. And even when tragedy does not occur, plots often devolve into heterosexist notions of sexuality, as with *The Kids Are All Right*. As lesbian scholars who encourage positive perspectives on the LGBT community, both in our teaching and our writing, we look forward to the time when mainstream queer films abound, films that resonate with original, complex characters, plots, and themes embracing the diversity and validity of the queer experience without relying on worn-out formulas and stereotypes.

## REFERENCES

Adler, A. (Producer) and Melnick, D. (Director). 1982. *Making love* [Motion Picture]. USA: Twentieth-Century Fox.

Anderson, J. 2010. "Interview: Lisa Cholodenko—Feelin' all right." *Combustible Celluloid*. www.combustiblecelluloid.com/interviews/lisac.shtml.

Avnet, J. (Producer), and D. Aaronofsky (Director). 2010. *Black swan*. [Motion Picture]. USA: Fox Searchlight Pictures.

Barnhurst, K. (Ed.). 2007. *Media queered: visibility and its discontents*. New York: Peter Lang.

Brillstein, B. (Producer), and R. Epstein and J. Friedman (Directors). 1995. *The celluloid closet* [Motion Picture]. USA: HBO.

Cholodenko, L. 2010. "Two moms and a baby." *Harper's Bazaar*, July 9 (1). http://www.harpersbazaar.com/magazine/feature-articles/lisa-cholodenko-the-kids-are-all-right-0810.

Cooke, Rachel. 2010. Interview with Lisa Cholodenko. *The Guardian*, October 3 (1). www.guardian.co.uk/film/2010/lisa-cholodenko.

Dyer, R. 1984. *Gays and Film*. New York: Zoetrope.

———. 2001. "Stereotyping." In M. G. Durham and D. Kellner (Eds.), *Media and cultural studies: Keyworks* (353–65). Malden, MA: Blackwell.

Ebert, R. 2004. "Review of Monster." *Chicago Sun-Times*, Jan. 1. http://rogerebert.suntimes.com/apps/pbcs.dll/article?AID=/20040101/REVIEWS/40310032/1023.

Gross, L. 2001. *Up from invisibility: Lesbians, gay men, and the media in America*. New York: Columbia University Press.

Levy-Hinte, J. (Producer), and L. Cholodenko (Director). 2010. *The kids are all right* [Motion Picture]. USA: Alliance Films and Focus Features.

Mulvey, L. 1975. "Visual pleasure and narrative cinema." In *The sexual subject: a screen reader in sexuality*, edited by M. Merck (1992), 22–34. New York: Routledge.

Proulx, A. 2011. "Interview about Brokeback Mountain." *Youtube*, April 18. http://www.youtube.com/watch?V=VpCaQSRwddd0.

Russo, V. 1981, 1987, 1995. *The celluloid closet: Homosexuality in the movies*. New York: HarperCollins.

Schamus, J. (Producer), and A. Lee (Director). 2005. *Brokeback mountain* [Motion Picture]. USA: River Road Entertainment.

Silverstein, M. 2013. "Interview with Donna Deitch, director of *Desert Hearts*." *Huffington Post*, http://www.huffingtonpost.com/melissa-silverstein/interview-with-donna-deit_b_111723.html.

Theron, C. (Producer), and P. Jenkins (Director). (2003). *Monster* [Motion Picture]. USA: DEJ Productions.

Towne, R. (Producer), and R. Towne (Director). 1982. *Personal best* [Motion Picture]. USA: Warner Bros.

Weintraub, J. (Producer), and W. Friedkin (Director). 1979. *Cruising* [Motion Picture]. USA: Lorimar Productions/United Artists.

Wyler, W. (Producer), and W. Wyler (Director). 1961. *The Children's Hour* [Motion Picture]. USA: United Artists.

Urdang, L. (Producer), and M. Mills (Director). 2011. *Beginners* [Motion Picture]. USA: Focus Features.

Vachon, C. (Producer), and K. Peirce (Director). 1999. *Boys Don't Cry* [Motion Picture]. USA: Fox Searchlight Pictures.

# FIVE

## To *Glee* or Not to *Glee*

### *Exploring the Empowering Voice of the Glee Movement*

### Lori Montalbano

"You are my hero." Four words. Four words that encapsulate the power of the message of *Glee*, the impact that it has on an audience, the power not only to entertain, but to help define a generation of acceptance. I heard my 13-year-old daughter speak these words as she came face to face with her hero, Chris Colfer—the actor who portrays the iconic character of Kurt Hummel on *Glee*. For her, Colfer has become a figure of inspiration for what can be . . . in her life and in the world. As an aspiring artist, my daughter identifies with the actor who has been intricately involved in defining and developing his televised character. I observed my daughter as she looked into Colfer's eyes and witnessed a connection that demonstrated not only identification, but also sincere appreciation.

The phenomenon that is *Glee* has established an important site of dialogue and contestation that allows multiple perspectives on life and love relationships that define us as human beings. It is this approach that separates *Glee* from other ratings giants. For adolescents, *Glee* offers a message of "acceptance" that allows important identification and individuation to occur. The power that is *Glee* resonates beyond the hour-long dramatic ride through the characters' lives, bursting through social media venues that keep the themes as well as the dialogue continuously open.

It is for this reason that *Glee* has been honored with accolades and awards for its unprecedented participation in televised rhetoric of both straight and LGBT adolescent experiences. Of note, for example, are the

GLAAD Media Awards of 2011, which awarded *Glee* with a tie for Outstanding Comedy Series for its portrayal of LGBT issues (Penn 2011). Producer Ryan Murphy claims that *Glee* is "about there being great joy to being different, and great pain" (Hedegaard 2010, 43). The rhetoric of acceptance promoted by *Glee* has resulted in a powerful message for contemporary American television. How can we account for this power? The *Glee* message is an ongoing social movement that has been created by the producers to integrate the lives and the messages promoted by the programming into the daily lives of their audiences—adolescents; young, aspiring artists looking for connections to characters that help them envision their own success in the performing arts; and members of the young LGBT community looking for a voice. In this chapter, we will explore the dynamic that is *Glee* and its impact on audience identification, acceptance, and understanding. That is, we explore the global message that the television program instills about the art of individuation. Relevant questions include: *What messages does* Glee *promote? What impact does this rhetoric have on the LGBT community? How does the rhetoric of* Glee *impact mainstream television? How does the rhetoric of* Glee *influence human experience?*

    *Glee*, according to Donahue (2010), "has sucked in young fans with its inventive mix of musical-theater brio, pop chart savvy and outsider empathy . . . generating substantial income across three platforms: TV, recording sales, and touring" (16). The producers of *Glee* have positioned the program strategically, well beyond its television timeslot. This has become the contemporary practice to retaining audiences. Wood and Baughman (2012) contend, "as a testimony to the convergence between television and the massive global network that is the Internet, television programmers have been cashing in on the 'enhanced television' phenomena with intentions of building viewer loyalty, widening audiences, and increasing retention (Fahey 2000; Griffin 1996)" (328). Further, Wood and Baughman (2012) contend that this convergence creates a participatory culture that is developed via transmedia storytelling by fans on Twitter and other social media venues. This cross-platforming technique facilitated by the producers and fans of *Glee* is manifested in tweeting by fans posing as characters and the *Glee* cast tweeting as their characters—and, on another level, as themselves. "These interactions are definitely transmedia storytelling but stick closely to the original narrative of the series, augmenting what happens in the program, rather than contradicting or ignoring it" (Wood and Baughman 2012, 336). This continual cross-platformed communication by and about *Glee* allows for an ongoing narrative sequence that situates the characters and audience in a relational configuration. This connection significantly reinforces the narratives of the characters as well as audience identification.

## METHODOLOGY

Multiple methods can be used to examine an audience's connection with a character. For *Glee* audiences, the connection can be explained by examining the concepts of convergence and identification, as well as applying a dramatistic analysis to the rhetorical significance of the *Glee* programming. To understand convergence, it is important to consider how empathy facilitates convergence. Pelias (1992) contends that through an empathic process, "a speaker and listener can come together" (93):

> They form a union or bond. The speaker becomes a part of the listener's affective world. The listeners take the speaker on an emotional level. Moving beyond a distanced recognition of the speaker's point of view, the listener merges with the speaker . . . emotions begin to correspond . . . convergence, then, is an act of identifying with the others' emotional state. (93–94)

For *Glee* audiences, this convergence moves beyond emotional empathy into identification that empowers them in the performance of their very lives. Herrick (2001) suggests that "rhetoric stresses commonality between a rhetor and an audience, something that . . . Burke termed identification" (9–10). This concept of identification is played out in significant ways through the narratives of the primary cast members of *Glee*, their experiences, and the context of the scene and plot development. To understand the impact of the dramatism imbedded in the *Glee* narratives, we will apply a pentadic analysis of the dramatistic process, including the elements of act, scene, agent, agency, and purpose. According to Burke, the *act* is that which has happened, "what took place, in thought or deed" (992). The scene refers to background or situation in which the act occurred. As for the agents, or the rhetors in this analysis, we will consider the primary characters of the show, focusing primarily on Kurt and Rachel, secondary characters, as well as their romantic counterparts. Burke describes agency as those strategies that are utilized by agents during the act, those words and actions used. We will examine this according to the overall purpose that lies in the motives of the action, and finally, examine how these actions become a catalyst for engagement.

## ACT

Imagine this: you walk down the hall, surrounded by your high-school counterparts. Your endorphins are pumping, feeling that unrivaled elation from performing an arousing musical set. Then, *bam!* You're drenched in a slushie for being an outcast, a member of the glee club. *That's high school*—the simultaneous unyielding desire to keep "undesirable" elements of the self invisible, yet trying desperately to shout it out loud and fit in. We all experience it to some degree. For the LGBT community, the reality is persistent, unrelenting, and often exponentially dangerous. This is the premise that propels *Glee*, as it examines the dynamic of sex and gender roles and relational dynamics, all while facilitating a voice that gets very little if any play in traditional televised programming. It is for this reason that simply the fact of *Glee*, or the *act* of *Glee*, becomes a significant arena for important social issues to play out, while simultaneously entertaining a wide-audience base. For our purposes, *act* will refer to the rhetorical words and actions of the characters of *Glee*, as well as the social media rhetoric that surrounds the show.

Dwight Conquergood (1991) states that "cultural performance becomes a venue for 'public discussion' of vital issues central to their communities, as well as an arena for gaining visibility and staging their identity" (187). The programming of *Glee* facilitates this venue through what Conquergood (1985) labeled a *dialogical performance* that "struggles to bring together different voices, world views, value systems and beliefs so that they can have a conversation with one another" (9). Further, Conquergood (1985) contends that "the aim of dialogical performance is to bring self and other together so that they can question, debate, and challenge one another" (9). Such engagement is manifested through the words and actions of the primary characters of *Glee*, the concurrent themes embedded in the episodes each week, and the indirect and direct interactions with the audiences or "Gleeks." The *Glee* arena has opened up dialogue surrounding adolescent themes of sexuality, self-esteem, and popularity, and has simultaneously touched on critical issues of suicide and domestic violence. Consider an episode in which Karofsky, a football player who displays a homophobic face, grapples with his own gayness and considers suicide, rather than face his ridiculing counterparts on the team. Coach Bieste, meanwhile, insists on the strength of her students yet remains in an abusive relationship until she shifts her perspective. This shift is facilitated by the student characters who compel her to change her submissive behavior by using her own rhetoric of empowerment.

What these examples have in common is the refuge or solace that the characters find in their classroom rehearsal space. They have membership in a club of outcasts. Their membership includes gays, straights, lesbians, bisexuals, socially ostracized adolescents, and students of diverse ethnicities and abilities. They all belong in the family that is *Glee*. This provides an important entrance into acceptance and identification with a wide range of audiences who are looking for a space to converge and identify.

Through each televised program, as well as the social media interactions that follow, the act of *Glee*—that is, the interactions and situations that are the act of this dramatistic process—allows for powerful agents to emerge.

SCENE

The scene is a small high school in Lima, Ohio. A teacher, Will Schuester, bored with the mundane activity of his daily teaching responsibilities coupled with the loss of his dreams of professional theater, lives vicariously through his students. Schuester forms a glee club that will welcome members from across the population of McKinley High. The atmosphere at McKinley is anything but supportive of this club. Through comedic representation of stereotypes, the ideology of the school is ultra-Midwestern, conservative, and lacking in spontaneity and spark. The students at McKinley are equally unaffected, with the exception of the handful of characters who enter our living rooms each week and who "shake up" the stale normalcy of the middle-America high school experience.

As the show progresses in its first season, we see characters audition for spots in the "out-group" that is the glee club. The sustainability of the choral program is directly tied to cooperation between the greatest antagonists. Imagine this scenario: recruiting football players who throw glee club members into trashcans, lock a young man in a wheelchair into a Port-a-Potty, and continually harass glee club members with slushies in their faces. Yet through it all, the glee club members break out in song, showing a talent and perseverance and love for performance that keeps us coming back for more.

AGENT

The primary characters of *Glee* include Kurt Hummel and Rachel Berry. Kurt is a young gay student who begins his high school experience by hiding his sexual orientation from his family, his friends, and the McKinley community. His character has a quiet and loving demeanor; his talent is breathtaking and seemingly innate. Immediately, as he makes his first on-screen appearance, we fall in love with his personality and feel a tremendous amount of empathy for his need to cover up his true identity. Over the course of many seasons, we witness Kurt grow into his ability to express who he is, reach out to a significant love interest (Blaine), and mature as he accepts and embraces who he is. We watch as his father discloses his acceptance when Kurt comes out. We see his glee club family simply love Kurt for being Kurt. Kurt ultimately represents a message of acceptance for members of the gay community as a valuable and heroic figure within popular culture.

Rachel is a sensationally talented, Broadway-bound, Jewish heterosexual. Raised by two fathers, Rachel has an open view of human relationships. She is a key player in the glee club. She is the obvious choice for most leads and solos, a dedicated artist, a good student, and consequential geek. Her passion and drive for her dreams are contagious, and her dreams seem quite attainable as she powerfully executes her passion as a vocal connoisseur. She represents a naiveté with which audiences like to empathize.

There are other pivotal characters that include the aforementioned Will Schuester (protagonist) and his controversial and outspoken antagonist, Sue Sylvester, coach for the Cheerios (cheerleading squad). Sue is the "Archie Bunker" of McKinley High. She is rude and brash. She is insensitive, often making very stereotypical and inappropriate racist, sexist, homophobic, and classist remarks. Her character is key in that she blatantly exposes the ridiculous nature of the negative hate speech and actions that typify the realities of individuals who actually hold such egregious attitudes.

Other key characters in the glee club include Quinn Fabray, a teen mother, Cheerio, and, ironically, the president of the celibacy club; Finn Hudson, Rachel's romantic counterpart, who struggles with his role as a jock on the football team and his simultaneous love of performing onstage; Santana and Brittany, lesbian lovers on the cheerleading squad; Sam, from a working-class household; Puck, a stereotypical "bad boy"; Mercedes, a strong and talented African American; Artie, a wheelchair-bound songster with a huge heart and a contagious smile; and Mike and Tina, an Asian couple whose talent becomes highlighted later in the *Glee* run.

Each week, we become intricately involved in the life drama and relational complications of the characters. The relationships convey many of the traditional dramas of adolescents' lives, including issues of popularity and sexuality. The relationships are multilayered and evolve around themed storylines and musical expression. The themes are often grounded in contemporary events: for example, the reduction of funding available for arts programs in public education. As in most televised programming, friends struggle, families interfere, and sexual partners change. As relational dynamics change, sexual orientations are often examined—for example, when Brittany dates Sam while she is actually in love with Santana. As the characters make sense of their lives and feelings, audience members participate passively through empathy and actively through social media venues.

## AGENCY

The agency of the *Glee* characters is exhibited through their interactions, their dialogue, and the themes embedded in the musical selections. To examine agency, I selected scenes from two episodes of *Glee*, Season 1, to analyze. In Episode 3, "Acafellas," Mercedes is feeling left out without a love interest. Kurt shows her attention, spends time with her, and lets her know that she is important to him. Mercedes misconstrues his intentions, believing that they are becoming a couple. What Kurt and the audience know is that Kurt is gay and sees Mercedes only as a friend. Their dichotomous feelings become apparent in a scene where Mercedes asks Kurt to make their relationship official and public. When he informs her that they are just friends, she begins to lash out against him, and in an action-packed and violent burst of song, she sings, "I smashed the windows out your car," believing that Kurt is looking at another woman. In fact, however, Kurt is looking at a male character, his eyes conveying feelings of love and lust. It is only later that Kurt discloses to Mercedes that he is gay, and what follows is the growth of a new and sustained friendship between the characters.

In Episode 4 from Season 1 ("Preggers"), we learn about Kurt's inability to share his sexual orientation with his father. To appease his father's narrow view of masculinity, Kurt joins the football team as a kicker. In this episode, Kurt saves the day by exhibiting his flamboyant and ultra-glee-club ritual of dancing to "Single Ladies (Put a Ring on It)" just before making a superb kick that propels the team to victory. The absurdities of these two scenes are no match for the strategies of inclusion that are embedded in the rhetoric. In this episode, we watch Kurt struggle until he finally converses openly with his father. Kurt states, "I'm gay." His father replies, "I know. I've known since you were three. All you wanted for your birthday was a pair of sensible heels. I guess I'm not totally in love with the idea [but] I love you just as much." These strategies, or agencies, move the conversation of acceptance forward through a dynamic and entertaining path.

PURPOSE

There seem to be many purposes of the *Glee* movement. One purpose is, of course, to entertain. This will always be a driving force behind any television production. Yet, the purpose reaches out across social media through the power of music, the rhetoric of the lyrics in the musical selections, and the situations and conversations of the primary characters. Within the larger purpose to entertain, gain ratings, and create a sustainable and profitable vehicle, there appears to be an equally compelling social movement that is being promoted by the rhetoric of this *Glee* movement. This purpose of Glee is to promote alternative rules of engagement, to facilitate a voice for all individuals—despite sexual orientation, ethnicity, socioeconomic status, or ability. With that purpose, *Glee* has become a site of dialogic engagement for issues of sexuality, relationships, culture, violence, suicide, and dreams. Consequently, *Glee* has become an arena for young audiences to rethink sexual stereotypes, the consequences of hate rhetoric, and the possibilities of a rhetoric of acceptance.

## DISCUSSION

*Glee* has positioned itself as a leader in television and social media programming. Using cross-platforming strategies, as well as a successful
strategy of identification, the *Glee* movement has garnered increased attention and provided a venue for increased dialogue regarding issues
that directly affect the LGBT community. This progress is significant
within the current, more traditional television line-up. The producers of
*Glee* have provided an arena for young audience members to participate
in the life experiences of the characters that represent *them*. The characters are diverse; they represent multiple perspectives and levels of understanding and experiences. The relationships among the characters provide a dialogic interaction that often tests issues directly affecting our
youth—including homophobic, racist, and sexist behaviors; stereotypical
thinking; bullying; and violence—by turning them upside down, con-
fronting them, and demonstrating how to overcome the obstacles they
present. The *Glee* message has become an empowering and important
one for all viewers, particularly for the adolescent LGBT community. As
a member of a "Gleek" household, I have witnessed the power of the
message first-hand, as I, too, laughed, cried, and sang along with the
compelling and talented characters of *Glee*.

## REFERENCES

Burke, Kenneth. 1990. "From a grammar of motives." In *The Rhetorical Tradition: Read-
    ings from Classical Times to the Present*, edited by Bizzell and Herzberg, 992–1018.
    Boston: Bedford Books of St. Martin's Press.
Conquergood, Dwight. 1985. "Performing as a moral act: Ethical dimensions of the
    ethnography of performance." *Literature in Performance* 5: 1–13.
———. 1991. "Rethinking ethnography: Towards a critical cultural politics." *Commu-
    nication Monographs 58*, 179–94.
Donahue, Ann. 2010. "Gleek love." *Billboard* 122 (18): 16–19.
Fahey, M. 2000. "Brands across the web." *Cable World* 25 (10): 18.
Griffin, J. 1996. "The Internet's expanding role in building customer loyalty." *Direct
    Marketing* 59 (7): 50–53.
Hedegaard, Erik. 2010. "*Glee* gone wild." *Rolling Stone* (1102): 42–49.
Herrick, James A. 2001. *The history and theory of rhetoric: An introduction*. Second edi-
    tion. Boston: Allyn and Bacon.
Pelias, Ronald J. 1992. *Performance studies: The interpretation of aesthetic texts*. New York:
    St. Martin's Press.
Penn, Denise. 2011. "GLAAD honors *Glee* and *Modern Family*." *Lesbian News* 36 (10): 14.
Wood, Megan M. and Linda Baughman (2012). "*Glee* fandom and Twitter: Something
    new, or more of the same old thing?" *Communication Studies* 63 (3): 328–44.

*Part II*

# Performances of Sexuality and Gender

# SIX

# A Pregnant Pause, a Transgender Look

## Thomas Beatie in the Maternity Pose

### Kristen Norwood

While the image may now be considered iconic in its own right, the image of Thomas Beatie (known as "The Pregnant Man") that appeared in *The Advocate* in 2008 referenced another iconic image, the pregnant nude in maternity pose. In doing so, the image was able to draw upon and challenge the meanings of this iconic image, as the body of Thomas Beatie starkly diverges from the bodies we typically see in such an image. In this chapter, I interrogate the particulars of the image to show how it is a visual text that is both rhetorically and politically significant. I argue that in asking the audience to view Beatie's engineered maleness in the same frame as his pregnant belly, the image achieves a *transgender gaze* (Halberstam 2005) that moves transgender politics forward.

### VISUAL RHETORIC AND THE ICONIC IMAGE

It is often said that a picture is worth a thousand words. This saying holds particular weight for scholars of visual rhetoric who analyze artifacts of visual culture as texts which are infused with, reflect, produce, and reproduce cultural discourses (Mitchell 1994). Attending to artifacts of visual culture allows for a critical consideration of the ways meaning is (re)created and circulated through visual modalities. Feminists have long argued that visuality, or "the conditions of how we see and make meaning of what we see," (Jones 2003, 1) is a primary way in which gender is culturally extolled. Visual images are never ideologically immune; in effecting particular meanings, they serve ideological purposes (Reynolds 1997).

If images are never neutral, the iconic image is especially so. An iconic image is reproduced in subsequent images through a recreation of the specific visual order of the original (Reynolds 1997). If images are never neutral, the iconic image is especially not, since it is reproduced in the context of recognizability; the image comes to represent a particular set of cultural meanings which are (re)appropriated when the visual order of the image is reproduced. Lucaites and Hariman (2001) explain that iconic images are "1) recognized by everyone within a public culture (2) understood to be representations of historically significant events (3) objects of strong emotional identification or response" (37).

The iconic image has the capacity to capture a fragment of a specific cultural moment. It acts as a public conversation piece and can come to be intimately associated with a particular cultural/historical event, a structure of feeling (Williams 1983). The rhetorical power of this iconic image lies in its ability to do the work that, at times, spoken or written discourse cannot do. It "focuses the viewer's attention on a particular enactment of the tensions that define the public culture . . . it repetitively conjures images of what is unsayable (e.g., because emotional) in print discourses otherwise defining the public culture" (Lucaites and Hariman 2001, 41). In this sense, visual rhetoric may be a valuable means for creating space for marginalized meanings to enter into public conversation.

## THE PREGNANT NUDE AND THE MATERNITY POSE

One iconic image represented in paintings and photography is the *pregnant nude*. Artists have painted pregnant nudes as early as the 1800s (Allara 1994). Allara argues that Alice Neel's series of pregnant nudes between the 1960s and 1970s were important feminist works in that they showed the female body in excess, in a state that was not appealing to the male gaze and therefore allowed for a female gaze. However, she argues that by the 1980s a new cultural ideal of fit pregnancy abounded, evidenced by maternity workout videos from Jane Fonda and books about how to keep the pregnant body firm and proportioned. The pregnant nude that once held potential to create new meanings for the allowable in the female form was reconfigured into a sexualized image, one that called for the pregnant body to (ironically) stay in shape. Allara argues that this pregnant perfection was epitomized in the pregnant nude photograph of Demi Moore that appeared on the cover of *Vanity Fair* magazine in 1991. Arguably, the circulation of this image was the catalyst for a new genre of photographs that depict pregnant nudes in what I call the *maternity pose*.

Most often, the maternity pose is recreated through the visual form that is seen in the Demi Moore photograph, with the woman turned to the side to both emphasize the pregnant belly and cleverly hide the genitals. One of her arms or a piece of fabric is used to cover the breasts, while the other arm cradles the stomach. The woman's face is serene; often, her gaze is directed toward the belly, or aimed up and away from the camera, creating a sense of far-away wonderment. The audience is presented with a female form that is both mother and sex object.

Following Demi Moore, other (fit and attractive) celebrities have appeared nude and pregnant in this recognizable pose, including Britney Spears and Christina Aguilera; but such images of serene yet sexualized pregnancy have dispersed into private culture as well, with many noncelebrities opting to have their pregnancies documented with (semi)nude photographs. An internet search for the phrase "maternity photography" results in a plethora of websites for photographers who specialize in such photos. The websites house pictures of pregnant women posing nude, covering breasts and genitals in ways similar to Moore. These photos, presumably hung in nurseries and living rooms, imply that the pregnant body has come to be seen as aesthetically pleasing.

As audience to such photographs, we do not see the messiness of a pregnant body. Instead, we see a contained protrusion of only the belly; the rest of the body remains trim and smooth. The strategic covering of the breasts and genitals serves as evidence that the pregnant female body is still a sexualized body—that there are parts of such a body that are indecent for public display. The things we see and do not see in the maternity pose speak to the ways in which pregnant bodies are culturally inscribed as feminine, sexual, acceptable, normal, and worthy of viewing, and are important for analyzing the image of Thomas Beatie, whose body took this visual code.

## THE BODY, SEX, AND GENDER

In differentiations between sex and gender, the body is often invoked as pre-given matter, marked naturally by sex and then culturally assigned a gender accordingly (Butler 1990; West and Zimmerman 1987). Butler (1993) problematizes this simple distinction, claiming that it is not enough to theorize gender as an interpretation of sex, because this leaves sex itself and the body under-theorized, resting too easily in the seemingly objective domain of biology/nature and thus outside of sociality and power. Naturalizing the sexed body has consequences for naturalizing difference. For certain corporeal configurations to be considered legitimate and therefore deserving of human subject-hood, others must exist outside of the realm of normality. That is, some bodies must fail in their materiality and be relegated to the abject. To have bodies that matter, you must have bodies that *don't* matter, which includes those that disrupt heteronormative scripts for sex and gender (Butler 1993).

Configurations of transgender, transsexual, and intersexed bodies qualify for what Butler describes as abjected. These bodies, unrecognizable against a dichotomized, heteronormative script for sexed/gendered bodies, are quite often denied legitimacy in social, legal, medical, and other cultural domains (Butler 2004). The heteronormative script prescribes particular ways that genitalia, secondary sex characteristics, appearance cues, and gender identity should align (Currah 2008). However, by way of physical conditions at birth, hormone therapy, surgery, and other means, bodies can depart from the strict binary of male or female. Currah argues, "trans people's bodies can confound conventional expectations . . . [they] have unexpected configurations in their particular *geographies*—for example, breasts with penises for some, male chests with vaginas in others—that produce a dissonance" (331). Bodies with nonconventional geographies become sites for alternative inscriptions of sex and gender. They exist as locations where discourses of biology, technology, and culture intersect and collide in ways that question what is possible for bodies, and what is considered real. One such body that has become a site for contestation is that of Thomas Beatie, also known as "The Pregnant Man."

## THOMAS BEATIE: MAN IN MATERNITY POSE

Thomas Beatie, a female-to-male transgender person who, in 2008, became pregnant with his first child, testified that he was once told by a reproductive endocrinologist to shave his facial hair and was later turned away because the physician and his staff were uncomfortable treating him. This anecdote relayed in an essay by Beatie that appeared in a 2008 issue of *The Advocate* shows outright resistance to a perceived misalignment of the body—a resistance that resulted in refusal of medical care. The fact that Beatie's beard kept him from reproductive care despite his female reproductive organs is testament to the material conditions considered allowable for a female and, conversely, a male body. The material of the male and the female are kept separate in our corporeal scripts, such that combinations of male and female materiality are unintelligible and problematic. One cannot *both* be pregnant *and* have facial hair. One cannot *both* be pregnant *and* not have breasts. One cannot *both* be pregnant *and* be a man. However, Thomas Beatie was indeed both pregnant and legally classified as male.

Public reactions to this story varied, but a common sentiment expressed on blogs was to deny Beatie's maleness, claiming that he was not *actually* a man if he was able to get pregnant (Currah 2008). This reaction to Beatie's news perpetuated the dichotomization of both sex and gender.

Male and female were placed in logical opposition to one another: if female, then not male, and vice versa. Specifically, Beatie's physical conditions were constructed as in contradiction to each other and in (partial) contradiction to his legal identity. The outward manifestation of the pregnancy, the belly, stood in blatant contrast to the legal identification of *male* and to Beatie's other gendered cues, like his full beard, short hair, and flat breasts. All of these conditions were presented to the public in the now recognizable photograph of Beatie that accompanied many, if not most, of the news articles about him. The photograph first appeared alongside Beatie's essay in *The Advocate* and became the image most often associated with the story, evidenced by a Google image search of his name.

In the photograph, we see an unfamiliar body taking on a familiar position. Beatie is presented to us as the iconic pregnant nude in the maternity pose. Read as a rhetorical text, the photograph of a pregnant female-to-male transgender person taking up the body position so well known to us as one that women (and, specifically, mothers) take is quite important for analyzing meanings of the body, of sex, gender, and of human possibility. In my analysis, I asked three questions of the image itself. First, "Why is Thomas Beatie presented to us as a pregnant nude in maternity pose?" Second, "In what ways does the image depart from the iconic image?" Third, "With what kind of body are we being presented in this image?" Next, I asked three questions about the effects of the image. First, "How are we called as an audience to view Thomas Beatie's body?" Second, "What does this image do with/for discourses of sex, gender, and the body?" and third, "What implications does the circulation of this image hold for transgender politics?" I now turn to the image with these questions in mind.

## The Iconic Image

The significance of the use of the iconic image should not be understated. Beatie positions his body as many women have before him. He is turned to the side to emphasize the pregnant belly, and the genitals are hidden from view. Beatie looks somewhere beyond the camera's frame with a serene gaze. His hand rests on his belly, directing the audience's attention toward it and showing Beatie's connection to the fetus inside. This is a meaningful visual code. For Demi Moore and others who followed, it is a statement that the female body can be sexual and beautiful in its pregnant excess (as long as the rest of the figure is contained). It at once shows the female as life-giver and sex object, as mother and provocateur. However, by placing a pregnant *man* in this pose, the audience is faced with juxtaposition. Are we to interpret Thomas Beatie as mother? As sex object? Are we to interpret this as a female body *because* it is presented in the visual code of female bodies before it and disregard the

many male cues? Or, is it that we are made to view Beatie this way so that
we must question what kinds of bodies can be legitimately presented in
this pose? It seems juxtaposition is the key in reading the image as a text,
and so it is important to note the elements of the image that offer contradiction.

### Departure from the Icon: With What Kind of Body Are We Presented?

The image presents us with many cues that exist in contrast to the
pregnant belly and the traditional maternity pose. First, Beatie's right
arm is not used to shroud his chest. Nothing covers the body where
female breasts would appear, as is expected from a (sexualized) iconic
maternity pose. Instead, the audience is presented with a lack of
breasts—a non-sexualized male chest, and therefore one is allowed for
public viewing. In this important way, the Beatie image departs from the
traditional maternity pose and so calls the audience's attention to this
important difference in his body and the bodies of pregnant nudes before
him. He removes the sexual objectification from the maternity pose and,
in effect, blocks the male gaze (Mulvey 1975). It is important, though, that
we still see Beatie shirtless. He has both a pregnant belly and a male
chest, and by viewing this material configuration we are forced to consider the body in seemingly contradictory and imaginative ways, and to
wonder what materiality exists (or doesn't) between his legs.

A closer look at Beatie's chest reveals two scars below the nipples.
Since no effort was made to conceal these, we are asked to view them in
the same frame as the pregnant belly. The scars remind us that this body
once had female breasts, but also that there was a choice made to remove
them—to use science and medicine to create male materiality and erase at
least this element of femaleness. The scars trace the history of, and stand
as a marker of agency in, his embodiment. It is not only these scars that
put discourses of science and medicine in play with discourses of sex and
gender, but the combination of these scars with the belly. The audience
must consider how a person who has had female breasts removed, and
has body and facial hair that signal "male," was able to become pregnant.
We might wonder, did he not want to be *fully* male or female? Is there a
legitimate space between in which one can exist? And if the scars represent a choice to erase femaleness, why would Beatie also choose to embody the epitome of femaleness by becoming pregnant? In what ways
did science and medicine intervene to produce not only this body but this
pregnancy? The image compels the audience to reconsider that sex and
gender are binary as well as what is and is not "real" regarding sexed/
gendered bodies.

These seemingly conflicting signs of maleness and femaleness marked
by the natural and the technological produce what Halberstam (2005)
calls a *technotopic aesthetic,* or a "collision of postmodern space and post-

modern embodiment . . . one that tests technological potentialities against the limits of a human body anchored in time and space, and that powerfully reimagines the relationship between the organic and the machinic" (103). Through the circulation of this image, Thomas Beatie's body becomes technotopic: a site of creation, of technological innovation, and of reimagining the possibilities of the body. Borrowing from Halberstam, it is "a body situated in an immediate and visceral relation to the technologies . . . that have marked, hurt, changed, imprinted, and brutally reconstructed it" (Halberstam 2005, 116). Beatie's material intersexuality constitutes an unstable embodiment, aided by technology that tests the limits of representation and recognition.

Adding to the ability of this image to test a viewer's episteme are other signs of maleness. Beatie not only lacks female breasts but has considerable hair under his arms, a beard and mustache, and a masculine hairstyle. He has a strong jaw and muscular shoulders. He wears a men's wedding ring on his left ring finger. In fact, if the pregnant belly were missing and we were not allowed to view the scars on his chest, we would likely interpret his body as only male. Or perhaps, if Beatie were not presented to us in the nude maternity pose, we might interpret his protruding abdomen as a "beer belly," which in some social groups is the epitome of masculinity (Coles 2007). Considering these alternative interpretations makes it even clearer why Beatie was presented to us in an iconic context. Beatie's ability to simultaneously embody the maternity pose and depart from it makes this image rhetorically significant.

## Transgender Gaze

Given all of the elements of this photograph—the nude body, the pregnant belly, the refusal to cover breasts, the chest scars, the body and facial hair, the wedding ring, the jaw-line, and the meanings these elements evoke—we must consider how the audience is called upon to view the body of Thomas Beatie. Beatie's postmodern embodiment challenges not only ideas about the legitimate, heteronormative sexed body, but also challenges ideas about the transsexual body. From the news articles about him, we know that Beatie was born female but is legally classified as male. Yet, his body has not been made to configure strictly to male or female.

Through the juxtapositions of his materiality and of the image, Beatie's is presented as a transgender body. Halberstam distinguishes between this and a transsexual body, arguing that, "If the transsexual body has been deliberately reorganized in order to invite certain gazes and shut down others, the transgender body performs self as . . . possibility . . . as an effect of deliberate misrecognition" (97). Because Beatie's body is presented to us as transgender, not easily placed in the category of male or female, the image produces a transgender gaze.

Halberstam discusses the transgender gaze as akin to Mirzoeff's (2002) transverse look. Both Halberstam and Mirzoeff describe these as ways of seeing that deconstruct compulsory heterosexual modes of being. Halberstam argues that an aesthetic of turbulence "inscribes abrupt shifts in time and space directly onto the gender ambiguous body, and then offers that body to the gaze as a site of critical reinvention. Within this turbulence we can locate a transgender look, a mode of seeing and being seen that is not simply at odds with binary gender but that is part of a reorientation of the body in space and time" (107). In illuminating the concept of the transgender look, Halberstam analyzes a painting by Jenny Saville of a transgender photographer named Del LaGrace Volcano. In Saville's *Matrix*, Volcano is painted nude, lying on a slab. If this were a photograph, we would imagine the camera positioned at the same level as Volcano's body, facing him and hovering to the left side of his right thigh, shooting him from bottom to top, so that the genitals are closest to the camera. Volcano looks over and around his body, toward the audience who is positioned to view the vagina first, then to trace up the body to see a pair of ample breasts, and then up to a face that seems to belong to a man. Halberstam reasons that at the point the audience comes face to face with the seemingly male head on the seemingly female body, we are compelled to look again at the vagina in an effort to reconcile the contradiction we observe. Halberstam argues that Volcano's "mutant maleness" (Volcano 1999, 25) is preserved in the portrait, not diminished. She claims, "in its flawed balance between maleness and femaleness, Volcano's body offers a map of the loss and longing that tinges all *transsexual* attempts to 'come home' to the body. But that same map locates the *transgender* body as a paradigm for the impossibility of bodily discomfort" (2005, 111; emphasis in original).

Halberstam concludes that by presenting Volcano's body in this way, the artist creates a transgender gaze. The audience cannot cleanly fit this body into either category and must see it as an alternative embodiment. This is precisely what we are called to do in viewing the image of Thomas Beatie. Together, the combination of the pose, the nudity, and the markers of male and female produce dissonance for viewers. Dissonance, as Stone (1992) argues, opens up space for multiple alterities. The abrupt shifts in time and space which constitute Beatie's body bring about a turbulence that forces the viewer to look up, down, and up again, and consider what kind of body is capable of being both biological mother and man. Through the transgender look, Beatie's body becomes a site for critical reinvention, for reimagining the possibilities of materiality, and in turn sex and gender.

## REPRESENTATION AND TRANSGENDER POLITICS

In her posttranssexual manifesto, Stone (1992) calls for transsexuals to cease attempts to pass as *either* male or female. By making the trans-body complicit with heteronormative notions of sex and gender, Stone argues the trans-identified person forecloses possibilities of polyvocality, and in effect commits violent erasures of subjectivity. She charges trans-identified persons to embrace intertextual bodies, because therein lies the "potential to map the refigured body onto conventional gender discourse and thereby disrupt it, to take advantage of the dissonances created by such a juxtaposition to fragment and reconstitute the elements of gender in new and unexpected geometries" (165).

Considering Beatie's body as a site of disruption brings us back to Butler's (1993) critique of the undertheorized sexed body. The way Beatie is presented to the audience, as an intersection of nature and culture, of biology and technology, of male and female, constructs this body as a site for theorization of sex and gender, as a site that protests simple distinctions and relationships between them. For example, a discourse of motherhood brought forth by the maternity pose at once feminizes Beatie's body and questions its femaleness. Things are further complicated by Beatie's essay, in which he said that he would be his daughter's *father*. With his image, Beatie calls on the audience to consider that the sexed body does not necessarily follow a linear path. The sexed body can veer from the genetic path, can come back to it again, and in doing so can create new possibilities. And with his claim to fatherhood—in spite of being pregnant—Beatie calls on us to consider that gender does not follow linearly from the sexed body, or more specifically, from its reproductive capabilities. *Even though* he will give birth to his daughter, he will not be her mother. The simple relationships between body and sex, and between sex and gender, are muddied through Beatie's materiality, and by the juxtapositions of his body and the gender identity he claims for himself. His taking up of the maternity pose is a performance.

### Transgender Politics

If iconic photographs "reflect social knowledge and dominant ideologies, shape and mediate understanding of specific events and periods . . . influence political behavior and identity, and provide inventional (figurative) resources for subsequent communicative action" (Lucaites and Hariman 2001, 37–38), we must consider what worth Beatie's photograph has for transgender politics. If the audience were called to look upon Beatie with a heteronormative gaze, his body would be abjected, and therefore his subject-hood would be diminished or denied. However, since this photograph is able to accomplish a transgender look, calling the audience to consider Beatie's body as a postmodern possibility, the image does not allow for this body to be so easily dismissed. The transgender look positions Beatie as a body that matters.

In Stone's (1992) posttranssexual manifesto, she claims that politically significant meanings will be opened up if trans-persons can "rearticulate their lives not as a series of erasures . . . but as a political action begun by reappropriating difference and reclaiming the power of the refigured and reinscribed body" (190). If this is true, then we can consider the representation of Beatie as a step toward this goal, as the image points to reinscription and rearticulation in the boldest form. It forces us to see how sex is written, unwritten, and rewritten on the body, and incites confusion that creates a space for questions, leading us closer to a re-evaluation of sex and gender. It is when faced with bodies that stretch our episteme that we can begin to re-evaluate human possibility and therefore work toward a reframing of transgender rights as human rights.

In this chapter, I have shown that, in the case of Thomas Beatie, a picture *is* worth a thousand words. The widely circulated visual artifact featuring Thomas Beatie is a rhetorically and politically significant text. By presenting Beatie in the image of the iconic pregnant nude in the maternity pose, refusing to hide the juxtapositions of his body, the viewing audience is made to see Beatie through a transgender look. It is through this look that discourses of sex, gender, and the body can be renegotiated, and through this renegotiation of bodies that transgender politics are implicated and moved forward. This image of Thomas Beatie may itself become an iconic image for the transgender community, a visual artifact that evokes a particular structure of feeling, which marks a significant time for transgender rights and recognition.

## REFERENCES

Allara, P. 1994. "'Mater' of fact." *American Art* 2: 6–31.

Beatie, T. 2008. "Labor of love." *Advocate.* http://www.advocate.com/news/2008/03/26/labor-love.

Butler, J. 1990. *Gender trouble: Feminism and the subversion of identity.* New York: Routledge.

———. 1993. *Bodies that matter: On the discursive limits of "sex."* New York: Routledge.

———. 2004. *Undoing gender.* New York: Routledge.

Coles, T. 2007. "Negotiating the field of masculinity: The production and reproduction of multiple dominant masculinities." *Men and Masculinities* 12 (1): 30–44.

Currah, P. 2008. "Expecting bodies: The pregnant man and transgender exclusion from the employment non-discrimination act." *Women's Studies Quarterly* 3/4: 330–36.

Halberstam, J. 2005. *In a queer place and time: Transgender bodies, subcultural lives.* New York: New York University Press.

Jones, A. 2003. "Introduction: Conceiving the intersection of feminism and visual culture." In *The feminism and visual culture reader,* edited by A. Jones, 1–7. New York: Routledge.

Lucaites, J. L., and R. Hariman. 2001. "Visual rhetoric, photojournalism, and Democratic public culture." *Rhetoric Review* 20: 37–42.

Mirzoeff, N. (2002). "The subject of visual culture." In *The Visual Culture Reader* (second ed.), ed. N. Mirzoeff, 3–23. New York: Routledge.

Mitchell, W. J. T. 1994. *Picture theory: Essays on verbal and visual representation.* Chicago: University of Chicago Press.

Mulvey, L. 1975. Visual pleasure and narrative cinema. *Screen* 3: 6–18.

Reynolds, L. J. 1997. "American cultural iconography: Vision, history, and the real." *American Literary History* 3: 381–95.

Stone, S. 1992. "The empire strikes back: A posttranssexual manifesto." *Camera Obscura* 29: 151–76.

Volcano, D. L. 1999. "On being a Jenny Saville painting." In *Jenny Saville: Territories*, 24–25. New York: Gagosian Gallery.

West, C., and D. H. Zimmerman. 1987. "Doing gender." *Gender & Society* 2: 125–51.

Williams, R. 1983. *The long revolution.* New York: Columbia University Press.

Wood, J. T. 2006. "Gender and communication in interpersonal contexts: Introduction." In *The Sage handbook of gender and communication*, edited by B. J. Dow and J. T. Wood, 1–7. Thousand Oaks, CA: Sage.

# SEVEN

# The Rhetoric of Sexual Experimentation

*A Critical Examination of Katy Perry's "I Kissed a Girl"*

## Brittani Hidahl and Richard D. Besel

In June 2008, singer Katy Perry exploded onto the music scene with her hit single "I Kissed a Girl." The pop song quickly leapt to number one on the Billboard charts, becoming the summer anthem for a generation of young people. Within weeks, it seemed that every mall and radio station across the country was blasting Perry's saucy song. Her music was catchy enough that even seven-year-old girls were soon mindlessly singing along to it, without comprehending the real meaning behind the lyrics. Perry began appearing on talk and radio shows worldwide, proving that she had successfully infiltrated the world of the pop elite.

While media journalists were busy glamorizing Katy Perry's feisty attitude and pinup girl outfits, many others were criticizing the song, including, not surprisingly, right-wing religious conservatives who proclaimed that it advocated a gay lifestyle. One church in Ohio even went so far as to post this message on its marquee: "I kissed a girl . . . and then I went to hell." When asked about the sign, Reverend Dave Allison said, "It's not something that is really a shock if you're a scriptural person. We meant that as a loving warning to teens. . . . The Scriptures tell us that you should not do what the song tells you to do. The Scriptures are not ambiguous on this issue" (Lecker 2008). Joanne Brokaw, a Christian music blogger from *Beliefnet*, expresses similar views, saying, "I just think it's interesting that seven years ago she had a Christian album and what she's doing now is clearly not Christian" (Marikar 2008). Because so many organized religions believe that homosexuality is a sin, it is no surprise that these religious figures are critical about Perry's flippant attitude toward what they consider the immoral behavior of a lesbian kiss.

It is mildly surprising, however, that much of the homosexual world is no happier about Perry's song, believing that she is simply promoting and perpetuating stereotypes. *The New Gay* asked Perry in an interview, "Isn't ["I Kissed a Girl"] kind of like those straight girls who make out at frat parties to get guys' attention?" (Rosen 2008). Perry's song contains controversial lines that can be interpreted offensively for those lesbians who struggle to disprove negative stereotypes. One angry blogger on *afterellen.com*, a site devoted to "news, reviews and commentary on lesbian and bisexual women in entertainment and the media," expressed her disgust with the song, stating, "Perry has told the press, 'It's about the magical beauty of a woman.' Hmm. I didn't really get that." (Perry's lyrics call attention to the anonymous, experimental nature of the kiss.) The blogger continues, "How flattering! Lesbians love to be science projects" (Bendix 2008). The one thing that homosexuals and religious advocates can agree on is that Perry's song does not set a good example, although their reasons differ greatly.

No matter which group one chooses to side with, it is clear that Perry's portrayal of the lesbian experience is different from mediated depictions of years past. Images of gays and lesbians have changed in the past several decades, although not to the extent one might expect. Gay activist Vito Russo's famous book-turned-movie *The Celluloid Closet* examines Hollywood's homophobia from the very beginning of film. In his book, Russo documented "how lesbians and gay men, throughout the early decades of filmmaking, were either rendered completely invisible or portrayed in vague and coded ways, most of which were negative" (Signorile 2003, 231). Hollywood has slowly been transitioning from portrayals of gays as villains and killers to portrayals of gays as everyday men and women—a struggle that will surely continue into future decades.

Hollywood is not the only media outlet that has been changing the way homosexuals are portrayed to the general public. In fact, "TV treatment of lesbians and gays roughly parallels that of Hollywood film" (Fejes and Petrich 1993, 399). Negative stereotypes of gays were inserted into television from its earliest days, much like the stereotypes found in film. However, beginning in the 1970s, gay characters began to be humanized a little more, due to the gay and lesbian community's demands for change. This progress has continued, but the presentation of homosexuals on television is still problematic. "Gays and lesbians rarely are presented as members of a larger homosexual community," state Fejes and Petrich, and "gays and lesbians are secondary or occasional characters who exist primarily in a heterosexual environment" (1993, 402).

Recent media transformations have not been as revolutionary as one might expect. In 1987, Celia Kitzinger, a lesbian psychologist and current associate editor of *Feminism and Psychology*, argued that the recent shift in psychological research from the view of homosexuals as intrinsically deviant (which dominated in the 1970s and 1980s) toward a liberal-humanistic view of lesbians and gay men as "just like heterosexuals" was not as positive and progressive as it seemed. Rather, she claimed that this viewpoint reinforced the dominant social order by "presenting same-sex sexuality as a matter of private lifestyle, thereby neutralizing its political challenge to heterosexuality" (Diamond 2005, 104). So while it might seem that media portrayals of homosexual men and women have finally given the gay community an opportunity to expose their real lives, in fact the portrayals reflect heterosexual views of the gay world. Diamond further argues that a close reading of contemporary media depictions reveals that "heteroflexibility" is packaged in a manner designed specifically to titillate young male viewers and presents same-sex experimentation as a means of confirming one's essential heterosexuality. We argue that the "bi-curious" monologue of Perry's "I Kissed a Girl" entrenches the societal expectation of heteronormativity—the view that heterosexuality is the natural and normal sexual identity for individuals. We also explain how Perry's work is damaging to lesbians who strive to prove that their love is just as valid and worthwhile as a heterosexual couple's, mainly because the song conforms to, rather than defies, heterosexual expectations.

Perry's first single, "I Kissed a Girl," from her 2008 album *One of the Boys*, was scheduled to be officially released on May 6, 2008, but the reaction from listeners was so strong that the single was made available for purchase on iTunes on April 29, a week before its intended release ("Hottie Katy Perry," 2008). The song rose to fame after it was featured on an episode of the show *Gossip Girl* ("Katy Perry biography," n.d.). Within its first week, the song ranked number twenty-four on the Billboard Pop Singles chart. It climbed to number one on the Billboard Top 100 and held the spot for seven consecutive weeks. The song was so popular that it managed to stay on the Billboard chart for twenty-three consecutive weeks. The song also topped charts in other countries, including Canada, the United Kingdom, and New Zealand ("Katy Perry—I kissed a girl," n.d.). The song was nominated for a Grammy in the category of Best Female Pop Vocal Performance, but was beaten out by Adele's performance of "Chasing Pavements" (Past Winners Search 2013).

"I Kissed a Girl" presents an often-disregarded and -ignored lifestyle, but not necessarily in the most favorable or most accurate manner. Perry's lyrical choices need to be analyzed in order to discern whether or not her portrayal of sexual experimentation is a fair representation of a lesbian lifestyle. Many people who are not familiar with this way of life base their judgments of lesbians on the stereotypes portrayed in the media. "The media are likely to be most powerful in cultivating images of events and groups about which we have little firsthand opportunity for learning," states communication and cultural studies scholar Larry Gross. "Lacking other sources of information, most people accept even the most inaccurate or derogatory information about a particular group" (Gross 2001, 11). Furthermore, "minorities share a common media fate of relative invisibility and demeaning stereotypes" (12). Therefore, it is important to know what stereotypes are being presented so that the gay community can support or defend these labels, as needed.

To argue that Perry's bi-curious narrative in "I Kissed a Girl" plays into the societal expectation of heteronormativity, and to explain how Perry's song is degrading to lesbians, we must first explore Perry's personal life and her musical career to understand how her upbringing influenced her career choices. From there, we will examine which sexual identity is present in Perry's song and how that identity is constructed within the artifact. We analyze Perry's lyrics for evidence that both supports and resists heteronormativity and use this evidence to prove the claim that this song is detrimental to the lesbian couple who is attempting to demonstrate to society that their relationship is as meaningful as their heterosexual counterparts. Finally, we offer an example of a song that portrays homosexuality in an appropriate and meaningful way, in an attempt to provide an alternative to Perry's flippant approach to this serious topic.

## THE RISE OF KATY PERRY

Katy Perry was born Kathryn Hudson on October 25, 1984, in Santa Barbara, California. The daughter of strict Christian pastors, Perry grew up singing in churches. Perry states that her mother used to ban her from listening to "secular" music. However, after Perry heard a Queen album at a slumber party, her view of music changed forever. Perry states, "Freddie Mercury was—and remains—my biggest influence. The combination of his sarcastic approach to writing lyrics and his 'I don't give a f**k' attitude really inspired my music" ("Katy Perry: Queen of Rock," 2008). Perry also claims to be influenced by Alanis Morissette, and she actually worked with Morissette's producer, Glen Ballard. Her recordings with Ballard won her the title of "The Next Big Thing" from *Blender* magazine in 2004 and eventually helped lead to her signing with Capitol Music in the spring of 2007 ("Katy Perry biography," n.d.).

Perry quickly made a name for herself in the music industry with songs like "Ur So Gay," "I Kissed a Girl," "Hot N Cold," and "Waking Up In Vegas." However, this is not Perry's first attempt to infiltrate the music industry. She released her self-titled debut album in 2001 under her real name, Katy Hudson, at the age of sixteen. This album featured songs written and co-written by Perry, but the subject matter was vastly different from that of her 2008 album, *One of the Boys*. An album review by *Christianity Today* editor Russ Breimeier hailed Perry as a promising Christian singer: "I hear a remarkable young talent emerging, a gifted songwriter in her own right who will almost certainly go far in this business" (Breimeier 2001). Breimeier's prediction may have proven correct in the long run, but not in the religious venue that he was expecting.

After her first attempt at an album flopped, Perry did not give up. She adopted the pseudonym "Katy Perry," so as not to be confused with actress Kate Hudson, and adopted a new persona. Her Christian fans were not too happy with Perry's sudden role reversal, however. "It seems like ever since the name change, she's gotten this rep as a party girl," Breimeier stated. "You can still hear some of the talent that was there before, but it just sounds like she's doing whatever she can to get noticed" (quoted in Marikar 2008). Perry did get noticed, and in a big way. Pop star Madonna commended Perry's 2007 hit "Ur So Gay" on the Johnjay and Rich Show on KRQQ, stating that it was her "favorite song" and encouraging them to "check it out on iTunes." Madonna also went on to mention the song to Ryan Seacrest, telling him he "had to hear it." Thanks in part to the good press by Madonna, Perry's song gained popularity quickly. In fact, the "Ur So Gay" music video had one million views within a week of appearing on MySpace ("Hottie Katy Perry," 2008). Perry's career only escalated from there, with the release of her album *One of the Boys* in 2008.

On May 15, 2008, the California Supreme Court ruled that "sexual orientation, like race or gender, does not constitute a legitimate basis upon which to deny or withhold legal rights" (Mears 2008). Overnight, gay marriage became legal in Perry's home state. Homosexual couples from across the country rushed to California to take advantage of the chance to validate their relationship in the eyes of the law. But while gay rights advocates were celebrating, other groups, such as the Protect Marriage Coalition and Concerned Women for America, were planning their retaliation. On November 4, 2008, California voters passed a state amendment banning same-sex marriage. In the aftermath of the election results, neither side has given up. Gay rights advocates continue to strive for equal protection under the law, and right-wingers are intent on keeping marriage a heterosexual institution. In a time when the political opinions on gay rights are so heated, it is easy to see how Perry's song stirred up controversy.

## THE ORIGINS AND METHODS OF QUEER THEORY

The origins of what is today known as queer theory can be traced back to the late 1970s. In the time period after the 1969 Stonewall riots, "homosexuality began to lose its essentialist and uniform connotation while homosexual desire began to be positioned in a social and historical context" (Dhaenens, Van Bauwel, and Biltereyst 2008, 336). This encouragement to change the ways of thinking about homosexuality would ultimately lead to radical changes in gay and lesbian studies. However, the development in queer theory was definitely not the beginning of the gay liberation movement. In fact, homophile movements in Europe as early as the end of the nineteenth century fought to "have homosexuality recognized as a natural human phenomenon" (Jagose 1996, 22).

Social constructivism emerged in queer theory as the dominant approach for discussing identity and sexual orientation from both historical and cultural angles. Two important principles emerged from this approach: first, socially recognized sexual orientations vary culturally and historically; second, in cultures where heterosexuality and homosexuality are acknowledged, sexual behavior can move between these categories or incorporate both (Dhaenens, Van Bauwel, and Biltereyst 2008). In America, where basic gay and straight sexual identities are recognized, many alternative sexual identities have emerged, including bisexual, queer, questioning, intersex, and pansexual, among others.

While many people in the gay community adhere to one of these identities, others prefer not to affix a label to their identities. This reflects a core message of queer theory: the concept of resistance. Resistance is a conscious refusal of labels that emphasizes a retreat from binary thinking about sexuality. Queer theory embraces all "non-straight" sexual identities, not strictly gay or lesbian, to reverse society's assumptions about sexuality and gender (Dhaenens, Van Bauwel, and Biltereyst 2008). Queer theory's promotion of individuality and tolerance of differences encourages societies to look beyond their norms and at least be tolerant, if not accepting, of alternative sexualities.

Another identity against which homosexuals struggle, especially in media portrayals of the gay community, is an extension of the common straight identity. This portrayal is termed *heteronormativity*: the view that heterosexuality is natural and normal for individuals and society. "Heteronormativity does not just construct a norm, it also provides the perspective through which we know and understand gender and sexuality in popular culture" asserts Didi Herman, a professor of law and social change at the University of Kent Law School (Westerfelhaus and Lacroix 2006, 144). The principle of heteronormativity privileges heterosexuality in much the same way that whiteness privileges whites or patriarchy privileges men. From a queer perspective, one of the prevalent difficulties facing gay portrayals in the media is how to be "out in culture," otherwise described as "how to occupy a place in mass culture, yet maintain a perspective . . . that does not accept its homophobic and heterocentrist definitions, images, and terms of analysis" (Creekmur and Doty 1995, 2). No matter what the outcome, however, increased exposure in the media does not always equal increased visibility for gays and lesbians.

Visibility is one of the LGBT movement's main slogans, and it is to this end that everything from buttons and bumper stickers to shirts and suspenders are emblazoned with the gay pride rainbow. Annual gay pride parades and festivals flourish in the streets of many cities. Through increased visibility, "the queer movement seeks to acquire social acceptance, freedom, and basic safety for sexual minorities" (Galewski 2008). While this is a noble goal, it is proving to be a long, uphill battle.

Along with this increased visibility comes an ongoing concern with the way popular culture supports the conventions of mainstream heteronormativity. Many activists feel that these representations of homosexuals in the media in fact tame and contain, if not outright exclude, queer sexuality. The pervasiveness of the strategic rhetoric of heteronormativity enables heterosexual norms to shape how our own sexuality and the sexuality of others are understood, and "influence[s] which forms of sexuality are sanctioned and which are proscribed" (Westerfelhaus and Lacroix 2006, 428). "The popular media provide audiences with powerful ritual experiences that tap into and promote the mainstream's sociosexual mythology. These mediated rituals perpetuate the heterosexist social order, often at the expense of queers and queer sexuality" (Westerfelhaus and Lacroix 2006, 430). Sexual experimentation is one such example of a ritual experience that often only serves to reinforce heteronormativity. "In popular culture, kissing a woman is only permissible and sanctioned if a woman is already an avowed heterosexual," states "Fatemeh," a blogger on the feminist blog *Feministe*. "This drags up the male fantasy of lesbian women that perform on each other to please him instead of each other." There are many slang terms to describe stories of this type of experimentation, including "bi-curious" and "LUG" ("lesbian until graduation"). However, many of these stories ultimately end with the woman focusing on dating men, "not because they were pretending same-sex desire before but because they are giving in to intense social expectations now" (Baumgardner 2007, 41).

Another problem with the media's representation of lesbians is that the portrayals tend to be very polarized. At one end, we see the intensely butch woman, with her manly hairstyle and cargo shorts. At the other end is the femme, the "lipstick lesbian" who is ultra-feminine with long, flowing hair and stiletto heels. Within the context of the LGBT counterpublic, a hierarchy of queerness has developed in which the "butch has been enshrined as 'the gospel of lesbianism, inevitably interpreted as the true revelation of female homosexuality.' Conversely, femme gender performance has been considered a retro assimilationism, an unbearable surrender, an unaccountable selling-out" (Galewski 2008, 280). With this perspective of the femme woman as not a "real" lesbian, the public's perception of lesbians is not helped when ultra-feminine women such as

Katy Perry write songs that further downplay the significance and increase the sex appeal for men of an attractive woman kissing another woman.

Queer theorists have investigated the impact that queer music can have on identity formation and maintenance in the gay community. Driver (2007) asserts that "girls not only reference and discuss music with explicitly queer messages; they also offer interpretations of visual, verbal, and sonorous languages exceeding heteronormative codes, used as a part of their ongoing identity work" (196). Clearly, queer music is a central part of gay life, as it provides gays and lesbians with positive role models who are not afraid to be "out and proud." Driver also believes that "hav[ing] access to queer music . . . helps queer youth to counter the heteronormative ethos of their social environment" (198). The challenge in analyzing Perry's song is that Perry is neither a queer artist, nor is she seeking to act as a voice for the queer community. Therefore, it is difficult to argue that Perry is providing lesbians with any sort of positive identity formation; neither is she aiding in the acceptance of a lesbian or bisexual identity by questioning. Instead, Perry's song is only, in the words of gay activists, "reinforcing stereotypes and trivializing lesbianism" ("Musician of the year," 2008, 87). One of the ways in which Perry trivializes lesbianism in "I Kissed a Girl" is through her construction of a bi-curious sexual identity.

## HETERONORMATIVITY AND SEXUAL IDENTITY IN "I KISSED A GIRL"

It is important to note that the bi-curious sexual identity in the song is not Perry's; rather, it is the sexual identity of the narrator. "I love my men," stated Perry in an interview with *The New Gay* (Rosen 2008). "I'm not a lesbian, but I can appreciate the beauty of women." Perry openly admits that the song is merely a fantasy; "it's a song about curiosity," she asserts.

Although Perry herself is heterosexual, it is clear that the persona in her song is not, or is at least questioning her sexual identity. The narrator openly admits to having a boyfriend, yet she kisses a girl and "like[s] it" — a fact that is asserted nine different times in the song. Her curiosity to explore other sexual identities is clearly expressed throughout the song. It is also evident that the narrator is unsure about her sexual identity and is at least questioning an alternative to the heterosexual orientation.

"I Kissed a Girl" both supports and resists the concept of heteronormativity. Although the song presents a bi-curious monologue, it does so in a way that favors heterosexuality over homosexuality. From the very first line, the narrator dismisses the girl-on-girl kiss as anything remotely meaningful. She emphasizes the spontaneity of the act, almost proclaiming guilt. The narrator is trying to defer blame for the kiss, which she goes on to explain meant nothing. Perry herself even asserts "the song is about an obvious curiosity. It's not about anything intense" (Pratt 2008).

The emphasis on how the act of one girl kissing another is illicit and inappropriate is one of the ways in which this song supports heteronormativity. The narrator implies that good girls do not kiss other girls. And if they do, they most certainly should not enjoy the experience. The narrator further pushes this point in her lyrics. She asserts that a same-sex kiss between women feels unnatural, immoral, and naughty, underscoring the pressure that heterosexual culture places on all people, assuming that being straight is the natural and right course, and that any other sexual orientation is deviant.

This song also defends heteronormativity through its downplaying of the significance of a kiss between two women. By the third line of the song, the narrator has again shifted blame for the cause of the encounter, justifying her bi-curious kiss with her consumption of alcohol. "Perry is basically assuming the position of drunk sorority girl #1, kissing drunk sorority girl #2 for shock value and/or to catch the attention of her boyfriend," claims Marissa Moss, cultural critic, writer, and political communication consultant for *The Huffington Post* (2008). This is an image that we see all too often today in our predominantly heterosexual culture: girls kissing girls to garner attention.

The significance of this same-sex kiss is further downplayed in the emphasis the song places on experimentation. Clearly, the narrator is simply slipping into a lesbian persona for an evening. By mentioning that she does not know the recipient's name and that the anonymity is unimportant she not only objectifies the woman who is the recipient of her kiss but all women in general. The narrator further compares the girl to an article of clothing. Are we to assume that women can be discarded as easily as a shirt or tried on like a pair of old shoes? In this sense, Perry is not only damaging the image of lesbians, but that of all women. The narrator implies that this kiss is trivial and ultimately forgettable, just like the girl she kissed. This statement also furthers the misconception and stereotype that all lesbians are promiscuous. The image of the lesbian as a party girl who has one-night stands is only supported by Perry's lyrical choice.

Although Perry's song overwhelmingly supports the social construct of heteronormativity, there are several ways in which it attempts to defeat the heterosexual norm. The emphatic restatement of "I liked it" reinforces the fact that for some women, a same-sex kiss is fulfilling and pleasurable. These true lesbians and bisexuals do not kiss other women for attention or because they are drunk, but because they truly enjoy the act. The narrator also admits that she enjoyed the kiss, a statement that lesbians might agree with wholeheartedly. Perry also makes a brief claim that lesbianism is natural and attempts to frame the same-sex kiss as an ordinary occurrence, an innocent act, which begs the question: If the kiss were not an innocent experimentation and was, in fact, a display of lesbian passion, would the kiss then become less innocent?

Perry does claim to be sensitive to gay issues. In an interview with the popular gay magazine *The Advocate*, Perry stated, "I guess it is a subject that is close to my heart. I have a lot of friends who are gay, and I have kissed a girl. I grew up in a very strict household where that was considered what you call 'an abomination'—and I f*cking hate that word" (Pratt 2008). Perry can claim to be "a friend to the gays" all she wants; however, her dismissive treatment of such a serious topic suggests otherwise. It is nearly impossible to see Perry's song as a good example of defying heteronormativity when there are so many superior examples of songs that address the same topic in much more effective ways.

## ALTERNATIVE VIEWPOINTS FROM LESBIAN SONGWRITERS

There are lesbian songwriters who have broached this topic with much more honesty and integrity than Perry. In fact, the song "I Kissed a Girl" is not an original concept. In 1995, openly bisexual singer Jill Sobule released a song with the very same title. (Perry's song is not a cover of Sobule's; it is simply a song on the same topic that goes by the same title.) However, Sobule's song was a more serious portrayal of sexual experimentation than Perry's adaptation. Sobule admits, "I played a show in Phoenix [in 1995] and there were a bunch of young girls with braces on their teeth, and they were yelling for the song. And I thought, this is so great, because I remember having braces on my teeth and having a crush on my best friend, and feeling so friggin' ashamed of it. If I would have heard a song like that, that would have made me feel much better" (Boehlert 1995).

Sobule's song quickly became a hit with lesbians and bisexuals everywhere because it celebrated kissing a girl. Her song is a firm proclamation that there is nothing wrong with kissing a person of the same sex and that the writer liked the encounter so much, she might repeat it. Sobule's lyrics bear similarities to Perry's at times. However, Perry's portrayal of the subject matter from a straight woman's perspective results in a very different, much more lighthearted song. When asked about Sobule's same-titled creation, Perry replied, "If my song directs traffic to Jill, that's awesome. She's deserving" (Montgomery 2008). And how does Sobule feel about Perry's take on the topic? "I don't feel precious about the title, but I've gotten tons of e-mails from annoyed fans," she tells *EW.com*. "Some think it's more of a Girls Gone Wild thing than anything shocking or empowering to true gay feelings" (Halperin 2008). It is honest songs by openly gay artists like Sobule that will help to correct the concept of heteronormativity.

## CONCLUSION

On the surface, Perry's song seems like a statement in support of lesbian relationships, based on the simple fact that it is a narrative about a same-sex kiss. However, once investigated in detail, it becomes evident that the lyrics actually reinforce heterosexual norms and perpetuate stereotypes. In the end, Perry is only trivializing lesbianism with her glib and superficial outlook. With so many negative stereotypes of homosexuals still perpetuated by the media, it is important for consumers to reject as many false and demeaning images of gays and lesbians as possible. One way of doing this is to not support media that treats queer relationships in such a dismissive manner. Perry's song only contributes to the stereotype that bisexuals are oversexed and do not know what they want, as well as the conception that lesbians cannot sustain meaningful and committed relationships. If consumers can keep songs like this from circulating to top spots on the billboard charts, perhaps they can start to dispel some of the unfair typecasts behind the songs.

To break free from the constrictive social pressure of heteronormativity, society needs to view same-sex encounters as "no big deal." Only once these experiences become commonplace and accepted can the norms of heterosexuality begin to be questioned. Perry's rhetoric does not take strides to break free of heteronormativity. In fact, because of her heavy support of the straight sexual identity, her song is actually degrading to lesbians. Instead of presenting a simple, honest narrative of a woman who kisses another woman and likes it, Perry downplays the experience through the use of alcohol and the underscoring of straight identity. The narrator is very clear on the fact that this kiss is simply an experiment and that its outcome does not matter. Throughout the song, same-sex encounters are made to seem frivolous and inconsequential. Thus, this song does damage to the progress of lesbians who are determined to prove that their love is the same as that of heterosexuals.

## REFERENCES

Baumgardner, J. 2007. "Lesbian after marriage." *The Advocate* 994: 40–43.
Bendix, T. 2008. "'I Kissed a Girl' version 2.0." *Afterellen.com*. http://www.afterellen.com/blog/trishbendix/i-kissed-a-girl-version-2.0.
Boehlert, E. 1995. "The modern age." *Billboard* 107 (20): 97.
Breimeier, R. 2001. " Katy Hudson (Red Hill Records)." *Christian Music Today*. http://www.christianitytoday.com/music/reviews/2001/katyhudson.html.
Creekmur, C. and A. Doty. 1995. *Out in Culture: Gay, Lesbian, and Queer Essays on Popular Culture*. Durham, NC: Duke University Press.
Dhaenens, F., S. Van Bauwel, and D. Biltereyst. 2008. "Slashing the fiction of queer theory: Slash fiction, queer reading, and transgressing the boundaries of screen studies, representations, and audiences." *Journal of Communication Inquiry* 32 (4): 335–47.

Diamond, L. 2005. "'I'm straight, but I kissed a girl': The trouble with American media representations of female-female sexuality." *Feminist Psychology* 15 (1): 104–10.

Driver, S. 2007. *Queer Girls and Popular Culture: Reading, Resisting, and Creating Media.* New York: Peter Lang Publishing.

"Fatemeh." 2008. "Katy Perry plays make believe." *Feministe.* http://www.feministe. us/blog/archives/2008/06/30/katy-perry-plays-make-believe.

Fejes, F. and K. Petrich. 1993. "Invisibility, homophobia, and heterosexism: Lesbians, gays and the media." *Critical Studies in Mass Communication* 10 (4): 396–422.

Galewski, E. 2008. "'Playing up being a woman': Femme performance and the potential for ironic representation." *Rhetoric and Public Affairs* 11 (2): 279–302.

Gross, L. 2001. *Up from invisibility: Lesbians, gay men, and the media in America.* New York: Columbia University Press.

Halperin, S. 2008. "Jill Sobule weighs in on Katy Perry's 'kissed a girl'." *Entertainment Weekly.* http://hollywoodinsider.ew.com/2008/06/katy-perry.html.

"Hottie Katy Perry warped tour dates/ new video." 2008. *Skope Magazine.* http:// skopemag.com/2008/05/12/katy-perry-warped-tour-dates-and-new-video.

Jagose, A. 1996. *Queer theory: An introduction.* Washington Square, NY: New York University Press.

"Katy Perry biography." n.d. *AceShowbiz.com.* http://www.aceshowbiz.com/celebrity/ katy_perry/biography.html.

"Katy Perry—I kissed a girl." n.d. *aCharts.us.* http://acharts.us/song/35582.

"Katy Perry: Queen of Rock." 2008. *The Daily Star.* http://www.dailystar.co.uk/playlist/ view/52458/Katy-Perry-Queen-of-rock.

Lecker, K. 2008. "Church turns pop lyrics into a bit of brimstone: 'Loving warning' about homosexuality isn't a hit with all who see it." *The Columbus Dispatch.* http:// www.dispatch.com/live/content/local_news/stories/2008/09/04/churchsign.ART0_ ART_09-04-08_B1_OTB7MRR.html.

Marikar, S. 2008. "Pastors' daughter turns pseudo-lesbian pop princess." *ABC News.* http://abcnews.go.com/Entertainment/Music/Story?id=5256149&page=1.

Mears, B. 2008. "California ban on same-sex marriage struck down." *CNN.* http:// www.cnn.com/2008/US/05/15/same.sex.marriage/index.html.

Montgomery, J. 2008. "Katy Perry dishes on her 'long and winding road' from singing gospel to kissing girls." *MTV Networks.* http://www.mtv.com/news/articles/ 1589848/20080623/katy_perry.jhtml.

Moss, M. 2008. "I kissed a girl." *The Huffington Post.* http://www.huffingtonpost.com/ marissa-moss/i-kissed-a-girl_b_112272.html.

"Musician of the year: Katy Perry" 2008. *Out Magazine* (180): 87.

Past Winners Search. 2013. *Grammy.com.* http://www.cbs.com/specials/grammys/ nominees.

Pratt, P. 2008. "Katy Perry isn't one of the boys." *The Advocate (Online Exclusive).* http:// www.advocate.com/arts-entertainment/music/2008/06/23/katy-perry-isn%E2%80%99t-one-boys.

Rosen, Z. 2008. "Katy Perry: The New Gay interview." *The New Gay.* http://www. thenewgay.net/2008/06/katy-perry-new-gay-interview.html.

Signorile, M. 2003. *Queer in America: Sex, the media, and the closets of power.* Madison: The University of Wisconsin Press.

Thompson, E., J. Thai, and E. M. Morgan. 2007, March 8. "Gender matters (sometimes): Differences in preferences and sexual experiences of bisexual and bi-curious women." Paper presented at the annual meeting of The Association for Women in Psychology, Golden Gateway Holiday Inn, San Francisco, CA.

Westerfelhaus, R. and C. Lacroix. 2006. "Seeing 'straight' through Queer Eye: Exposing the strategic rhetoric of heteronormativity in a mediated ritual of gay rebellion." *Critical Studies in Media Communication* 23 (5): 426–44.

"Who's That Girl?" 2008. *Capital Music Group.* www.katyperry.com.

# EIGHT

# Queer Male TV Commentators

## Kinjo-no-Obasan *in Advanced Capitalism*

## Kimiko Akita

The inclusion of effeminate or feminized or gay male guests and cross-dressing commentators on Japanese TV talk shows, daytime variety shows, and "light-news" programs has become increasingly common, accepted, and popular, with a certain nostalgic appeal. Such men—once denigrated as *okama* (homosexual, but literally, "rice pot") but now called *new-half*, a queer[1] term with a more positive connotation in mainstream culture—have become staples of popular Japanese TV programming, respected for their opinions and perspectives, rather than for the sheer entertainment value of what was once considered their deviance.

It took many years and a historical and cultural path different from that of the West for queer men on Japanese TV to achieve their current status of urbane, intellectual, and critical commentators respected by male and female viewers of all sexual orientations. These queer men are readily identifiable by fashion and makeup (often, like Miwa Akihiro, Matsuko Deluxe, *Ikko*, Mittsu Manglove, and Haruna Ai, wearing women's clothes) or speech style (such as Piiko, Kariyazaki Shogo, and Kaba-chan, who affect a feminized speech and cross-dress) or the critical comments they offer about sex, life, and politics (for which Miwa, a Nagasaki survivor, is famous). Their TV commentating is usually a side job, complementing their primary occupations as actors, singers, writers, choreographers, flower artists, or even beauticians.

In this study of queer male TV commentators, I unpack culture-bound meanings of gender and sex in Japan; offer a brief history of queer performers in Japan; analyze the speech style, demeanor, and behavior of these commentators; and conclude with a discussion that situates this phenomenon in advanced capitalist consumption of media. I focus specifically on Miwa Akihiro (born in 1935) and Matsuko Deluxe (born in 1972), both of whom are transgender and transsexual TV commentators with regular weekly TV shows. Miwa uses *okusama* (high-class wife's) speech style and Matsuko uses *obasan* (ordinary middle-aged women's) speech style. I discuss why these two different queer performances successfully turn both of them into *kinjo no obasan* (middle-aged women who live in the neighborhood).

## GENDER AND SEX IN JAPAN

Gender and sex are culturally bound. In the West, scholars tend to dichotomize sex (biological) vs. gender (nurture) and treat them as autonomous analytical categories (Pflugfelder 1992). The modern Western construction binds gender closely with biological sex (353). In Japan, notions of gender and sex are ambiguous, transitional, and fluid. Buddhist notions such as reincarnation and karmic retribution have influenced gender construction as more malleable (Pflugfelder 1992; Robertson 1992). One may be born female but could be reborn male. This also helped create the idea that "both normative and non-normative behavior, the ordinary and the strange, are more closely knit than the Judeo-Christian system" (Pflugfelder 1992, 353–54).

According to Foucault (1980), the East follows an *ars erotica* (the idea that truth is drawn from pleasure itself, understood as a practice), which is similar to sensual pleasure, and sexual experience. Easterners generally avoid talking about sex openly because the knowledge of sex is to remain secret, even sacred. On the other hand, Westerners, who once followed the idea of *ars erotica*, have adopted *scientia sexualis* (the idea that confession produces truth) and understand sex as an abstract concept. Westerners generally refrain from talking about sex because of the shame associated with it. Sex can be revealed through confession, which enables people to find the truth (57–58).

Japan was temporarily induced to replace its cultural ideal of *ars erotica* with *scientia sexualis*. Beginning with the Meiji Restoration in 1868, Japan's modernization—influenced also by missionary Christianity and militarism—resulted in Western heteronormativity subtly and temporarily seeping into the culture (see Miwa 1998, 273). A psychiatric style of reasoning was introduced to Japan from European and U.S. models, which derived from German sexology, focusing on the psychosexual pathology of the individual (Pflugfelder 1992, 350). Homosexuality in Japan, then, was briefly considered abnormal (Robertson 1992, 428). Sensual pleasure became a dirty secret, something to feel shameful about. Only from the Meiji Period (1868–1912) to the early Showa Period (starting in 1926), while the Japanese underwent dramatic cultural transformations from their traditions under Western (and Christian and militaristic) modernizing influences, did notions and attitudes about gender and sex become oppressed, oppressive, and culturally confused. Between the late nineteenth and mid-twentieth centuries, homosexuality was considered abnormal and immoral in Japan. For instance, in the 1920s, *Takarazuka* male-role performers and fans were considered abnormal (Robertson 1992).

But Western heteronormativity does not culturally suit true Japanese society. Both ancient Japanese (pre-Meiji) and modern Japanese (postwar) have tended historically to be more tolerant than Westerners have been of the very idea of transgenderism and transsexuality. Japanese homophobia finally began to gradually dissipate after World War II. After a highly visible government crackdown on female and male prostitution in Tokyo in 1948, during the Occupation, newspapers began writing articles that exposed the fate of socially oppressed and economically desperate *dansho* (male prostitutes) (Abe 2010, 55). The *dansho* disdained the derogatory label *o-kama* (a derogatory expression for homosexuals) with which society had saddled them and they resisted its use, simply identifying themselves as "women" (55).

By the early 1990s, Japan was experiencing a "gay boom" (McLelland 2000). A wide range of media projected a positive "imagery of Japanese queer male culture" targeting heterosexual women (Suganuma 2007). This positive image appealed to women, a great many of whom were unhappy with Japanese patriarchy (Hirano 1994). *Takarazuka* male-role performers, who had once been considered abnormal, came to be identified as "asexual" (Robertson 1992, 433). Rather than viewing these orientations from afar as something foreign or alien, the Japanese now tend to treat them with familiarity and affinity.

GENDER-BENDING PERFORMANCE IN JAPAN

Unlike in the West, gender in Japan is defined by the performative aspects of gender (Abe 2010; McLelland 2006; Pflugfelder 1992; Robertson 1992). For an example, *kabuki* (all-male theater) performers have been highly respected for centuries. *Takarazuka Revue* (all-female theater) performers also have been respected and admired for decades. Whereas Westerners may be more conscious of the sexual orientation of actors who are performing in differing gender roles, what the Japanese care about is the aesthetic of the gender performance of the actors, especially the performance of those playing the opposite gender.

*Torikaebaya Mongatari* (The Changelings) was a Japanese tale of unknown authorship from the Heian Period (794–1185), probably written in the twelfth century, that dealt with gender and sex transformation. The half-brother and half-sister—children of the same father, but different mothers—at the center of the story confound, confuse, and ultimately fool those around them by living contentedly under the guise of the opposite sex. Horton (1984) observed that after critics of the Meiji Period (1868–1912) renounced the tale as decadent, it received little scholarly attention until the mid-1900s, with the first translation into English (Willig 1983) only three decades ago (Gatten 1984). Pflugfelder's (1992) analysis of *Torikaebaya* was informed by the Buddhist notion that gender is not permanent, but rather that gender identity reflects an individual's disposition. Pflugfelder found that through temporary androgynous performances, the characters in the story empowered themselves and inspired awe in the reader/audience. Pflugfelder argued that Buddhist traditions helped shape the initial conception of intersexuality in Japan.

Robertson (1992) analyzed the *Takarazuka Revue*, an all-female theatrical troupe founded in 1913. From her study, she extrapolated that gender identity is achieved by one's gender performativity and that gender is transitional: "transformation is not part of a particular role but precedes it" (423). Butler (1990) challenged the Western belief that prioritizes biological sex before gender and sexuality, asserting instead that gender is achieved through gender performance.

## QUEER MALE TV COMMENTATORS IN JAPAN

Today's queer male TV commentators in Japan express femininity through their attire, hairdos, accessories, demeanors, and speech styles. Many of them wear fashionably feminine clothes; behave elegantly, coquettishly, and femininely; and speak *onna-kotoba*—considered feminine speech. Abe (2010) argued that Japanese queers engage in a "transgression of gender appropriate linguistic practice" (150) through the manipulative use of *onna-kotoba* (feminine speech) and *otoko-kotoba* (masculine speech) to create and speak *o-ne-kotoba* (honorific *o* + older sister or woman; an imitation of feminine speech), an effeminate speech style used by homosexual men and/or transgendered individuals. This performative speech style helps gay men achieve their gender identity, but Abe's theory does not neatly explain the social construction of the queer male TV commentators, who usually choose either the ordinary speech style or the highly polished speech style of women and use it consistently.

The queer male TV commentators' feminine performativity makes them appear different from ordinary men and strange to viewers informed by Western notions of heteronormativity. These queer men's performativity, however, helps Japanese viewers feel closer to them. Based on Walter Benjamin's (1979) idea of alterity, primitivism, and the resurgence of mimesis with modernity, I argue that the queer male commentators' respectful mimicking of ordinary or high-class women's demeanor and speech style helps them transform into *kinjo-no-obasan*: middle-aged women neighbors who could be found on every corner in postwar Japan, women who talked loudly and forthrightly, offering their candid opinions to anyone and everyone.

Many queer men in Japan, including those performing in high-profile media roles, have adopted *o-ne-kotoba*, an imitation of feminine speech (for example, use of a particular pronoun, frequent use of sentence final particles, use of interjections) (Abe 2010). Their speech style is much more diverse than standard feminine speech (57). The queer male commentators have become popular not only among female viewers, but also among male viewers. Female TV viewers feel an affinity to queer commentators because of their feminine demeanor and speech. Male TV viewers identify, partly, with the queer commentators since they are of the same biological sex and because they admire their direct and assertive way of speaking, which only men are permitted and encouraged to follow in Japan.

## FINDINGS AND ANALYSIS

Miwa Akihiro and Matsuko Deluxe are extremely popular queer male TV commentators in Japan. Miwa uses *okusama* (high-class women's) speech style while Matsuko uses *obasan* (ordinary middle-class and middle-aged women's) speech style. Both speak candidly, assertively, and critically.

### "Miwa no yu" ("*Miwa's bathhouse*")

This five-minute show airs from 7:55 to 8:00 p.m. every Wednesday on NHK-TV. Miwa always stands facing the women's locker room of a bathhouse. About a half dozen women with lobster-red skin, who are wrapped in big towels after having just finished bathing, listen attentively to Miwa's advice about politics, culture, fashion, makeup, relationships, friendship, courtship, and work. With a feminine demeanor and refined feminine speech style, Miwa talks directly to the younger women. His advice is full of wisdom and compassion for the women in the locker room on the show's set, as well as for the audience at home.

### "5 p.m. ni muchu!" ("*Crazy about/devoted to 5 p.m.*")

This 60-minute news show airs live, Mondays through Fridays, on Tokyo Mix (Tokyo Metropolitan TV Station). On Mondays, Matsuko Deluxe and Wakabayashi Fumie comment on politics and social issues. Matsuko and Fumie act as if they were sisters or school chums.

*"Matsuko & Ariyoshi no ikari shintou" ("Matsuko & Ariyoshi's Angry New Party")*

This 60-minute talk show airs Wednesday nights from 11:15 p.m. to 12:15 a.m. on TV Asahi. Matsuko Deluxe and Ariyoshi Hiroyuki respond to questions mailed in by viewers. These are read by Natsumi Miku, who acts as secretary to Matsuko, acting as a political party leader, and Ariyoshi, the political party manager.

Miwa appears as a fashionably dressed, high-class woman with the most elegant feminine demeanor. Miwa's sharp and intellectual advice sounds confident, convincing, and comforting to the viewers, who seek affirmation and direction in their lives. Miwa's approach is top-down, as a strict mentor: perhaps a mother, aunt, grandmother, or teacher. On the other hand, Matsuko's ordinary feminine speech style and down-to-earth demeanor attracts viewers seeking a peer's advice from a sister, an aunt, or a friend in a middle-aged female neighbor. Miwa and Matsuko successfully perform this range of roles, transforming into whoever the viewers need them to be.

Expressing transgression against the Japanese feminine normative speech style via their assertion and directness, both Miwa and Matsuko appear heroic, especially to women, because they courageously express what viewers themselves typically cannot or would not say, for the sake of maintaining harmony in their lives and social and work circles. Ironically, because Miwa and Matsuko are men, their assertiveness is tolerated and considered more credible. If Miwa and Matsuko were women biologically, viewers would criticize their assertiveness and discredit their advice. Their transgression against gender-appropriate speech style and demeanor displays a power that appeals to viewers and captures their hearts.

## DISCUSSION

Altman (1996) assumed that change such as sexual liberation is brought to the non-West only from the West. McLelland (2006) argued that both Western and non-Western cultures have been transformed, mutually hybridizing them. I reject Altman's Orientalist (see Said, 1978) interpretation and McLelland's simplistic mutual hybridizing interpretation. In the advanced capitalist society of today, global power has become more de-centered or recentered (Allison 2006; Baudrillard 1975). The fandom for queer men may proliferate from a remote island in the Southeast (see The International Transsexual Beauty Pageant held annually in Pattaya)[2] and be shared globally from someone's Twitter or YouTube account via the Internet.

Modernist distinctions (private/public, inside/outside, self/other) disappear in advanced capitalism (Allison 2006, 15). Consumers can bring the *kinjo-no-obasan*, the sharp-tongued older neighborhood woman on the corner, into their homes on large-screen, high-definition TV or through an iPad, iPod, or iPhone. Consumers can control when, how, and where to watch Miwa's and Matsuko's shows. With blurred lines dividing the private and the public, Miwa and Matsuko have become *kinjo-no-obasan* (intimate) consumers.

Japan has progressed postwar, thanks to modernization, Westernization, and urbanization. As a result, the number of intergenerational families has dwindled and the number of nuclear families has increased. Traditional extended families and closely knit neighborhoods with *kinjo-no-obasan* have disappeared. Lévi-Strauss (1963) argued, however, that the unconscious nature of collective phenomena (culture and tradition that appear to have vanished), which he called "the primitive unconscious," is never lost or forgotten. Lévi-Strauss believed that events in the historical past survive in our consciousness only as myth, contemporaneously, as part of a single synchronous totality (Leach 1970). This myth has been "actively produced and shaped by it . . . [both] conscious and consciously manufactured" (Allison 2006, 24) and survived despite urbanization and industrialization.

Benjamin (1979, 1999) studied the magical power and fantasy energy that emerge from mimesis embedded with commodities and new technologies. The industrial world has become re-enchanted on an unconscious level (Benjamin 1999), which seems to correspond with Lévi-Strauss' idea of the primitive unconscious. What appears to be unconscious is in fact a myth that remains in our consciousness. I argue that the queer male TV commentators' mimetic performance of producing and reproducing *kinjo-no-obasan* exudes a magical power of consolation, comfort, and stimulation for viewers. On the other hand, the mass mediation of the queer commentators' performance does not represent exactly who they actually are in person or who the *kinjo-no-obasan* of the old days once were.

Taussig (1992) built on Walter Benjamin's (1979) idea of alterity, primitivism, and the resurgence of mimesis with modernity. Taussig (1992) called the *mimetics of alterity* "the nature that culture uses to create second nature, the faculty to copy, imitate, make models, explore difference, yield into and become Other" (xiii). It became crucial, in terms of the Japanese male commentators' alterity, for them to be watched, respected, and appreciated through a medium of mass communication: specifically, their televised image. Their mimetic faculty allows them to "'become and behave like something else.' The ability to mime, and mime well, in other words, is the capacity to Other" (19). Over the years, the queer male TV commentators have engaged in mimetic performativity (speech style, demeanor, content of their talk). As a result, their performance of *kinjo-no-*

*obasan* has come to represent what a *kinjo-no-obasan* of old days is believed to be.

Taussig (1992) identified "the surfacing of 'the primitive' within modernity as a direct result of modernity" (20). The surviving myth of *kinjo-no-obasan* and relationship with *kinjo-no-obasan* are commodified and fetishized. And consumers engage in the mimetic activity of turning on the TV, recording Miwa's and Matsuko's programs, and perhaps watching them later. The "magic of mimesis" (Taussig 1992) has exuded not only magical fantasy but also alterity: someone (a commodity and fetishized representation) who we are not or they are not. Because a new creation—alterity—allows one to preserve tradition (Akita 2009), a myth can survive only as a fetishized commodity. The queer commentators and their viewers allow themselves to be consumed by capitalism, accepting the fetishized value of the modern *kinjo-no-obasan* and any relationship to her. Consumers seek to connect with the queer commentators, just as their ancestors sought to relate to their *kinjo-no-obasan*. However, the queer male TV commentators are not, in reality, the *kinjo-no-obasan* of old, but merely a mass-mediated representation.

## REFERENCES

Abe, H. 2010. *Queer Japanese: Gender and Sexual Identities through Linguistic Practices.* New York: Palgrave Macmillan.

Akita, K. 2009. "A story of *tansu*, a chest of drawers: Japanese women's love, hope, and despair." *The Journal of Public and Private in Contemporary History* 4: 17–33.

Allison, A. 2006. *Millennial Monsters: Japanese Toys and the Global Imagination.* Berkeley, CA: University of California Press.

Altman, D. 1996. "On global queering." *Australian Humanities Review* (July): 1–7. http://www.australianhumanitiesreview.org/archive/Issue-July-1996/altman.html.

Baudrillard, J. 1975. *The Mirror of Production.* St. Louis, MO: Telos Press.

Benjamin, W. 1979. "Doctrine of the similar," translated by K. Tarnowski. *New German Critique* 17: 65–69. (Original work composed in Berlin, early 1993).

———. 1999. *The arcades project.* In *The Arcades Project*, edited by R. Tiedemann, translated by H. Eiland and K. McLaughlin. Cambridge, MA: Belknap Press of Harvard University Press.

Butler, J. 1990. *Gender Trouble: Feminism and the Subversion of Identity.* New York: Routledge.

Foucault, M. 1980. *The History of Sexuality: Vol.1: An Introduction,* translated by R. Hurley. New York: Vintage Books.

Gatten, A. 1984. "Review." *Harvard Journal of Asiatic Studies* 44 (1): 257–66.

Hirano, H. 1994. *Anti-heterosexism.* Tokyo: Pandra.

Horton, H. M. 1984. "Review." *Journal of Asian Studies* 43: 773–75.

Leach, E. 1970. *Claude Lévi-Strauss.* New York: Penguin Books.

Lévi-Strauss, C. 1963. *Structural Anthropology, Vol. 1,* translated by C. Jacobson. New York: Basic Books.

McLelland, M. 2000. *Male Homosexuality in Modern Japan: Cultural Myths and Social Realities.* Richmond, UK: Curzon Press.

———. 2006. "Japan's original 'gay boom.'" In *Popular culture, globalization and Japan,* edited by M. Allen, & R. Sakamoto, 158–73. New York: Routledge.

Miwa, A. 1998. *Jinsei note* [Notebook on life]. Tokyo: PARCO Press.

Pflugfelder, G. 1992. "Strange fates: Sex, gender, and sexuality." *Torikaebaya Monogatari. Monumenta Nipponica* 47 (3): 347–68.

Robertson, J. 1992. "The politics of androgyny in Japan: Sexuality and subversion in the theater and beyond." *American Ethnologist* 19 (3): 419–42.

Said, E. 1978. *Orientalism.* NY: Random House.

Suganuma, K. 2007. "Associative identity politics: Unmasking the multi-layered formation of queer male selves in 1990s Japan." *Inter-Asia Cultural Studies* 8 (4): 485–502.

Taussig, M. 1992. *Mimesis and Alterity: A Particular History of the Senses.* New York: Routledge.

Willig, R. F., translator. 1983. *The Changelings: A Classical Japanese Court Tale.* Stanford, CA: Stanford University Press.

## NOTES

1. I use the term *queer* here as an empowering antonym to "heteronormative."

2. Haruna Ai, a Japanese transsexual TV personality and singer, won the "Miss International Queen 2009" transsexual beauty pageant. This annual beauty pageant is held in Pattaya, Thailand (8.6 square miles). See http://www.missinternationalqueen.com/index.htm.

*Part III*

# Living in the Margins

# NINE

# The Construction of Queer and the Conferring of Voice

*Empowering and Disempowering Portrayals of Transgenderism on* TransGeneration

## K. Nicole Hladky

In 2005, the Sundance Channel aired *TransGeneration,* a documentary miniseries about four transgender college students. The show gained attention for its groundbreaking focus on a population that, historically, had been marginalized and/or ignored in many scholarly and popular discourses (Dow and Wood 2006). Authors, scholars, and advocates mentioned the show in articles, book introductions, course syllabi, and programs for awareness workshops and events. The series even received a Gay and Lesbian Alliance Against Defamation (GLAAD) Media Award for Outstanding Documentary in 2006.

Despite the show's popularity, no known published work has systematically examined the content of the series. In a chapter in his book *Not Remotely Controlled: Notes on Television,* cultural critic Siegel (2007) discusses the show and admonishes critics for largely ignoring it in their reviews and acclaims. An article by Siebler (2010) includes *TransGeneration* as an example of a television show that portrays "transqueers" in ways that "reinforce the idea that there is no such thing as 'trans' people who are healthy and happy with who they are" (324). Though both authors draw examples from the television show to support their arguments, neither examines the series as a whole.

The importance of mediated portrayals of marginalized populations cannot be ignored. Gross (2001) points out that "when previously ignored groups or perspectives do gain visibility [in media], the manner of their representation will reflect the biases and interests of those powerful people who define the public agenda" (4). Moreover, media effects scholars have long argued for the role of television and other forms of mass media as educational tools (for a comprehensive overview, see Bryant and Oliver 2009).

In light of the implications for how marginalized populations are portrayed in media, this study utilizes a grounded theory approach to investigate the ways in which *TransGeneration* portrays transgenderism and how this representation empowers and/or silences transgender individuals. The results of the analysis reveal that, though the series does present a number of the complexities surrounding transgenderism, it nonetheless limits transgender individuals by the prescriptive view of transition it reinforces through the portrayal of its transgender characters.

Media effects research, according to Bryant and Zillmann (2009), emerged in the late nineteenth and early twentieth centuries in response to "the development of a worldview of a mass society of fragmented individuals who served as the hapless consumers of mass media messages" (11). Though the passivity of media consumers and the strength of media effects have been challenged over time, media effects scholars nonetheless recognize the role of mediated portrayals as educational tools capable of shaping individuals' beliefs (for a comprehensive overview, see Bryant and Oliver 2009). Perse (2001) has argued that "much of the empirical research published in the major mass communication journals concerns the effects of the mass media" (1). Given the expansive scope and well established nature of this area of research, this literature review will focus primarily on media effects research related to the LGBT population.

Early studies of media portrayals of the LGBT population linked the virtual absence of LGBT individuals on television and in films to the invisibility of this group in society at large (Gross 1991; Kielwasser and Wolf 1994). As the presence of LGBT characters in media increased, studies turned to examining the ways in which the portrayals of these characters influenced viewers' attitudes toward the LGBT population. Though some researchers found that viewing television shows featuring LGBT characters could improve attitudes toward this population and decrease prejudice (Adelman, Segal, and Kilty, 2006), others cautioned that portrayals which stereotype or sensationalize gays, lesbians, bisexuals, and transgenders could, in fact, reinforce prejudicial beliefs. Siebler (2010), for example, suggested that "positive attitudes toward any group of people who are traditionally marginalized or persecuted is always a step forward, but only when people are seen as individuals instead of a static identity associated with that group marked as outside the norm will we acheve social justice" (328). Similarly, Levina, Waldo, and Fitzgerald (2000) found that participants exposed to a pro-gay video held significantly more positive attitudes toward gay men than individuals exposed to an an anti-gay video. Other studies have found similar effects (for recent examples see Calzo and Ward 2009; Schiappa, Gregg, and Hewes, 2006).

In light of the popularity of the Sundance Channel's television show *TransGeneration*, research on media effects, and the goals of this study, the following research question is addressed:

RQ1: How does the television show *TransGeneration* portray transgenderism?

## METHOD

I employed a basic grounded theory approach, modeled after Strauss and Corbin (1990), to address my research question. The following section will provide more information about the text analyzed, the television show *TransGeneration*, and the procedures used to analyze the data.

Text: I chose to analyze the television series *TransGeneration* because of the attention it received after its release and its widespread availability to popular audiences via the Sundance Channel and Netflix. Chen and Waterman (2007) contend that, though considered a premium channel because of its lack of advertising support, the Sundance Channel is provided by many carriers in the basic cable package. The authors also point out that the providers offering the Sundance Channel only as a premium channel typically do so at lower rates than other paid channels such as Showtime and HBO. Individuals with a paid Netflix subscription can also view the show for free online or by ordering the episodes on disk. Through this venue alone, the show has received over 45,000 viewer ratings.

World of Wonder produced *TransGeneration* in cooperation with the Sundance Channel. The documentary series aired beginning in September 2005 and consisted of eight episodes. The first and last episodes lasted approximately 54 minutes each, and all other episodes lasted between 25 and 27 minutes each. The television show followed four transgender college students: Gabbie, Lucas, Raci, and T.J. Gabbie, a sophomore computer science major at the University of Colorado–Boulder, and Raci, a freshman English major at California State–LA, both identified as male-to-female transgender persons. Lucas, a senior neuroscience major at Smith College, and T.J., a graduate student in Student Affairs Administration at Michigan State University, identified as female-to-male transgender persons. The series showcased different aspects of the characters' transitions, from crossdressing to hormones and, in one case, sex reassignment surgery.

## ANALYSIS

Strauss and Corbin (1990) propose three stages of coding for their basic grounded theory approach: open, axial, and selective. This method of analysis, according to the authors, provides "the framework for taking observations, intuitions, and understandings to a conceptual level" and "the guidelines for the discovery and formulation of theory" (Strauss and Corbin 1997, 182). Before I could begin the coding process, I watched all episodes of *TransGeneration* twice and noted any instances in which characters on the television series discussed transgenderism or issues related to transition—for example, hormone usage or restroom usage. I described all instances in detail, marked their placement in the series, and denoted them on separate sheets of paper so that they could be easily distinguished during coding.

Following Strauss and Corbin's (1990) recommendations for coding, I first divided all noted instances of discussions about transgenderism and transition into groups of similar observations (open coding). Then, I refined the categories created during open coding by looking for similarities and differences in observations (axial coding). Finally, I reexamined the resulting categories and developed themes of observations (selective coding). The following section describes the themes that emerged during selective coding.

## RESULTS

Four major themes resulted from the open, axial, and selective coding stages proposed by Strauss and Corbin (1990): Process, Intersection, Stigma, and Prescription.

*Process*

Data coded within the Process theme featured portrayals of transgenderism that emphasized the physical, emotional, and psychological aspects of transition, including identity development, hormones, and gender reassignment. This theme contained the largest number of instances, as *TransGeneration* frequently depicted the physical, emotional, and psychological components of transition. First, all of the transgender characters on the show manipulated their bodies in some way to represent their chosen gender identity. For example, a scene from the second episode shows Gabbie walking to the pharmacy with a friend to pick up hormones. As they walk, Gabbie discusses the hormones and their effects while her friend asks her questions about them. Hormones play a predominant role on *TransGeneration*, with three of the four main characters taking them at some point on the show. Hormones are not, however, the only physical aspect of transition that is emphasized. One main character, Gabbie, and two minor characters, Kasey and Cate, undergo some kind of surgery on the show: sex reassignment surgery for Gabbie, a double mastectomy for Kasey, and an orchiectomy (removal of the testicles) for Cate. *TransGeneration* also portrays a number of non-medical interventions that characters employ in the physical process of their transition — for example, breast binding and "packing" (wearing a penis-like object in one's pants).

In addition to these physical processes, the show heavily emphasizes transition as an emotional process. The characters frequently discuss their past, their struggles with gender identity, and their current emotional states, which range from elation to frustration with family members and friends. In the third episode, for example, Lucas writes a letter to his father in which he describes the emotions he has experienced thus far in life that have led to his decision to transition. Each character also often mentions his or her desire to feel like a man or woman and to be the person he or she is meant to be. Typically, these desires are linked to their ability to experience true happiness.

Discussions of the psychological component of transition also appear on *TransGeneration*. Early in the television series, Gabbie describes a contemplated suicide during her freshman year at the University of Colorado. She first recalls the psychological torment that she experienced as she struggled with her gender identity and then goes on to discuss her progression since that incident. The characters on the show also discuss their relationships with therapists and bring up the diagnosis of Gender Identity Disorder (GID).

It is important to note that the show provides examples of the ways in which the physical, emotional, and psychological processes of transition relate to each other. While visiting his mother and brother in the second episode, Lucas discusses Gender Identity Disorder (GID). Specifically, he points out to his family that, though diagnosed psychiatrically by a therapist, GID is treated physically with hormones and potential surgeries. Other characters also discuss the relationship between hormones and/or surgery and changes in their emotional states.

*Intersection*

Data that fit the Intersection theme emphasized the connection between the characters' transitions and other aspects of their lives, including their cultural background, socioeconomic status, and religious beliefs. The show constructs the main characters as diverse individuals whose unique life circumstances influence their transitions. One example of the intersectionality of identities showcased on *TransGeneration* involves the character Raci, a hearing-impaired immigrant from the Philippines. The show emphasizes the ways in which Raci's position as a transgender individual differs from others on the show because of her inability to afford legally obtained hormones and her isolation from peers at school. Similarly, Lucas's status as a full-time student at an all-female university influences the degree to which he is able to transition while in school. It also informs his decision to withdraw from advocacy efforts during his last year of school because of his struggle to find the place of a male student on an all-female campus. The portrayal of the characters on *TransGeneration* illustrates the multifaceted nature of identity by focusing on aspects of the characters' lives that extend beyond their gender identity.

*Stigma*

The Stigma theme included any examples of *TransGeneration*'s portrayal of transgenderism as a socially unacceptable condition. These portrayals emerged from comments made by both main characters and minor characters. Although no characters express any explicit beliefs that critique transgenderism, the show does include some comments that reflect the stigma attached to transgenderism. Raci often expresses a fear that her classmates will see her as a freak if they discover that she is transgender. In addition, her aunt, with whom she lives, explains that, though her family loves Raci, they do not encourage her transgenderism and accept it only because they have no choice. The show also features several comments by friends, family members, and strangers that express ignorance of and clear discomfort with transgenderism. This discomfort is illustrated when Gabbie visits her grandparents' church for a Sunday service in the fourth episode. This episode features a scene in which women from the congregation discuss Gabbie's transgenderism after her grandmother explains it to them. During this conversation, the women make jokes at Gabbie's expense and appear to be clearly uncomfortable. Despite its overall positive portrayal of transgenderism, *TransGeneration* does not ignore the existing stigma against transgender individuals.

*Prescription*

Instances coded within the Prescription theme included comments endorsing or discounting a specific view of transition, a particular action by a character, or a certain belief about transgenderism. Though each character on *TransGeneration* experiences a different journey in his or her transition, the show seems to imply, both through the portrayals of the characters that it features and the comments from friends, family, and other transgender individuals that it includes, that certain journeys are more acceptable than others. By doing this, the show prescribes or advocates for a particular view of transition.

One way that the show endorses or discounts a particular approach to transition is through the comments that other individuals make about the main characters and their actions. An example of a character whose approach to transition is discounted throughout the show is Gabbie. As the only character on the show who receives sex reassignment surgery, Gabbie is heavily criticized by her friends and family. They continually accuse her of being selfish and unrealistic about the changes that sex reassignment surgery will bring. Because Gabbie undergoes sex reassignment surgery too quickly, her character faces criticism that makes it clear to viewers that her choice is incorrect.

The show also prescribes an acceptable view of transgenderism in the way in which it frames characters' stories. For example, the story of T.J., the only character who does not take hormones on the show, continually features disclaimers about his obligation to return to his home country of Cypress once he graduates to fulfill the demands of his scholarship. These disclaimers typically occur before, during, or after discussions of his transition and his decision not to take hormones or move forward with any type of sex reassignment. By including these disclaimers, the show provides a reason T.J. has not moved along in his transition and implies that, if not for this obligation, the next logical step should be to take hormones. Thus, though *TransGeneration* includes diverse characters in various stages of transition, certain approaches to transition, particularly those characterized by a progression from gender identity struggles, to therapy, to hormones, and finally to potential surgery, all in a specific timeframe, emerge as more acceptable than others in the ways in which they are framed.

## DISCUSSION AND IMPLICATIONS

This research considered the portrayals of transgenderism featured on Sundance Channel's documentary mini-series *TransGeneration* and found that the show portrayed transgenderism as a physical, emotional, and psychological process, as a part of the character's lives that intersected with other identities, as a stigmatized condition, and as a prescriptive process. Though the television show generally depicted transgenderism as a complex phenomenon and empowered its characters with positive portrayals, this project revealed some ways in which it problematized viewers' perceptions of transgender individuals.

The Process theme revealed several important components of the characters' transitions: the physical, the emotional, and the psychological, and the ways in which these components overlap. Transgender care providers agree that "transition . . . occurs across psychological and physical planes" (Israel, Tarver, and Shaffer, 2001, 29–30). As such, it is important to address the various ways in which individuals experience transition.

By providing a multifaceted view of transition that responds to the demands of transgender advocates for a more comprehensive understanding of transgenderism, *TransGeneration* begins to empower transgender individuals.

The second theme, Intersection, illustrated *TransGeneration*'s depiction of its characters as diverse individuals whose transitions remain imbedded in unique life circumstances. Crenshaw (1989) first called attention to the importance of intersectionality in her research on black women's employment in the United States. LGBT researchers have acknowledged the importance of an intersectional approach to research on and depictions of gay, lesbian, bisexual, and transgender individuals. Meem et al. (2010) proposed that "intersectionality allows us to see an even more complex picture of how individuals are included or excluded by considering their queerness in its relationship to other identity categories, such as race, class, age, and nationality" (204). The authors go on to argue that intersectionality further empowers the LGBT community by encouraging a view of LGBT individuals that considers more than their sexuality. *TransGeneration*'s focus on the intersection among its characters' identities empowers transgender individuals by promoting a complex portrayal of transgender individuals that acknowledges more than just their gender identity. The television show, however, does not ignore popular societal stereotypes against transgender individuals.

Stigma, the third theme, reflected the disadvantaged position of transgender individuals and the issues they face in today's society. *TransGeneration* illustrates these disadvantaged positions, first, by the comments that transgender individuals make about transgenderism and the struggles they face, the fears they experience, and the ways in which they are stereotyped by others. The show also demonstrates stigma against transgender individuals through its portrayals of clearly uncomfortable cisgender individuals as they talk about transgenderism or interact with transgender individuals. In terms of the effects of these portrayals, however, it should be noted that the manner in which *TransGeneration* presents stigma typically serves to empower transgender individuals. On the show, characters continually overcome adversity, defy transgender stereotypes, and stand up to their fears of rejection. The inclusion of these portrayals thus calls into question the veracity of the presented stigma against transgender individuals. Additionally, the cisgender individuals exhibiting discomfort toward transgender individuals are made to look ignorant on the show, questioning the validity of the stigmas they hold. This approach to the presentation of stigma positively portrays transgender individuals as capable of overcoming the barriers they face and critiques those who propagate negative views of transgenderism. Though *TransGeneration* generally depicts transgender individuals positively, the last theme problematizes the show's portrayals of transgender individuals.

The fourth theme, Prescription, detailed the ways in which *TransGeneration* endorsed particular views of transgenderism and approaches to transition. The results of the analysis indicate that, though *TransGeneration* includes individuals at various points in their transition, the comments included on the show and the ways in which the characters' stories are framed indicate to viewers which approaches to transition are preferred. Siebler (2010) has presented a similar critique of *TransGeneration*, proposing that on the show "the body *must* match the gender . . . the young people who are profiled must 'pass' as male or female, and the only way to do that is via hormones and surgery" (323). Though this analysis acknowledges that certain characters on the show, such as T.J., do not take hormones or undergo surgery, it does reveal the ways in which the show's framing of these issues and the inclusion of critiques from friends and family discredit certain approaches to transition. Siegel (2007) similarly contended in his analysis of the show that the characters' journeys "are strictly foregrounded in the medical technologies of surgery, drugs, and counseling, which has the effect of both normalizing their fate and turning it into an illness that can be cured, or repaired." The implications for such a narrow view of transition, according to Siebler (2010), include reinforcement of the myth that all transgender individuals are born in the wrong body and the propagation of the belief that transgender individuals who choose not to undergo hormone treatment or surgery should be viewed as freaks. In light of this critique, it is crucial to acknowledge the ways in which *TransGeneration* might potentially disempower transgender individuals, particularly those embodying a queer notion of gender.

This project provided a systematic analysis of a popular television series' portrayal of transgenderism. The results respond to and problematize previous researchers' examinations of the show. In light of the popularity of *TransGeneration* and the complexities revealed in this analysis, future research attempting to seek the response of viewers, both transgendered and cisgendered, could be beneficial. Additionally, research investigating other popular mediated portrayals of transgender individuals could provide more information about the ways in which viewers come to learn about this population.

## REFERENCES

Adelman, M., E. A. Segal, and K. M. Kilty. 2006. "Introduction: Transforming LGBTQ inequalities in the twenty-first century." *Journal of Poverty* 10 (2): 1–4.

Bryant, J. and M. B. Oliver. 2009. *Media effects: Advances in theory and research*, third edition. New York: Routledge.

Bryant, J., and D. Zillmann. 2009. "A retrospective and prospective look at media effects." In *The SAGE handbook of media processes and effects*, edited by R. L. Nabi and M. B. Oliver, 9–18. Thousand Oaks, CA: Sage.

Calzo, J. and L. Ward. 2009. "Media exposure and viewers' attitudes toward homosexuality: Evidence for mainstreaming or resonance?" *Journal of Broadcasting & Electronic Media* 53: 280–99.

Chen, D., and D. Waterman. 2007. "Vertical ownership, program network carriage, and tier positioning in cable television: An empirical study." *Review of Industrial Organization* 31 (1): 227–52.

Crenshaw, K. 1989. "Demarginalizing the intersection of race and sex: A Black feminist critique of antidiscriminatory doctrine, feminist theory, and antiracist politics." *University of Chicago Legal Forum*, 139–67.

Dow, B. J., and J. T. Wood, editors. 2006. *The Sage Handbook of Gender and Communication*. Thousand Oaks, CA: Sage.

Gross, L. 1991. "Out of mainstream: Sexual minorities and the mass media." *Journal of Homosexuality*, 21 (1–2): 19–46.

Gross, L. P. 2001. *Up from invisibility: Lesbians, gay men, and the media in America*. New York: Columbia University Press.

Israel, G. E., D. E. Tarver, and J. D. Shaffer. 2001. *Transgender Care: Recommended Guidelines, Practical Information, and Personal Accounts*. Philadelphia: Temple University Press.

Kielwasser, A. P., and M. A. Wolf. 1994. "Silence, difference, and annihilation: Understanding the impact of mediated heterosexism on high school students." *The High School Journal*, October/November 1993, December/January 1994: 58–77.

Levina, M., C. R. Waldo, and L. F. Fitzgerald. 2000. "We're here, we're queer, we're on TV: The effects of visual media on heterosexuals' attitudes toward gay men and lesbians." *Journal of Applied Social Psychology* 30 (4): 738–58.

Meem, D. T., M. Gibson, J. F. Alexander, and M. A. Gibson. 2010. *Finding Out: An Introduction to LGBT Studies*. Thousand Oaks, CA: Sage.

Perse, E. M. 2001. *Media Effects and Society*. Mahwah, NJ: Lawrence Erlbaum Associates.

Schiappa, E., P. Gregg, and D. Hewes. 2006. "Can one TV show make a difference? Will & Grace and the parasocial contact hypothesis." *Journal of Homosexuality* 51: 15–37.

Siebler, K. 2010. "Transqueer representations and how we educate." *Journal of LGBT Youth* 7 (4): 320–45.

Siegel, L. 2007. *Not Remotely Controlled: Notes on Television*. Philadelphia: Basic Books.

Strauss, A., and J. Corbin. 1990. *Basics of Qualitative Research: Grounded Theory Procedures and Techniques*. Newbury Park, CA: Sage.

———. 1997. *Grounded Theory in Practice*. Newbury Park, CA: Sage.

# TEN

## "Born This Way"

### Biology and Sexuality in Lady Gaga's Pro-LGBT Media

### Shannon Weber

"[S]uddenly it becomes poisonous and something else because there are some people in this world that believe being gay is a choice. It's not a choice[;] we're born this way." —Lady Gaga, defending the queer themes in the music video for "Telephone," March 2010

In contemporary discussions about same-sex desire in the United States, it is common for pro-LGBT[1] individuals and groups to promote the idea that sexuality should be accepted at least in part because it is something that cannot be "helped" or "changed." Mirroring this idea is the trend in popular media of locating gayness within a specific narrative that centers on and privileges biological determinism. In this framework, sexuality is portrayed as lifelong, unchangeable, often involving varying degrees of regret (the "I would be straight if I could!" defense), and determined at birth or in early childhood. The assumption here is that to be pro-gay is to embrace biological determinism, whereas to connect sexuality with choice, agency, change, and/or social constructionism is linked with anti-gay Christian Right rhetoric (Weber 2012).

I borrow Lisa Duggan's term "homonormativity" to argue that such a popular framework for articulating same-sex desire ultimately becomes what I call "biological homonormativity." Biological homonormativity is a variation of a regulatory "politics that does not contest dominant heteronormative assumptions and institutions but upholds and sustains them while promising the possibility of a demobilized gay constituency" (Duggan 2003, 179). In this case, the heterosexist assumption is that no one would choose to be gay if she or he could help it and that gayness is second in preference to heterosexuality. For the sake of political unity against the Christian Right, identity becomes neatly biological, which leaves out the voices of people who experience their same-sex desire as something *other* than lifelong, unchosen, and primarily or solely biological.

I argue that popular musical performer and iconoclastic queer heroine Lady Gaga deploys biological homonormativity both for exciting as well as deleterious ends. On the one hand, her music, public aesthetic, and political messages provide a powerful affirmation in favor of the rights of LGBTQ people to exist, express themselves, and be treated equally. Her public advocacy in favor of marriage equality, the repeal of Don't Ask Don't Tell, the importance of ending teen bullying and suicide, and the essential beauty and diversity of queer and trans youth is something certainly unmatched by the "progressive" president of the United States, Barack Obama. Since her quick rise to fame in 2008, Gaga has proven to be a force to reckon with in her direct critique of the Christian Right's homophobia and in her embrace of same-sex desire, conveyed through political rallies as well as what some would consider to be deceptively danceable pop songs.

On the other hand, in her enthusiasm for promoting LGBT-friendly messages, Gaga reasserts the hegemony of biology in understanding the identities and experiences of LGBTQ people. Her much-needed popular media rebuttal of the Christian Right unfortunately flattens out the nuances of sexuality, thus perpetuating the current "culture war" framing of gayness I have outlined. It is these tensions I explore, neither to wholly valorize nor merely reject Gaga, but to critically engage with Gaga's messages and what they tell us about the ongoing American political debate surrounding LGBT rights.

## GAGA FOR THE GAY COMMUNITY (AND VICE VERSA)

Gaga, who affectionately refers to her proudly marginal and alienated youth fans as "little monsters," has widely publicized the fact that it was the early support of the gay community that aided her rise to fame. In an interview with *MTV.com*, Gaga explains, "The turning point for me was the gay community. I've got so many gay fans and they're so loyal to me and they really lifted me up. . . . Being invited to play [the San Francisco Pride rally], that was a real turning point for me as an artist" (Vena 2009). This early support influenced Gaga, who identifies as bisexual, to make public advocacy for LGBT people a cornerstone of her musical and media persona. During the 2009 LGBT National Equality March in Washington, DC, which Gaga called the "single most important moment of [her] career," she took to the podium and publicly called out President Obama during her speech, saying, "Obama, I know that you're listening." She then shouted into the microphone, to cheers and applause, "*Are you listening?*" Gaga continued, "We will continue to push you and your administration to bring your words of promise to a reality. We need change *now*. We demand actions *now*." In addition, she chastised House Representative Barney Frank for his prior lack of support for the march, ultimately exiting with the words "Bless God, and bless the gays!"

Similarly, in response to a teenage fan in Tennessee who had been sent home from school for wearing a "I Heart Lady Gay Gay" shirt in April 2010, Gaga reached out on the popular social networking site Twitter to tweet "You're perfect the way God made you" (Kaufman 2010), again invoking God while also making use of an ontological explanation for gayness. Later that year in September, after Gaga took four gay members of the military to the MTV Video Music Awards as her dates and tweeted to Democratic House Majority Leader Harry Reid to repeal Don't Ask Don't Tell, Reid wrote back with a favorable message. Gaga thanked him "from all of us, like u, who believe in equality and the dream of this country. We were #BORNTHISWAY" (ladygaga 2010), using a Twitter hashtag[2] to invoke both a biological explanation for queer identities as well as a reference to her new album, which, tellingly, is titled *Born This Way*.

## BORN THIS WAY

In November 2010, Lady Gaga revealed the name of her newest album, *Born This Way*, upon accepting an award for Video of the Year at the MTV Video Music Awards. The following February, Gaga premiered the title track "Born This Way" at the Fifty-third Grammy Awards, in which she used heightened biological metaphors to publicize the song on the red carpet. Gaga arrived on the red carpet inside an egg-like capsule she referred to as a "vessel," which she claimed she "incubated" inside for seventy-two hours prior to the Grammys, as a way to meditate on the messages of "Born This Way" (Ward 2011). She then burst out of the egg onstage to sing the song that Elton John has termed "the anthem that's going to obliterate 'I Will Survive' in queer popularity for the twenty-first century" (Savage 2011).

The imagery of the egg is a quite literal and direct illustration of the position that gayness is an inherent biological trait, echoing controversial studies such as that conducted by biologist Simon LeVay on the hypothalamuses of heterosexual and gay men (1991). Ruth Hubbard and Elijah Wald (1999) argue that LeVay and a few other prominent pro-gay scientists employed problematic and at times distorted methods in collecting and analyzing data in the hopes of justifying the existence of gayness, despite the complex multitude of factors that may contribute to one's sexual identity. Indeed, LeVay himself pointed out the several limitations of his 1991 study in his later book *Queer Science* (LeVay 1996), but this did not stop his work from being taken up in public discourse to argue for a straightforward understanding of gayness as biological. Gaga's use of the egg as well as the lyrics of "Born This Way" follow the same paradigmatic alignment of pro-LGBT positions with belief in the biological origins of sexuality. Gaga's "birth" from the egg onstage during her first performance of the song, as well as her "Mother Monster" birthing imagery in the "Born This Way" music video, further solidify this connection.

Granted, Gaga's firm positioning of LGBT people, along with people of color and individuals with disabilities, within the realm of biology is a strong and powerful statement given the context of the contemporary American political landscape. "Born This Way" takes aim at the hegemony of the Christian Right's anti-gay discourse, indicating that God created LGBT people and does not consider marginalized sexual or gender identities to be an abomination. Gaga also alludes to "the religion of the insecure," an obvious jab at homophobic religious practices, and affirms that she must "be [her]self, respect [her] youth."

The potency of Gaga's critique is confirmed in the response to the song found on the blog of the notorious Christian Right organization Focus on the Family. After asserting that he "[is] not inclined toward celebrity psycho-analysis [sic]," Focus on the Family writer Jim Daly (2011) nevertheless attacks Gaga's personal character, declaring that her celebrity persona is itself not "born this way" and that "the message found within the lyrics of *Born This Way* is in stark contrast to the message of the Gospel." In an even harsher and perhaps panicked critique of "Born This Way," Kelly Boggs (2011) of *Baptist Press* calls Gaga "a Pied Piper leading her fawning fans down a primrose path of deception concerning aberrant sexuality." The power of the homophobia behind these sentiments cannot be taken lightly, especially given the continued operation of "ex-gay" conversion camps such as Exodus International,[3] which provide an apt example of what Eve Sedgwick calls "gay-genocidal" agendas (Sedgwick 1990, 40). In fact, Boggs mentions that "[t]here are also countless numbers of people who once were homosexual but who no longer are so" and ultimately provides further information at the end of his article for how to contact the Southern Baptist Convention's ex-gay ministry.

In this climate of cultural warfare, where any mainstream stance in favor of LGBT people often becomes of necessity linked to biology in defending LGBTQ rights from the "sinful chosen lifestyle" rhetoric of the Christian Right, Gaga's message should rightfully be commended. Her lyrics and persona, while not embraced by all LGBTQ people, have been taken up by many queer and trans youth who find inspiration in her words and deeds, sometimes even life-saving inspiration. One young man, Benji, wrote a post in a discussion forum on Gaga's official website titled "Lady Gaga Saved My Life" (HausDJ 2011). Identifying himself as one of the queer homeless youth portrayed in the documentary film *Queer Streets*, Benji discusses how he was homeless on the streets of New York City, addicted to meth and HIV positive, and staying at Sylvia's Place, an "emergency over-night shelter for self-identified gay, lesbian, bisexual, and transgender youth from 16 to 23 years of age" named after Stonewall Riots veteran Sylvia Rivera ("Sylvia's Place" 2011). He writes,

> [I]t wasn[']t that long ago that I was on the street leading a life that was going nowhere and quite literally, I had nowhere to go . . . but whenever I hear Lady Gaga I was not in this world but another! A world without prejudice or hate! And I do know I am not without flaw, and Mother Monster [Gaga] made me take a step back and look at myself for once and truly gave me "the fame" I so desperately needed! . . .When I heard [the album] *The Fame* for the first time, I escaped the horror of my head and the shady dealings of my past and I fel[t] it! . . . I seen her front row the other night in Atlantic City, NJ at Boardwalk Hall and never in my life did I ever think I would be so close to her for a whole show! My only goal left now in life is to meet her and get my family out of the trailer park. Quite literally . . . I would put an LOL but it[']s the truth. That[']s all. Love, Benji[.] (HausDJ 2011)

Such candor is testament to the very real impact that Gaga has on the everyday lives of some at-risk and marginalized youth.

Given the immense value of Gaga's pro-LGBT advocacy, one might question what value there is in an academic critique of Gaga's use of biological determinism. I am in agreement that too often in this era of postmodernism and queer theory, academics participate in the deconstruction and demonization of valuable social and political phenomena without contributing meaningful alternatives or fully legitimating the intense significance for marginalized populations of that which is under deconstruction. That is not my aim here. Rather, I wish to examine what, and who, is elided in biological determinist advocacy of LGBTQ people. In critically engaging with the pro-gay representation of sexuality in the media, it is important to consider the underlying homophobia and transphobia that produce the reactionary, biologically driven defense of LGBT people.

## THE "BAD ROMANCE" OF BIOLOGY AND SEXUALITY

While biology is used in certain contexts to advance the causes of some marginalized groups, it has also been used against them; for example, the eugenics movement promoting white supremacy and the elimination of children of color, or the attempt to genetically screen for and selectively abort fetuses with disabilities (Hume 1996; Hubbard 2006). This fraught historical relationship between scientific authority and the marginalized must be at the forefront of any discussion regarding the use of biology in advancing the rights of LGBT people. As Nancy Ordover argues, the queer community has historically used biological determinist arguments in what she terms "the science-as-savior prism" and that "[o]f all the groups targeted by biological determinism, queers seem to be the only ones who have looked to eugenics to deliver us from marginalization" (Ordover 2003, 60). That being said, it also is important to highlight the ways in which Gaga's use of biological determinism both leaves out some LGBTQ people's experiences as well and fails to fully grapple with the underlying heterosexism present in the idea that LGBT people are only acceptable if they were born that way.

The idea that gay people are gay because they were born that way is well-documented and, indeed, is experienced by many gay people, especially gay men, as a valid way of describing their identities. Many gay men report the traditional narrative of having been gay since they can remember, of feeling "different" from other little boys, and even of attempting to change their feelings to no avail. The testimonies of gay men subjected to failed ex-gay conversion therapy speak to this shared experience (Toscano 2008; *Perry* 2010; Rix 2010). However, as Lisa Diamond (2008) points out, this dominant narrative premised in male experience leaves out the voices of some women who have experienced their identities as more sexually fluid, including those women who have experienced a shift in sexuality later in life. For such women, they may not necessarily identify as "born this way," but as Diamond writes, they have often "been written off as atypical and inauthentic, not only by researchers, but also by many subsets of the gay/lesbian/bisexual community" (257). In this context, lyrics such as Gaga's further render certain queer people's experiences invisible even while trying to promote queer visibility.

Vera Whisman (1996) also explores the standpoints of queer people who do not necessarily experience their sexual identities as originating in biology. Whisman interviews a woman who says, "I'm not going to spend a lot of time forgiving myself or forgiving anybody else because I started out straight, damn it. Okay? I say to people, 'You're going to have to take me as I am. I am converted, if you wish, okay? I used to be straight, now I'm gay. *I'm sorry if it would make you happy that I was born this way, but I wasn't'*" (62; emphasis mine). Additionally, individuals who may experience shifts in sexuality depending on environmental factors are left out of the biological narrative, such as students at single-sex high schools and colleges, individuals in juvenile detention centers and prisons, or, in E. Patrick Johnson's (2008) example, members of the military. Transgender people, too, may fall outside the biological model; for example, when a trans man has not necessarily felt inherently "like a man" his whole life (Spade 2000), or when trans men experience a change in sexual attraction as they go through the transition process (Devor 1997; Dozier 2005).

Claiming legitimacy for LGBT people based on being "born this way" fails to grapple with the homophobia/transphobia, heterosexism/cissexism, and heteronormativity inherent in such a proposition. Heterosexuality and cisgender identities (as opposed to gay and transgender ones) remain the unspoken standard, and any identities and experiences challenging that standard become excusable when they are presented as something that cannot be changed, something that *happens to* or *has always already happened to* an individual rather than something that one could experience, desire, pursue, explore, or cultivate. The individual remains passive rather than an agent of his or her own sexual desire, emotions, and thought processes, and the idea that no one would *want* to be LGBT if she or he could help it is reiterated, even if implicitly or unwittingly. No reasons are given for what is good, enriching, or even preferable about same-sex desire or pursuing a gender identity other than the one assigned to a person. While Gaga is entirely correct in singing that LGBT people are in the right, this should not be so mainly because of a biological origin.

There are undoubtedly concrete advantages to deploying biological determinism in the fight for LGBT rights in the United States. One is the ability of an individual to explain to her family that her same-sex desire is not "just a phase"—even though some people's sexuality does in fact shift after coming out, for example from lesbian to bisexual or vice versa—and that her sexuality is simply a manifestation of how she was born. The use of religious discourse to argue in favor of God's acceptance, as Gaga does in "Born This Way," remains particularly important for individuals whose families subscribe to certain religious ideologies that tell them that same-sex desire is a sin. The ability to believe in an inclusive God may also be important for queer individuals who themselves are religious. Still, when speaking to one's family, if being gay or transgender is what makes a person legitimately *happy,* regardless of how it came to be, that circumstance in itself is significant. After all, when an individual converts to a different religion that his family might not approve of, the arguments in favor of acceptance are usually about how fulfilled the person is in his new path, not that he was genetically predisposed to be Jewish or Muslim or Wiccan and would follow the religion of his parents if only he could help it.

Additionally, the use of biological determinism has been used as a legal strategy in the attempt to argue that gay and lesbian people deserve to be classified as a "suspect class," akin to women and people of color, in order to apply strict scrutiny, thus making potential discrimination harder to justify under law. The use of biological determinism in arguing for strict scrutiny can be seen as key since one prong of suspect classification is immutability, or the enduring, non-changing nature of the identity at hand. However, to be seen as immutable does not necessarily imply that one's identity is biological; as the Iowa Supreme court ruled in *Varnum v. Brien*, the unanimous 2009 ruling legalizing same-sex marriage in the state,

> [C]ourts need not definitively resolve the nature-versus-nurture debate currently raging over the origin of sexual orientation in order to decide plaintiffs' equal protection claims . . . we agree with those courts that have held the immutability "prong of the suspectness inquiry surely is satisfied when . . . the identifying trait is 'so central to a person's identity that it would be abhorrent for government to penalize a person for refusing to change [it].'" (*Varnum* 2009, 43–44)

In other words, as in my argument about discussing one's identity with family, it does not matter *why* someone is gay, but rather that it is an important, central, and meaningful aspect of someone's life that should not be expected to change simply because of another's disapproval. Finally, there are other legal pathways of approaching discrimination against gays and lesbians, such as arguing that treating same-sex couples differently based on the gender of the individuals involved constitutes gender discrimination. Although this legal strategy is not often argued, the use of it in the future may provide a fruitful way forward that is not reliant on biological determinism.

## CONCLUSION: MOVING FORWARD IN PRO-LGBT PERSONAL, LEGAL, AND MEDIA ADVOCACY

Lady Gaga undoubtedly remains a dedicated and inspirational advocate for LGBT equality as well as for many disempowered and marginalized youth in general. She speaks to the experiences of many LGBT people and works as an in-your-face counteractive force to challenge the hegemony of the Christian Right. The importance of such an all-star figure in the continued battle for the positive recognition and celebration of LGBT lives cannot be overstated, especially during a time in which we hear that even the most devoted and determined of Gaga's "little monsters" are susceptible to suicide, as was the case for fourteen-year-old Jamey Rodemeyer in September 2011 after severe bullying that lasted for years ("Lady Gaga Wants" 2011).

According to *The Huffington Post*, Rodemeyer's mother, Tracy Rodemeyer, planned to bury her son in a "Born This Way" t-shirt. Gaga responded to the child's suicide with anguish, tweeting, "Bullying must become illegal. It is a hate crime," and then announcing that she was planning to meet with Obama to "#MakeALawForJamey." Just a few days later, she performed a rendition of her popular song "Hair" as a tribute to Jamey at the iHeartRadio Music Festival in Las Vegas, including photos and videos of him on stage and asking the audience to put

, to be empowered and
to make a difference in the world. Together, we will move towards acceptance, bravery and love" ("Our Mission" 2011).

While Gaga has acted to help fill a tremendous gap in addressing the
life-or-death realities of bullied, harassed, and marginalized youth, I
would like to suggest that there may be alternative frameworks in media
and popular culture advocacy that do not rely on invoking biology in
order to advocate for accepting difference. Songs such as Jill Sobule's
1999 "I Kissed A Girl" speak to this potential, as do the lyrics and music
video from Katy Perry's 2010 song "Firework." Gay pop singer and
*American Idol* star Adam Lambert's 2011 song "Aftermath" approaches a
framework that avoids biology, advising queer people to learn to accept
themselves. The lyrics are not explicitly biological, and the song focuses
more on self-love and overcoming adversity, similar to Gaga's message
but lacking the "born this way" language.

Overall, it is important to acknowledge and appreciate the contributions of LGBT-friendly media icons despite their limitations. However, it
is also important to continually imagine even better and more-inclusive
media representations. The higher the standard is set for LGBTQ people
to be portrayed in celebratory, non-pitiable ways in the media, the more
LGBTQ people will be valued on our own terms rather than in spite of
our non-heterosexual and/or non-cisgender status.

## REFERENCES

Boggs, K. 2011, January 28. "FIRST-PERSON: Lady GaGa promotes a gay myth."
    *Baptist Press*. January 28. Message posted to http://www.bpnews.net/BPFirstPerson.
    asp?ID=34551.
Daly, J. 2011, March 9. "Lady Gaga Was Not Born This Way." *Focus on the Family*.
    Message posted to http://www.focusonlinecommunities.com/blogs/Finding_Home/
    2011/03/09/lady-gaga-was-not-born-this-way.
Devor, H. 1997. *FTM: Female-to-Male Transsexuals in Society*. Bloomington: Indiana Uni-
    versity Press.
Diamond, L. 2008. *Sexual Fluidity: Understanding Women's Love and Desire*. Cambridge:
    Harvard University Press.
Dozier, R. 2005. "Beards, Breasts, and Bodies: Doing Sex in a Gendered World." *Gender
    and Society* 19 (3): 297–316.
Duggan, L. 2003. *The Twilight of Equality? Neoliberalism, Cultural Politics, and the Attack
    on Democracy*. Boston: Beacon Press.
Eckholm, E. 2012, July 6. "Rift Forms in Movement as Belief in Gay 'Cure' Is Re-
    nounced." *The New York Times*. http://www.nytimes.com/2012/07/07/us/a-leaders-
    renunciation-of-ex-gay-tenets-causes-a-schism.html?_r=2&smid=tw-nytimes&seid=
    auto.

HausDJ. 2011, Feb. 23. "Lady Gaga Saved My Life." [Online Forum Comment]. http://www.ladygaga.com/forum/default.aspx?cid=454&tid=480670.

Hubbard, R. 2006. "Abortion and disability: Who should and should not inhabit the world?" In *The disability studies reader*, edited by L. J. Davis, second edition, 93–103. New York: Routledge.

Hubbard, Ruth, and Elijah Wald. 1999. *Exploding the Gene Myth: How Genetic Information Is Produced and Exploited by Scientists, Physicians, Employers, Insurance Companies, Educators, and Law Enforcers*. Boston: Beacon Press.

Hume, Joan. 1996, Jan. 26. "Disability, Feminism and Eugenics: Who has the right to decide who should or should not inhabit the world?" Paper presented at the Women's Electoral Lobby National Conference, University of Technology, Sydney, Australia.

Johnson, E. Patrick. 2008. *Sweet Tea: Black Gay Men of the South*. Chapel Hill: University of North Carolina Press.

Kaufman, Gil. 2010, April 8. "Lady Gaga Supports Teen Sent Home For 'Lady Gay Gay' T-shirt." *MTV.com*. http://www.mtv.com/news/articles/1635666/20100408/lady_gaga.jhtml.

ladygaga. 2010, Sept. 14. "God Bless and Thank you @HarryReid." *Twitter.com*. Message posted to http://twitter.com/ladygaga/status/24503132373.

"Lady Gaga defends controversy over new video." 2010, March 21. *Press Trust of India*. http://movies.ndtv.com/Ndtv-Show-Special-Story.aspx?page=2&ID=119&StoryID=ENTEN20100135641&.

"Lady Gaga Wants To Make Bullying Illegal Following Jamey Rodemeyer's Suicide." 2011, Sept. 22. *The Huffington Post*. http://www.huffingtonpost.com/2011/09/22/lady-gaga-wants-to-make-bully-illegal_n_975653.html.

LeVay, Simon. 1991. "A difference in hypothalamic structure between homosexual and heterosexual men." *Science* 253, no. 5023 (Aug. 30, 1991): 1034–37.

———. 1996. *Queer Science: The Use and Abuse of Research into Homosexuality*. Cambridge: MIT Press.

Mazur, Kellie. 2011, Sept. 25. "Lady Gaga tributes Jamey Rodemeyer in concert." *WIVB.com*. http://www.wivb.com/dpp/news/local/lady-gaga-tributes-jamey-rodemeyer-in-concert.

Ordover, Nancy. 2003. *American Eugenics: Race, Queer Anatomy, and the Science of Nationalism*. Minneapolis: University of Minnesota Press.

"Our Mission." 2011. *Born This Way Foundation*. http://bornthiswayfoundation.org/pages/our-mission.

*Perry v. Schwarzenegger*. 2010. American Foundation for Equal Rights. 1504-1522. http://www.afer.org/wp-content/uploads/2010/01/Transcript-from-Wed.pdf.

Rix, Jallen. 2010. *Ex-Gay No Way: Survival and Recovery from Religious Abuse*. Forres, Scotland: Findhorn Press.

Savage, Jon. 2011, Feb. 13. "Lady Gaga's new gay anthem." *The Guardian*. http://www.guardian.co.uk/music/2011/feb/14/lady-gaga-gay-anthem.

Sedgwick, Eve. 1990. *Epistemology of the Closet*. Berkeley: University of California Press.

Spade, Dean. 2000. "Mutilating Gender." *Makezine*. http://www.makezine.enoughenough.org/mutilate.html.

"Sylvia's Place." (2011). *QueerStreets.com*. http://www.queerstreets.com.

Toscano, P. 2008. *Doin' Time in the Homo No Mo' Halfway House: How I Survived the Ex-Gay Movement!* [DVD]. Available from http://www.quakerbooks.org/doin_time_in_the_homo_no_mo_halfway_house.php.

*Varnum v. Brien*. 2009. http://www.iowacourts.gov/wfData/files/Varnum/07-1499%281%29.pdf.

Vena, J. 2009, May 7. "Lady Gaga on success: 'The turning point for me was the gay community.'" *MTV.com*. http://www.mtv.com/news/articles/1610781/lady-gaga-on-success-turning-point-me-was-gay-community.jhtml.

Ward, K. 2011, Feb. 15. "Lady Gaga says she stayed incubated in Grammy 'vessel' for 72 hours." *PopWatch: Entertainment Weekly.* http://popwatch.ew.com/2011/02/15/lady-gaga-egg-72-hours.

Weber, S. 2012. "What's wrong with be[com]ing queer?: Biological determinism as discursive queer hegemony." *Sexualities* 15(5/6): 679–701.

Whisman, V. 1996. *Queer by Choice: Lesbians, Gay Men, and the Politics of Identity.* New York: Routledge.

## NOTES

1. Throughout this paper, I use "LGBT" when referring to the enumerated identities of lesbian, gay, bisexual, and transgender, especially because many mainstream advocacy groups (and gay people themselves) do not embrace the reclaimed term "queer." I use "LGBTQ" when referring to the possibilities for sexual and gender diversity that may extend beyond LGBT.

2. A hashtag refers to the use of the character # followed by a word or phrase, which on Twitter creates a searchable database in which all tweets containing the same hashtag may be easily found and ranked in popularity. Twitter keeps track of the most popular "trending" topics on any given day and lists them on their main webpage.

3. Despite the fact that Exodus International President Alan Chambers publicly announced in July 2012 that ex-gay "reparative therapy" does not work to change one's sexual orientation, including his own same-sex desire, and that it is in fact harmful to gay and lesbian people, this news has hardly come without controversy for many churches affiliated with the organization who remain committed to the pursuit of heterosexual conversion. See Eckholm (2012).

# ELEVEN

# First But (Nearly) Forgotten

## *Why You Know Milk But Not Kozachenko*

## Bruce E. Drushel

In early 1974, Kathy Kozachenko was elected to the city council in Ann Arbor, Michigan, making her the first openly gay elected official in the United States. She joined two other gay members of the city council, both of whom had self-disclosed their sexuality after their elections two years before. Kozachenko's accomplishment preceded by more than three and a half years a similar election in San Francisco that brought Harvey Milk to that city's board of supervisors. Between the elections of Kozachenko and Milk, no fewer than three other openly gay candidates were elected to office. Even so, a number of otherwise credible sources, including the redoubtable *Washington Post*, have inaccurately identified Milk as the nation's first openly gay elected official, and Kozachenko was able to rate no better than one among eight runners-up in the respected lesbian magazine *Curve*'s 2010 awards for trailblazing lesbian politician, political pioneer, and political newcomer.

In attempting to unravel the mystery behind this example of collective historical amnesia, the author has proposed as possible elements of an explanation four distinct but interrelated factors: the overshadowing effects of Milk's tragic assassination by a fellow city supervisor less than a year into his term; Milk's talent for self-promotion; the status of San Francisco as a major media market and, therefore, its ready access to national exposure; and the more generalized phenomenon of lesbian invisibility. The present analysis will interrogate and assess each of those factors with the aim of arriving at a more definitive answer to why Koza-chenko's noteworthy accomplishment has been largely overlooked.

## A CASE OF MISTAKEN IDENTITY, AGAIN (AND AGAIN)

On November 26, 2008, *Washington Post* reporter Ann Hornaday (2008) became the latest in a line of good journalists to get an important piece of queer history wrong. In her review in the paper's *Style* section, she praised the just-released Gus Van Sant film *Milk* for its poignancy in telling the story of the first openly gay elected official in the United States, Harvey Milk. *Milk* may have been poignant, but Milk was not the first. Other sources, too, have made the same error, including the Asso-ciated Press, *San Francisco Weekly*, and *The Portland Mercury* (Grant 2009). Nor, for that matter, was Hornaday the first *Post* reporter to make the mistake. On January 23, 1995, Mark Adamo, writing that time about an-other tribute to Milk, the then-new opera *Harvey Milk*, also incorrectly identified Harvey Milk as the first (Adamo 1995). In its "Correction" (1995) two days later, the *Post* named the true first self-identified LGBTQ person to be elected in the United States: Kathy Kozachenko. In 2008, perhaps even more embarrassed, and deservedly so, the *Post* waited three days and allowed LGBTQ historian Ron Schlittler (2008) to correct the record. Even Urvashi Vaid (1995), former executive director of the National Lesbian and Gay Task Force, a leading queer political organiz-ing group, incorrectly credited the Massachusetts state legislature's Elaine Noble with the distinction in her book *Virtual Equality*, even though Kozachenko's election preceded Noble's by some ten months.

For the record, Kozachenko was elected to the Ann Arbor City Coun-cil in January 1974, making her the first openly gay public official to be "out" at the time of her election (Sitaramiah 2004; Schlittler 2008; Grant 2009; Schlittler 2009; Stanton 2010; Jenkins 2011). Kozachenko ran as a candidate from the Human Rights Party and won the contest for the seat representing the city's second ward by fifty-two votes (Heflin 2007). She later moved to Pittsburgh but remained active in LGBTQ causes (Wech-sler 1980). Elaine Noble, who, like Milk, is frequently identified as having been first, actually became the second candidate who was openly gay at the time of the election to win her race. She was elected to the Massachu-setts House of Representatives in November 1974, after a hard-fought campaign during which bullets were fired through the windows of her campaign headquarters (Schlittler 2008).

Allan Spear was the third openly gay candidate to be elected. Actual-ly, he was first elected to the Minnesota Senate in 1972, more than a year ahead of Kozachenko, and therefore has the distinction of being the first to serve after he came out. But he did not publicly disclose his sexuality until midway through his first term and then was re-elected, this time as an openly gay man, in 1976 (Schlittler 2008). Jim Yeadon, who was voted onto the Madison, Wisconsin, city council in April 1977, also preceded Milk, who in turn became the fifth openly gay elected official in November of that year.

Perhaps more astonishing than the mainstream media's continual erroneous reporting is the queer media's seeming willingness to disregard Kozachenko's accomplishment. While the influential LGBTQ news magazine *The Advocate* published items about her shortly after her election ("This time" 1974) and a year and a half later (Baker 1975), in its recent issue celebrating forty-five years of publishing, its reporters noted the significance of both Milk (Grindley 2012) and Noble (Garcia 2012) as early pioneers, but failed to mention Kozachenko. And in its "First Annual *Curve* Lesbian Awards," that magazine chose former HUD Assistant Secretary Roberta Achtenberg as Politician, state senators Sheila Kuehl and Tammy Baldwin as Politician/Pioneers, and Houston city official Laura Spanjian as Politician/Newcomer, relegating Kozachenko to the status of "finalist" in all three categories, along with seven others (2010).

While it would be far simpler to credit all of these errors (as well as no doubt countless others that have been made in the media over the years but never reported) to sloppy reporting and lax editing, they instead may point to a pair of more serious underlying issues: first, that even basic events in the history of the lesbian, gay, bisexual, transgender, and queer movement are not well-known or even easily discovered from conventional credible sources, and second, that skillful use of media by individual public figures, along with the media's own tendency to represent people in ways that render some visible and others nearly invisible, plays a key role in *a history*; that is, they may determine the history that is known as opposed to the one that is correct.

## EXPLAINING COLLECTIVE AMNESIA

The elections of both Kozachenko and Milk received scant coverage nationally and particularly outside of major urban areas, perhaps because the press discounted such groundbreaking events as anomalies confined to famously progressive Ann Arbor and San Francisco, and perhaps because their local elected offices seemed disconnected from state or national politics. Kozachenko and Milk received somewhat more coverage in the national LGBTQ media, but not a sufficient amount to make them household names—even in queer households.

## DYING TO BE FAMOUS

Ironically, the circumstance that most thrust Harvey Milk into the national political consciousness was his own murder. On Monday morning,

November 27, 1978, Milk was shot and killed in his city hall office by fellow supervisor Dan White. Minutes before, White also had shot and killed Mayor George Moscone for his failure to reappoint White to the board after White's petulant resignation earlier in the month. The shootings occurred in the late morning—early enough to be covered in many afternoon newspapers and network television newscasts that day, and as front-page news in daily national newspapers, including the *New York Times* (Turner 1978), the following day. *NBC Nightly News* devoted roughly the first quarter of its half-hour broadcast to the story the day of the killings, giving roughly equal time to the deaths of Moscone and Milk (Westfeld 1978). The major U.S. national news magazines provided more analytic coverage, with *Time* connecting the event thematically with the mass-suicides in Jonestown, Guyana, which had claimed the lives of dozens from the Bay Area just days before ("Nation" 1978). Not surprisingly, the story made many media outlets' listings of the top news stories of 1978, including UPI Radio's *Recap 78* (Futz 1978).

## SELF-PROMOTION

There can be little doubt that the success of political figures of the last 150 years has been owed, to a large extent, to their treatment by and adroit use of the news media. The specific personal attributes and skill sets required have varied with the mix of media predominating during a particular period. Meyrowitz (1985) compares these media (and other contexts) to "stages" on which a politician "performs" and argues that the stages become most visible when a candidate either violates their structures or fully exploits them.

Harvey Milk, in many respects, epitomized the performing in Meyrowitz's metaphor, even going so far as to welcome a guest to his City Hall office with, "What do you think of my new theatre?" (Shilts 1982). Milk has been variously described as a "savvy politician" (Streitmatter 2005, 58) and as having "a flair for the theatrical" (Shilts 1982, 202), attributes which would seem to equip him to exploit the stages provided by the media. His use of the press played upon knowledge of both the substance of information they might use and the style of presentation that would guarantee its use. During campaigns, he created groups supporting his candidacy, such as Veterans for Milk, that were headed by friends and whose most important function was as the basis for distribution to newspapers of press releases about their creation (Shilts 1982). When he was finally elected to the San Francisco Board of Supervisors, his careful staging of news events proliferated, prompting an aide to a fellow supervisor to complain, "Every time you pick up the paper, there's Harvey doing something new. How in the hell does that guy do it?" (202).

Milk also used popular obsession with his identity as a gay man, and its possibilities as the basis for novelty and humor, to get coverage. Once, when Mayor George Moscone was out of town and the rotating designation of acting mayor reached him, he called a press conference declaring himself the first openly gay (acting) mayor in the country (Shilts 1982). Later, when he appeared at the grand opening of a friend's delicatessen, he told the crowd, "I am the only mayor who is cutting the ribbon and then wearing it" (202–3). His association with memorable lines in the press extended to those originating with journalists, such as the columnist who called him the "number one most ineligible bachelor of San Francisco" (203).

Two specific cases, one before his election as supervisor and one soon after, illustrate Milk's skills at self-promotion. The first suggests a political figure who understands professional practices among journalists and how to exploit both their availability and the conventions in news value. In 1975, two news events coincided to bring throngs of national and international media to San Francisco (Luzer 2009). The first was the arrest of heiress, kidnapping victim, and alleged terrorist sympathizer Patricia Hearst. The second was a visit by President Gerald Ford and his attempted assassination in Union Square by Sara Jane Moore. At a critical moment, Moore was rushed and thwarted in her attempt by ex-marine Oliver Sipple, a friend of Milk's. Milk tipped off longtime *San Francisco Chronicle* columnist Herb Caen that Sipple was a gay man, believing that the story would advance both Milk's political ambitions and the gay rights movement. Though Caen never identified Sipple as gay, his references to a well-known gay bar as Sipple's favorite, associating Sipple with Milk, and his mention of breaking (gay) stereotypes allowed readers to draw their own (correct) conclusions:

> One of the heroes of the day, Oliver "Billy" Sipple, the ex-Marine who grabbed Sara Jane Moore's arm just as her gun was fired and thereby may have saved the President's life, was the center of midnight attention at the Red Lantern, a Golden Gate Ave. bar he favors. The Rev. Ray Broshears, head of Helping Hands Center and Gay Politico Harvey Milk, who claim to be among Sipple's close friends, describe themselves as "proud—maybe this will help break the stereotype." Sipple is among the workers in Milk's campaign for supervisor. (Caen 1975, 33)

Milk also complained to the *Los Angeles Times* that the president never had thanked Sipple for saving his life, speculating that Ford did not want to associate himself with a gay man (Streitmatter 2005). Ford subsequently sent Sipple a thank-you letter on White House stationery, and Sipple made a press appearance to express his own appreciation for the gesture.

In the other instance, with news of his election to the Board of Supervisors scarcely cold, Milk immediately began using the media in what might have been the first tentative steps in a campaign for mayor. Milk campaign manager Anne Kronenberg related a story of Milk's effort to get a "pooper scooper" ordinance passed in San Francisco after he was elected supervisor. According to Kronenberg, Milk believed that whoever could solve the pet waste problem in the city could be elected mayor. TV news footage of the event showed Milk concluding his press conference in a park and stepping in dog feces he had strategically placed in his path before reporters arrived (Epstein 1984).

## MEDIA MARKETS

While media technologies of the era, such as cable television, did much to equalize access to content between urban markets and smaller towns, differences still were apparent in the pervasiveness of local news coverage and the ubiquity of local media culture that accompanies it. San Francisco of the 1970s was by any measure a major media market, with more than three million people. The market included four large daily newspapers (two in San Francisco and editorially aggressive nearby competitors in Oakland and San Jose), a half-dozen local television stations with local news and public affairs programming, and dozens of local radio stations, many of which also maintained local newsgathering efforts. In addition, several specialized publications, including those focusing on the LGBTQ communities, were available. As Shilts (1982) noted, the *San Francisco Chronicle* and *Examiner* both were editorially conservative papers but based their coverage on populist perceptions. Because editors perceived that their readerships liked stories about gays, such stories proliferated, and a high-profile gay public official such as Milk (particularly) made for good copy.

Ann Arbor was hardly a media backwater, with its population of more than 100,000, situated near the major Detroit market and the smaller Toledo and Lansing markets. Yet, it had little indigenous media itself—a small daily newspaper in the city and another serving the University of Michigan campus, as well as eight small radio stations (Murray 2009). But because it tended to be overshadowed by larger cities in the region, had media outlets that were not owned by large national groups, and was considered primarily a university town, local events and issues tended to remain local.

As Olien, Donohue, and Tichenor (1995) have observed, college towns such as Ann Arbor tend to be characterized by more homogenous social structures that lack mechanisms for challenging authority. This includes press coverage of conflicts that, when they do occur, tend to focus on external, not internal, players. Because residents of smaller cities are less anonymous than those in more populous areas, the author reasons that they tend to encounter each other more often informally and in multiple capacities. These regular encounters foster the settlement of intergroup differences interpersonally rather than in the media. Small cities are also characterized by greater acceptance of authority, if not always of the specific decisions those in authority make. Therefore, any controversy over the election of an openly lesbian city council candidate would be less a subject for even local press coverage, unless external groups either supported or contested her bid, or unless her campaign platform contained controversial planks.

The local media culture in Ann Arbor was likely different from that in San Francisco. If reporting in San Francisco was characterized by industry veterans with a more populist agenda, the trade in smaller Ann Arbor was more likely characterized by a mixture of longtime residents inured to the progressive politics of the Ann Arbor/University of Michigan communities and newcomers to the profession unlikely to be well-integrated into their new home, to engage with non-journalism members of the communities, or to involve themselves in local politics (Bunch 2008).

## LESBIAN INVISIBILITY

Social awareness of sexual behavior between people of the same sex is, of course, quite old; social awareness of minority sexuality as a form of identity is much more recent, dating by most accounts to the study by social scientists of sexual behavior in the late-nineteenth century. Paradoxically, the increased awareness of sexual minorities led to a greater urgency for their concealment. Faderman (1999) has noted that, while notable women of the 1800s would have felt no need to keep secret their most intense feelings for others of their sex, their twentieth-century biographers did and even sought to find a hidden man at the root of their despondency at the unhappy ending of a relationship or affair. What might better be termed a "visibility gap" in the nascent queer communities, but which often is called "lesbian invisibility," began to widen in the 1950s, following publication of Alfred Kinsey's groundbreaking studies of sexual behavior in men (1948) and women (1953). Though both studies found evidence of homosexuality in a significant part of the adult male and adult female populations in the United States, homosexuality as early as the 1950s became publicly the domain of white middle-class men (deJong 2006).

The popular media, especially concerning their preoccupation with Kinsey's work, were instrumental in the divide. According to deJong (2006), media can marginalize certain groups because they have the ability to create or perpetuate stereotypes. Women, both straight and queer, had been perceived historically as limited in their capabilities and agency, a perception frequently codified in the West in laws concerning political participation, property ownership, and rights in marriage, and tacitly accepted in the workplace and other social institutions. Gross (1991) has argued that media treatment of sexual minorities is in many respects an extension of dominant culture's broader construction of gender, wherein those who are systematically ignored are symbolically annihilated. Patriarchal society did not feel threatened by the prospect of sexually deviant women, but it did feel threatened by sexually deviant men. Thus, gay men flourished in the media and lesbians did not.

When the media do represent lesbians, they do so in roles supporting the "natural order," and therefore lesbians are negatively and narrowly stereotyped (Gross 1991). Even as the visibility gap began to narrow in the 1990s—and, in fact, flip in lesbians' favor, according to Gross (2001)—only certain types of representations were repeated and legitimized, leaving in place the relative invisibility of other types, including the more masculine "butch" (Kessler 2008).

The significant role assumed by media representations in popular culture means that what Gross (1991) called annihilation can become something of an inescapable spiral: according to Cooper (2009), their particular lack of representation in popular culture means that rural lesbians resemble their straight neighbors more than they do their urban counterparts. In turn, social scientists' work on lesbians in the United States has focused on those in urban and progressive areas, owing to the relative difficulty in identifying and reaching them elsewhere. Similarly, film historian Vito Russo (1981) observed that, historically, many lesbians were invisible even to themselves, and therefore that their sexuality was ill-defined and rendered invisible because it was seen as purely psychological.

## HOW TO FORGET HISTORY

Journalism has been called "The First Draft of History" ("The Educational Value" 1905). I wish to argue that queer history, already incomplete and inaccurate because the mainstream media were unaware of it or chose to ignore it, and because anti-sodomy laws and social stigma have conspired to discourage queers themselves from documenting it, is particularly in danger from misreporting and misimpressions owing to the ways in which media outlets report the news and the ways in which audiences process the events they witness through the media. And we should make no mistake about it: when history has not been written down or otherwise documented, and when (as eventually and inevitably happens) those who witnessed it no longer are around to relate it accurately, it is left to the whims of the unmotivated and the agendas of those with a stake in its manipulation. The implications are more substantive than a misidentified picture or a sentence that should read differently.

When the history of which we are aware changes—becomes more complete and more detailed—it transforms our understandings both of ourselves and of the path(s) the ancestors in our "chosen" families (as many queers view fellow members of the LGBTQ communities) have traced. Sometimes, it answers more basic questions while raising new and provocative ones. As an example, scholars are rediscovering accounts of LGBTQ uprisings throughout the United States that anticipated the one that tends to receive the most attention, namely, the 1969 Stonewall uprising in Greenwich Village. Scholars have documented at least twenty-three disturbances in the decade leading up to Stonewall, including a large-scale riot that destroyed Compton's Cafeteria in San Francisco in 1966 (Silverman and Stryker 2005) and a riot at a doughnut shop in Los Angeles in 1959 (Faderman and Timmons 2006). These "resurrected" histories answer the question of how the Stonewall uprising seemingly came out of nowhere to launch the nascent gay rights movement—which it didn't—but also raise the question of why it alone is the one that was remembered.

Specifically concerning the elections of "out" lesbian and gay candidates, understanding by the mainstream electorate of the pervasiveness of LGBTQ officeholders has the potential to alter their perception of its normalcy. Sitaramiah (2004) reported that, as of 2004, the Gay and Lesbian Victory Fund, which funds the candidacy of queer politicians and tracks their success, could point to more than 270 self-identified lesbians and gays who had been elected; by 2012, that number nearly had doubled to well over 500 ("The Victory Fund" 2012). The less isolated the phenomenon is perceived to be, the more an individual can imagine it happening. As the volatile 2012 Republican presidential primaries demonstrated, perceived electability can have a role in an eventual election.

And what is true in the present and in the future could have a bearing on the past, as well. A new generation of historians is providing fresh insights into the personal histories of elected officials from long ago. And while queer theory and its conceptualization of identity as both provisional and contingent cautions us about applying contemporary understandings of language when we attempt queer readings of texts from the past, understanding queerness among elected officials to be more than an isolated oddity lends credibility to the possibility that past officeholders—including those in very high office—might also have been gay. Though evidence of Abraham Lincoln's queerness may rely upon misinterpretations of his correspondence or upon time-bound standards for acceptable gender behavior, arguments that his predecessor, James Buchanan, lived, spoke, and was spoken of in ways that would today mark him as a gay man may be more persuasive in a world in which the queerness of a councilperson, state legislator, cabinet member, congressperson, or senator is widely known.

And this possibility has significance well beyond the world of politics. Repeated studies involving diverse populations support the assertion that straight individuals who claim close associations with one or more

LGBTQ persons are less likely to harbor homophobic attitudes and generally more likely to be accepting of queer people than those who profess no such relationships (Herek 2000). There also seems to be a relationship between youth and acceptance: younger people tend to be less homophobic than older people, perhaps because they are more likely to know self-identified sexual minorities, but perhaps because they are more likely to have seen "out" queers in the media—both scripted characters from fictional television and film (for example, *Will & Grace, Buffy the Vampire Slayer, Dawson's Creek,* and *The L Word*) and real people in nonfiction television and documentaries (such as Ellen DeGeneres, Pedro Zamora, Rosie O'Donnell, RuPaul, and Greg Louganis.) Clearly, people "know" public figures in ways that are different from the way they "know" close friends and casual acquaintances; yet, figures representing sexual minorities can't help broadening the worldview of those with otherwise-limited contact with queers. Similarly, figures such as Emmett Till, Cesar Chavez, and Ryan White made personal and concrete issues such as racism, farmer workers' rights, and HIV/AIDS, which to many were abstractions and easily misunderstood. "Knowing" Barney Frank, Tammy Baldwin, Sheila Kuehl, and Tom Ammiano as queer elected officials and as historic figures provides yet another substantial link to queer communities and their histories.

Ultimately, having access to one's history helps legitimize one's identity. Soon after the Stonewall uprising brought increased visibility to the gay rights movement, Dank (1971) argued that gays and lesbians could not be conceptualized as minorities (and presumably, be worthy of equal treatment) since their parents did not socialize them to their identity group as members of other minorities do. While the limitations of this argument (the first being that mainstream media has tended to ignore the histories and accomplishments of African Americans, women, and those from non-Judeo-Christian faiths as well) seem more obvious today, more than four decades after it was made, its fallacy belies a greater truth: that the health and integrity of a subculture depend upon someone for the accurate transmission of its history. If that task cannot be performed by a biological family, it falls to the chosen family; and because of the discontinuities and dispersions in that group, the media must play a role.

## REFERENCES

Adamo, M. 1995, January 23. "Opera: A brave and brilliant 'Harvey Milk.'" *Washington Post*, B-1.

Baker, K. 1975, June 18. "Kozachenko: City councilperson." *The Advocate*, 13.

Bunch, W. 2008. "Disconnected." *American Journalism Review* 30 (4): 38–45.

Caen, H. 1975, September 24. "In this corner." *San Francisco Chronicle*, 33.

Cooper, M. 2009. "Rural popular culture and its impact on lesbian identity." In *Queer identities/Political realities*, edited by B. E. Drushel and K. German, 113–27. Newcastle-upon-Tyne, UK: Cambridge Scholars Publishing.

"Correction." 1995, January 25. *Washington Post*, A-3.

Dank, B. 1971. "Coming out in the gay world." *Psychiatry* 34: 180–97.

deJong, M. J. W. 2006. "From invisibility to subversion." In *News and Sexuality*, edited by L. Casteneda and S. Campbell, 37–52. Thousand Oaks, CA: Sage.

Epstein, R. (Director). 1984. *The Times of Harvey Milk*. [DVD.] San Francisco, CA:Telling Pictures.

"The educational value of 'news.'" 1905, December 5. *The State* [Columbia, SC], 5.

Faderman, L. 1999. "Who hid lesbian history?" In *The Columbia reader on lesbians and gay men in media, society, and politics*, edited by L. Gross & J. Woods, 241–45. New York: Columbia University Press.

Faderman, L., and S. Timmons. 2006. *Gay L.A.: A history of Sexual Outlaws, Power Politics, and Lipstick Lesbians*. New York: Basic Books.

"The first annual Curve lesbian awards." 2010, October. *Curve* 20 (8): 22.

Futz, B. (Reporter). 1978, December 30. "Assassination of Harvey Milk and George Moscone." *Recap 78*. [Network Radio Feature.] Washington, DC: United Press International Audio Network.

Garcia, M. 2012, March 14. "Our hall of fame: Elaine Noble." *The Advocate*.

Grant, J. 2009, January 21. "Think Harvey Milk was the first openly gay politician? Think again." *Queerty*. http://www.queerty.com/think-harvey-milk-was-the-first-openly-gay-politician-think-again-20090121.

Grindley, L. 2012, March 14. "Our hall of fame: Harvey Milk." *The Advocate*.

Gross, L. 1991. "Out of the mainstream: Sexual minorities and the mass media." *Journal of Homosexuality* 21 (1/2): 19–46.

Gross, L. 2001. *Up from Invisibility*. New York: Columbia University Press.

Heflin, C. 2007, August 13. "City Council candidates uncontested." *Ann Arbor News*, A-3.

Herek, G. M. 2000. "The psychology of sexual prejudice." *Current Directions in Psychological Science* 9 (1): 19–22.

Hornaday, A. 2008, November 26. "By delivering poignant depth, 'Milk' hits the stirring heights." *Washington Post*, Style.

Jenkins, B. 2011, June 2. "The history of Motor City pride." *Between the Lines 1922* (715): 25.

Kessler, K. 2008. "Mommy's got a gal-pal: The victimized lesbian mother in the made-for-TV movie." In *Televising Queer Women: A Reader*, edited by Rebecca Beirne, 33–48. New York: Palgrave MacMillan.

Kinsey, A., W. Pomeroy, and C. Martin. 1948. *Sexual Behavior in the Human Male*. Philadelphia, PA: Saunders.

Kinsey, A., W. Pomeroy, C. Martin, and P. Gebhard. 1953. *Sexual Behavior in the Human Female*. Philadelphia, PA: Saunders.

Luzer, D. 2009. "The gay man who saved Ford's life." *Gay & Lesbian Review Worldwide* 16 (4): 23–26.

Murray, S. 2009. "Ann Arbor News to close in July." *Ann Arbor News*, March 23.

"Nation: Another day of death." 1978, December 11. *Time*.

Olien, C. N., G. A. Donohue, and P. J. Tichenor. 1995. "A guard dog perspective on the role of media." *Journal of Communication* 45 (2): 115–32.

Russo, V. 1981. *Celluloid Closet*. New York: Harper & Row.

Schlittler, R. 2008, November 29. "Gay officials who blazed trails." *Washington Post*, A-13.

Schlittler, R. 2009, November 11. "Out and elected in the USA: 1974–2004." *OutHistory*. http://www.outhistory.org/wiki/Out_and_Elected_in_the_USA:_1974-2004.

Shilts, R. 1982. *The Mayor of Castro Street: The Life and Times of Harvey Milk*. New York: St. Martin's Press.

Sitaramiah, G. 2004, March 28. "Council's 3 gays break ground; City seen as leader on rights issues." *Saint Paul Pioneer Press*, A-1.

Stanton, R. J. 2010, October 19. "Ann Arbor City Council condemns Andrew Shirvell's attacks on Chris Armstrong." *Ann Arbor.com*. http://www.annarbor.com/news/annarbor-city-council-condemns-andrew-shirvell-for-attacks-on-openly-gay-u-m-student/.

Streitmatter, R. 2005. "The Oliver Sipple story." In *News & Sexuality*, edited by L. Castaneda and S. Campbell, 55–72. Thousand Oaks, CA: Sage.

Stryker, S., and V. Silverman. (Directors.) 2005. *Screaming Queens: The Riot at Compton's Cafeteria* [DVD]. San Francisco: Frameline.

"This time, gay candidate wins as a gay." 1974, May 8. *The Advocate*, 9.

Turner, Wallace. 1978, November 28. "Suspect sought job." *The New York Times* , 1.

Vaid, Urvashi. 1995. *Virtual Equality: The Mainstreaming of Gay & Lesbian Liberation*. New York: Anchor Books.

"The victory fund: A brief history." 2012. *Gay and Lesbian Victory Fund*. http://www.victoryfund.org/our_story/history.

Wechsler, Nancy. 1980. "'Relaxed, Spirited' march in Pittsburgh." *Gay Community News* 7 (49): 3.

Westfeld, Wallace. (Executive Producer.) 1978, November 27. NBC Nightly News [Television Broadcast]. New York: National Broadcasting Company.

*Part IV*

# Queer Issues

# TWELVE

## "Is She a Man? Is She a Transvestite?"

### *Critiquing the Coverage of Intersex Athletes*

### Rick Kenney and Kimiko Akita

In August 2012, twenty-one-year-old South African sprinter Caster Se-menya won the silver medal in the women's 800 meters at the XXX Olym-pic Games in London. Despite criticism that she had either been mis-judged or intentionally lost a race she should have won, Semenya's finish as the second-fastest woman in the world at track's most grueling sprint event represented a triumph for herself and for a nation that supported her along the steps of one of the most difficult journeys any athlete has had to endure. For it was three years earlier that Semenya, then eighteen, was accused by competitors at the World Athletics Championships in Berlin of being not a woman, but a man. Semenya was subsequently suspended from international competition until her sex and athletic eli-gibility could be determined, leaving her gold medal at the 2009 event tarnished, at least temporarily.

Semenya's story should resonate with anyone interested in and con-cerned about media representations and explanations of complex issues of sex and gender in general, and about sex testing and persons who are intersex. In 2006, twenty-five-year-old Santhi Soundarajan of India won the silver medal in the women's 800 meters in Qatar at the Asian Games, which is second only to the Olympics for sheer size of athletic competi-tion (Shapiro 2012). Two days later, Soundarajan was ordered to leave the Games, having failed a sex-verification test that determined she was not a woman. Soundajaran, however, received little attention in Western me-dia until the sports cable TV and Internet juggernaut ESPN, in a feature timed to the opening of the London Olympics in 2012, included an update on her whereabouts.

Semenya, on the other hand, attracted global media interest in 2009 because of the sensational rumors swirling around her (Clarey and Kolata 2009; CNN 2009; Vinton 2009; Knapp 2009; Smith 2009; "Mother" 2009). Press and broadcast reports replete with misconceptions, anonymous sources, and leaked information fueled speculation around the sporting world and sparked anger in South Africa. A month after the race, the *Daily Telegraph*—an Australian tabloid newspaper owned by now-disgraced media magnate Rupert Murdoch—reported the supposedly confidential results of Semenya's test (Hurst 2009). She was finally cleared in July 2010 to return immediately to international competition and won a women's race in August that year (Motshegwa and Imray 2010; Zinser 2010). Semenya's presence at the London Games in 2012 renewed the controversy about her sex when the media raised the specter that the issue might haunt her again. Indeed, new rumors—about whether she was undergoing a treatment that was transforming her, *softening* her into a woman—arose in the media narrative that explained her runner-up finish (Broadbent and Fearon 2012; Greer 2012; Ralph 2012; Squires 2012).

This chapter discusses the respective controversies surrounding the sexual identity of both Caster Semenya and Santhi Soundarajan. These athletes' stories—the ultimate unwanted public exposure of individuals, writ large on global scripts—provide a rich text for the ethical critique of media coverage of intersex individuals. We first describe how Soundarajan's and Semenya's stories emerged in the mass media and situate their cases in a historical context of sex testing of athletes. We then discuss the problematic amoral journalistic craft values that drove media to chase down information about the most private, intimate details of these individuals' lives and then to publicize those details. Finally, we propose an alternate, non-Western ethical theory that focuses on notions of mutuality, trust, and privacy that better protect individual rights in an increasingly complex world of sexual identities.

## SANTHI SOUNDARAJAN

Soundarajan was raised in Kathakurichi, a rural village in southern India, in a 20-by-5-foot hut without running water or electricity (Shapiro 2012). Her parents earned $4 a week working in a brickyard in another town, while Soundarajan cared for her four younger siblings. When she was thirteen, her grandfather bought her shoes and taught her to run on a field of dirt. Her running ability became, literally, a meal ticket, paying for hot lunches and tuition at her high school. She earned a scholarship to a college in a nearby town, then transferred to a school seven hours away.

There, she began to set national records and, in 2005, won a silver medal at the Asian Athletics Championships in South Korea. In 2006, she won the silver again at the Asian Games in Doha, Qatar.

The next day, the Indian Athletic Federations team doctor took a blood sample from Soundarajan without explaining to her why (Shapiro 2012). He next brought in a panel of IAAF medical experts, including a gynecologist and an endocrinologist, to examine her. A day later, she was dismissed from the Games, again without explanation. Soundarajan learned why along with the rest of the world: News reports broadcast a few days later announced that she had been stripped of her medal because "she was not really a woman."

## CASTER SEMENYA

Mokgadi Caster Semenya grew up in the rural village of Fairlie, in Limpopo (South Africa's northernmost province), as one of five children, and played soccer as a child, growing to love the running that the sport required (Smith 2009). After Semenya won the 2009 World Championships at age eighteen, her rivals began questioning whether she had a physical condition that might give her an unfair advantage over other women (Clarey and Kolata 2009). Some outright called her a man. Semenya and her family steadfastly maintained that she was a woman who had been raised as a girl ("Mother" 2009).

In August 2009, a reporter inquired about rumors circulating at the World Championships: that questions had arisen over Semenya's sex after her victory performance in the African junior championships three weeks earlier, and that she had been required to undergo gender-verification testing (Levy 2009).Violating its own confidentiality policies, the International Association of Athletics Federation (IAAF) confirmed the rumor (Longman 2009). Semenya's world championship was overshadowed, and she was suspended from competition while tests were conducted and officials pondered which sex she was. Semenya had first come to the attention of the IAAF when she cut more than seven seconds off her best time in the 800 meters at the African Junior Championships on July 31, in the world's fastest time of 2009. Saying the dramatic increase in her performance "obliged" it to test Semenya for possible doping violations, the IAAF at first found nothing but then asked her to undergo sex-verification testing, too (Clarey and Kolata 2009).

## SEX TESTING

The IAAF stopped conducting mandatory tests on all athletes in 1992 but has retained the right to test them. The tests were dropped from Olympics sports in 1999 because they were not only controversial but also scientifically complicated. Since IAAF does not generally conduct sex-verification tests based on its own hunches, the challenge must come from another athlete or team—or through suspicion raised during specimen collection for doping control. Just before the 2012 Games, the International Olympics Committee implemented new criteria, defined by levels of androgens and not by chromosomes, DNA, or genitals (Shapiro 2012).

In Soundarajan's case, unbeknownst to her, the chaperone for a routine doping test at the 2006 Asian Games had "noticed something unusual" when Soundarajan was urinating (Shapiro 2012). For Semenya at the World Games in 2009, it turned out that someone "within the IAAF community"—perhaps her rivals—had questioned Semenya's sex: "Just look at her," Russian Mariya Savinova was quoted as saying. "These kind of people should not run with us. For me, she's not a woman. She's a man," Italy's Elisa Cusma told journalists (Clarey and Kolata 2009).

Soundarajan said that the four doctors who examined her at the 2006 Asian Games did not speak to her in Tamil, her native tongue, leaving her confused (Shapiro 2012). The Indian Athletic Federation's team doctor, Kumar Mendiratta, said that Soundajaran was addressed in English, which she speaks, but not fluently. It shocked Soundarajan when the media reported that she had a condition known as Androgen Insensitivity Syndrome, meaning she had a Y chromosome and was genetically male, even though she had external female genitalia. Soundarajan has a deep voice and a flat chest and had never menstruated—not uncommon for female runners. Humiliated, she returned to her rural Indian village, fell into depression, and attempted suicide by ingesting poison: "Everyone looked down on me. . . . Everyone was looking at me in this new way: Is she a man? Is she a transvestite? It's very hurtful. It ruined my life and my family's life" (Shapiro, 2012).

During the 2009 World Games, Semenya had been subjected to similar medical testing—including her first gynecological examination—on suspicion that she was not a woman. IAAF plainly violated its own policy of confidentiality as well, by confirming to reporters that an investigation into her sex was under way. South Africans reacted angrily, saying that reports of the investigation had spoiled Semenya's moment of triumph: "We condemn the motives of those who have made it their business to question her gender due to her physique and running style," said the African National Congress, South Africa's ruling party (Clarey and Kolata 2009). Semenya did not speak to the news media after her Berlin victory or after the medal ceremony, but her father, Jacob, told South Africa's *Sowetan* newspaper, "I raised her and I have never doubted her gender. She is a woman, and I can repeat that a million times" (Smith 2009).

By the London Olympics, Semenya clearly had the South African media on her side, but other news outlets appeared skeptical or even antagonistic. Australia's *Daily Telegraph* asserted that Semenya "knew she had blown her first Olympic final by starting out too slowly" (Pye 2012). Australia's *Herald Sun* called her strategy in the 800 final of hanging back in the pack and coming on strong with a final runner's kick "bizarre." BBC commentator Colin Jackson wondered aloud whether Semenya had been "slightly anxious about winning, after all that torment that followed her win in Berlin in 2009. That may have had a mental scarring on her" (Ralph 2012). Typically, one journalist attributed the media's skepticism to the ubiquitous, anonymous "they":

> Caster Semenya . . . according to some accounts, was required to take oestrogen to correct her excess of testosterone before she could be accepted to compete as a female in London. It is not the first time pundits have wondered if Semenya is happy to run well, but not be the centre of attention after dominant victories. Another theory is that rumoured hormone therapy may have dulled her brilliance, but she showed with her heat run she is still capable of exceptional times. (Ralph 2012)

Yet another writer suggested the opposite:

> Compared to the other athletes, who looked tired out, Semenya looked as if she had a lot left in her legs, and it left one thinking she could have challenged for the title had she run a different race tactically. (*SouthAfrica.info* 2012)

## THEORIES OF MEDIA ETHICS

This chapter considers two distinctly different, if not diametrically opposite, theories that one might apply to media coverage of the Soundajaran and Semenya stories: 1) the traditional utilitarian model that news media generally follow, and 2) normative principles based on mostly overlooked ideas articulated more than eighty years ago by the Japanese ethicist Tetsuro Watsuji, who represents, for the West, perhaps the most influential Eastern philosopher of the past century. This chapter will argue for the superiority of Watsuji's (1937, 1996) notions of mutuality, privacy, and publicity in making ethical journalistic decisions about publishing the most intimate secrets of sexual identity that involve not only highly complex science, but also the fragile psyches of naive athletes thrust into the spotlight on the stage of global sports.

### Utilitarianism

Media reports explicitly represent a tension in the dynamic of power over control of information about oneself: who has the right to access it and who has the right to disseminate it? Some journalists argue that disclosure and debate about the details of a person's embarrassing private facts—though generally a violation of privacy law, if not public sensibilities—may serve a greater social good, a moral utility. But traditional news media's amoral craft values of prominence, conflict, and controversy often fail to adequately meet fundamental ethical obligations of minimizing harm, especially to society's most vulnerable. Media members who respect privacy rights of those they cover know that, legally and ethically, they must be careful not to intrude unduly while gathering news that might violate someone's privacy, let alone publish it.

Utilitarianism is the most pervasive theoretical foundation for media ethics in the West. Journalists are continually making ethical decisions on a cost-benefit basis. News judgment—deciding to cover some stories while rejecting others, ranking and placing stories and photographs throughout a newspaper—is most often a utilitarian act. It reflects what editors think will be of most interest and usefulness to the greatest number of readers, viewers, or listeners. But utilitarianism poses major problems for media. Reporters and editors cannot predict outcomes, nor is it always clear how to identify the stakeholders: those with a moral claim in the ethical decision, those who will be most directly affected by that decision. Utilitarianism implies that the majority always wins, often at the expense of the minority or the individual. The utilitarian approach to journalism favors the publication of information, honoring truth as the primary ethical principle, outweighing the individual in the principle of minimizing harm. The weight of utilitarianism's moral obligation in balance favors the majority: readers, viewers, listeners—audiences—who rely on journalists for information. Utilitarianism does not acknowledge that individual rights might be violated for the sake of the greatest good.

When media coverage threatens to expose someone's private medical facts—information that could not only potentially embarrass that person but also place her or him in society's cultural crosshairs—the ethical quandary in balancing the truth and harm principles becomes more complicated. At special risk from unwanted publicity are certain groups such as the young, the disabled, and those marginalized from mainstream society because of differences sometimes out of their control, such as gays, lesbians, transgendered, and intersex persons. Many at-risk groups and individuals have long endured social inequalities and public prejudices; those problems are not produced by media coverage alone. But media practices may perpetuate stigmas through the traditional reproduction of ideas and the construction of social realities.

So when does the public have a legitimate interest—a real need to know? The sports world offers a unique field for studying an individual's privacy rights regarding medical facts. Unlike most persons, athletes are often placed under the brightest of media spotlights. An individual athlete's health is considered newsworthy in media coverage of sports. But what about an athlete's genetic makeup in general?

## Watsuji's Communitarianism

Tetsuro Watsuji (1937, 1996), who lived from 1889 to 1960, formulated notions of trust in a combined five volumes written about ethics, which he predicated on an ontology of community and relationalism long before the rise in the West of Communitarianism as it is known today. Watsuji saw all human existence as based on social and communal life with its sense of sincerity in relationships and thus emphasized a principle of social relationism emphasizing *"ningen,"* or the "betweenness" of persons. Watsuji asserted that the interrelationships of individuals form the basis of our humanity and, therefore, our community. This notion of "betweenness" further suggested that we must acknowledge our relationship to one another and that the best, most ethical way to do this is to begin from a basis of trust.

Watsuji (1937, 1996) distinguished between what is and should be public or private, maintaining that "against an instance of mere widespread publicity, the family or group is still private" unless or until we choose, of our own free will, to "reveal our happy existence to the public" and enter the "public domain" (147). In elaborating on the idea of publicity, Watsuji noted that a "typical source of public information in the modern world is the press:" specifically, "newspapers" (150). Our "private existence," when "published or reported" in the press, was "exposed to the sun," and "loses in privacy" (151). Concerning rumors, Watsuji asserted:

> We do not mean . . . that this kind of publicity keeps the authentic features of things exposed to the sun. Rather, it may even be a place where the authentic features are kept hidden. What a rumor or a newspaper report repeats day after day is to enter the private sphere that refuses publication . . . and brings it to public awareness against the wishes of those who would prefer to keep it private. Publicity . . . hides its authentic features by means of a "lie" disguised as authenticity. (151)

Under Watsuji's formulation of communal ethics, then, privacy accrues even greater significance since it would be too easy to allow the individual to become subsumed by the interests of greater society. To prevail, then, the individual and her rights must be considered just that much more carefully, leading us to the principle of publicity: Do we succumb to the temptations of rumor and innuendo and unfounded or premature reports of "news"? Watsuji pointed out that in such cases, the exposure to sunlight is undesirable; forced exposure would certainly present an ethical problem.

## DISCUSSION

Santhi Soundarajan and Caster Semenya should have been able to trust that their coaches, medical doctors, and the IAAF would value and protect their privacy and favor that over publicity about intimate information regarding their biological sexual identity. Furthermore, they should have been able to trust that news media would act ethically and, likewise, operate from a mutual position of trust in their relationships.

Although Watsuji's formulation of ethics clearly states that the individual matters in the context of community, this does not mean that the individual does not matter. In fact, the community might be said to mutually exist because of its many individuals. Therefore, both Soundarajan and Semenya mattered most in their respective cases and held the strongest moral claim. Their families, however, might be said to have been equal stakeholders. Each family represented the nucleus of community, according to Watsuji's formulation. Their families' humanity was bound up in that of each woman, and vice versa. Each family's right to privacy about the intimate information of Soundarajan's and Semenya's genetic makeup—and by extension, theirs—superseded any claims other stakeholders (competitors, fans, officials) might have had. Because of Soundarajan's and Semenya's belonging to another community—intersex persons—the principle of mutuality presented another intriguing argument about whose moral claims must be considered most highly.

Ethical consideration of the Soundarajan and Semenya cases following Watsuji's thinking would have led journalists to understand that Soundarajan and Semenya "owned" their stories and the related narrative because their private medical information belonged to them and only them all along. Journalists acting under Watsuji's principle of mutual trust should have come to the reporting of these stories from a much less aggressive, accusatory, and judgmental position—one of humility that respected Soundarajan's and Semenya's dignity as well as their own. Their respective claims of being women were factually legitimate when considering how to label their gender, were that even necessary to have done.

## CONCLUSION

The Soundarajan and Semenya stories unveiled conventional media practice and ethics that further marginalize and reduce minoritarian moral claims in favor of majoritarian interests. Media coverage revealed some of the problems of journalism that depend on timeworn utilitarian tradition. These case studies also introduced and illuminated Watsuji's (1937, 1996) principles of mutuality, privacy, and trust, that suggest ways in which journalists and other media professionals—as well as activists, advocates, or anyone who cares about the dignity and respect due all beings—might identify and include in their deliberations those underprivileged sources and resources that can most helpfully add to the conversation and enhance people's understanding of complex sex-and-gender issues.

Journalists' professional orientation, including usage and word choice according to unyielding conventions of "style," tends toward traditional and timeworn craft values that threaten to overwhelm ethical principles. Scholars have noted that bias is often contested over language used to convey controversial ideas in mass media. Examples over the years have included word binaries such as "prolife" versus "prochoice," "refugee" versus "evacuee," and "the right to live" versus "the right to die" (Kenney and Dellert 2007). Consumers of mainstream media are unlikely to have a substantial understanding of transgender, transsexual, or intersex identities, so the language used in communicating narratives involving those concepts is of critical importance (Kenney 2008).

The Semenya and Soundajaran stories offer a rich site to begin discussion about not only the craft accuracy of reporting on complex controversies of sex and gender, but also the ethical implications of language choice. Although news organizations are wise to research and debate internally which terminology is correct and how and when to use it, there is a further issue regarding who gets to decide which words become custom in stories about gay/lesbian/bisexual/transgender issues. Intersex and transgender activists are not likely going to stand by—nor should they—and allow the media to construct labels and definitions on their own. At stake may be their "right to self-definition" (Kenney 2008).

## REFERENCES

Broadbent, R. and M. Fearon. 2012, August 24. "Smooth Semenya puts controversy behind her with Olympic debut." *TheTimes.co.uk*.http://www.thetimes.co.uk/tto/sport/olympics/athletics/article3501562.ece.

Clarey, C., and G. Kolata. 2009, August 21. "Gold is awarded, but dispute over runner's sex intensifies." *The New York Times*, B9.

CNN. 2009, August 20. "Women's world champion Semenya faces gender test." http://edition.cnn.com/2009/SPORT/08/19/athletics.worlds.berlin.semenya/index.html

Greer, G. 2012, August 25. "The dangerous sport of unnatural selection." *The Age*, 48.

Hurst, M. 2009, September 11. "Caster Semenya has male sex organs and no womb or ovaries." *The Daily Telegraph*. http://www.dailytelegraph.com.au/sport/semenya-has-no-womb-or-ovaries/story-e6frexni-1225771672245.

Kenney, R., and C. Dellert. 2007. "An ethics of caring and media coverage of Terri Schiavo." *Journal of Mass Media Ethics* 21 (2 and 3): 215–17.

Kenney, R. 2008. "The real gender-bender: The curious case of coverage of the Steve Stanton story." *Florida Communication Journal* 37 (1): 1–12.

Knapp, G. 2009, August 20. "Drug testing trumped by gender testing." *The San Francisco Chronicle*, B1.

Levy, A. 2009, November 30. "Either/or: Sports, sex, and the case of Caster Semenya." *New Yorker*. http://www.newyorker.com/reporting/2009/11/30/091130fa_fact_levy.

Longman, J. 2009, November 20. "South African runner's sex-verification result won't be public." *The New York Times*, p. B10.

"Mother of 800m winner Caster Semenya dismisses gender questions." 2009, August 20.        http://www.telegraph.co.uk/sport/othersports/athletics/6059875/Mother-of-800m-winner-Caster-Semenya-dismisses-gender-questions.html.

Motshegwa, L., and G. Imray. 2010, July 6. "Caster Semenya cleared to run after 11-month gender saga." http://www.huffingtonpost.com/2010/07/06/caster-semenya-to-be-clea_n_636202.html.

Pye, J. 2012, August 13. "A silver lining for Semenya." *The Daily Telegraph*, 60.

Ralph, J. 2012, August 13. "Doubts cast on her will to win." *Herald Sun*, 74.

Shapiro, S. 2012, August 1. "Caught in the middle: a failed gender test crushed Santhi Soundarajan's Olympic dreams." Accessed August 15, 2012, http://espn.go.com/olympics/story/_/id/8192977/failed-gender-test-forces-olympian-redefine-athletic-career-espn-magazine.

Smith, D. 2009, August 20. "Caster Semenya sex row: 'She's my little girl,' says father." *The Guardian*. http://www.guardian.co.uk/sport/2009/aug/20/caster-semenya-sex-row-athletics.

*SouthAfrica.info*. 2012, August 12. "Caster takes silver as team SA shines." *Africa News*.

Squires, N. 2012, August 12. "Caster Semenya: I didn't run from the win." Express. Accessed August 15, 2012, http://www.express.co.uk/posts/view/339274/Caster-Semenya-I-didn-t-run-from-the-win.

Vinton, N. 2009, August 20. "Gender test ordered for fast woman." *New York Daily News*, 65.

Watsuji, T. 1996. *Watsuji Tetsurō's Rinrigaku, Ethics in Japan*, translated by S. Yamamoto and R. Carter. Albany: State University of New York Press. (Original work published in 1937).

Zinser, L. 2010, July 7. "South African is cleared to compete as a woman." *The New York Times*, B13.

# THIRTEEN

## The Commercial Closet

*How Gay-Specific Media and the Imagery of "the Closet"*
*Erases the LGBT Community from the Mainstream Gaze*

### Kristin Comeforo

In 1969, New York City police raided the Stonewall Inn in Greenwich Village, touching off the Stonewall Riots and, in many ways, the gay rights movement. The chant of "Gay Power!" energized participants on Christopher Street and in the Village but also made visible an LGBT community that was at once discriminated against *and* a powerful constituency that would fight for its rights. In giving meaning to the movement, visibility also served to give meaning to a concept, which, while present, had gone somewhat unstated or concretized: "the closet." Stonewall gave birth to both the notion of the closet and coming out—holding the latter as "the first essential step towards freedom" (D'Emilio 2000, 35).

Visibility comes through a variety of vehicles, with mainstream media and its advertising serving as pervasive and powerful sources. While traditionally conceptualized as operating under economic imperatives, morals and ethics have increasingly come to bear on advertisers and their practices, leading some to argue that the former operates under the guise of the latter (Jhally 1990; Williamson 1982). In regard to the LGBT market, for instance, economic decisions to reach these consumers through gay-specific media are conflated with moral and ethical achievements. This chapter will argue that LGBT advertising is a double failure: not only does it renege on its moral imperative to represent the LGBT community and provide visibility, but it also fails to deliver on its economic imperative to adequately target these consumers and convince them to purchase the sponsoring brand. Both of these failures are derived from notions of "the closet," which are embedded in LGBT advertising strategy and render LGBT folk invisible both to themselves and to mainstream audiences.

## THE LGBT MARKET

For a market that is becoming increasingly coveted, many of the "facts" that contribute to its attractiveness take form, largely, as "myths." Population estimates, for instance, appear to be all over the map, ranging from 2 to 10 percent of the adult population. Lameck and Witeck (2011) cite research from Packaged Facts, which found the LGBT population to be 16 million in size, and with $743 billion in buying power. Gary Gates, from the Williams Institute on Sexual Orientation Law and Public Policy, however, found a significantly lower 9 million LGBT population, or approximately 3.8 percent of the overall population (Leff, 2011). Regardless, other "facts" contribute to the infatuation with the LGBT market.

Although the "gay affluence myth" has definitively been debunked, Shullman and Kraus (2011) find that there are indeed affluent LGBT folk who are, when compared to their non-LGBT counterparts, a unique and attractive market. The 2.4 percent of the 14,405 participants who described themselves as LGBT were found to be not only "more affluent" but also younger and more likely to be social and cultural leaders (for example, active voters, theater/museum/concert-goers) than non-LGBT affluents. LGBT affluents were also more likely to use new media platforms such as smartphones and tablets, be interested in new and luxury products and brands, and be willing to pay more for brands that (a) fit their values and beliefs (for example, organic or environmentally friendly) and (b) deliver higher quality (Shullman and Kraus 2011). Further, LGBT consumers have been found to be more brand-loyal (Tuten 2005) and more likely to actively advocate for or against brands they feel address, or do not address, issues that are important to them (Witeck and Combs 2006).

## COMPETING STRATEGIES

In approaching the market, the easiest, safest, and therefore most readily adopted strategy is to avoid the segment completely. This decision, however, is becoming more and more costly, and thus more brands are seeking ways to reach out to LGBT folk while not offending their mainstream consumer base. As a result, brands have tested the LGBT waters in several ways, ranging from low involvement/attention, to higher involvement/ more specific strategic initiatives.

The lowest form of involvement with LGBT audiences occurs when a brand runs a mainstream advertising execution in a gay-specific media. Engagement with the target market, essentially, is reduced to a mere media buy. Absolut vodka adopted this strategic position in 1981 when it began courting the LGBT market by placing ads on the back covers of a variety of gay interest magazines. The first ad to run was the mainstream "Absolut Perfection" ad, featuring the iconic Absolut bottle, capped with an angelic halo (Elliott 2011).

As brands become more involved in their appeals to the market, they may employ a "gay vague," "gay window," or "purposive polysemy" strategy, which calls for the embedding of implicit or ambiguous gay cues in mainstream communications (Puntoni, Vanhamme, and Visscher 2011). This provides a somewhat middle ground in terms of involvement/attention to the target market. During the mid to late 1990s, Absolut used this type of strategy, running its Absolut Au Kurant and Absolut Haring ads in both mainstream and gay media. LGBT audiences could read gay pride into the purple laces and leather of the corset (Au Kurant ad) and the hallowed space held by Keith Haring as a famed "out" artist and AIDS activist. The cues supposedly picked up and appreciated by the LGBT audience remain invisible to the hetero audience, thus preserving its perception of the brand. This veiling of LGBT cues, or sequestering them to the subtext, is a relatively obvious way in which advertising not only serves as *a closet for* LGBT folk but also serves *to closet* the community.

The most involved and overt appeal to LGBT consumers comes through a gay-specific strategy. Brands may choose to develop LGBT-specific messages and deploy them in either mainstream or LGBT-specific media. The 2009 Gay Press Report (Prime Access and Rivendell Media 2010) suggests that brands adopting a gay-specific strategy are far more likely to do so via gay-specific media—a point supported by findings that ad revenue in the gay and lesbian press grew more than ten times faster than that of the mainstream press (7). From 1996 to 2009, ad revenues grew by 377 percent in gay-specific titles, while general market consumer magazines saw increases of 17 percent. Similarly, almost 90 percent of the ads in national LGBT magazines were gay-specific, indicating that national brands are tailoring their messages, and committing, to the market (7).

While viewers and consumers of gay media are nearly 100 percent LGBT-identified, these media not only fail to deliver mainstream visibility, but also, some have argued, visibility among LGBT audiences. Gay media, on the whole, are thought to deliver less than 50 percent of the overall LGBT population (Angelini and Bradley 2010; Oakenfull and Greenlee 2005). Increased advertising and visibility in gay media does not necessarily result in increased visibility of LGBT folk, thus revealing the complex relationship between visibility/closeting inherent in LGBT advertising practice.

Absolut's evolving relationship with the LGBT market finds the brand currently in a gay-specific strategic position. In fact, 2011 marked the thirty-year anniversary of the love affair Absolut has been having with the LGBT market. To celebrate, the brand launched a $4 million campaign under the theme "Absolut Outrageous" that included advertising, events, and social media executions (Elliott 2011). The cornerstone of the campaign was a print ad, which ran in gay publications—*Out, The Advocate,* and *Instinct*—along with mainstream titles, *Vanity Fair* and *Vogue,* and delivered a "fantastic image featuring closets, divas, disco turntables, the performance artist Amanda Lepore, and unicorns" (Elliott 2011, paragraph 9).

## ABSOLUT OUTRAGEOUS: UNDER THE LENS

Press musings surrounding the campaign referred to the ad created by David LaChapelle as, "a visual cornucopia of iconic gay images . . . [that] draws viewers into a menagerie of icons and symbols that represent life and cocktails . . . perfected" (*Echelon* 2011). This menagerie consists of a closet, depicted in the shape of an Absolut bottle, positioned as the optical center of the ad. The closet is empty, save a lone hanger. It is outlined in pink and stands ajar, with a variety of fantastic images tumbling out below.

Among these fantastic images is an oversized roller skate, atop which two male "drum majors" are poised—one perched on the other's shoulders—both waving batons which leave vibrant neon trails in their wake. We also see two cowboys in flamboyant costumes striking a dance-like pose, while two very feminine cowgirls recline in a romantic embrace slightly below. There is an elegant, bedazzled, drag queen-esque woman, reminiscent of Marilyn Monroe or Anna-Nicole Smith, reclining on a life-sized hotdog, and an African American 1970s-style disco "girl" dancing near a purple double turntable. Positioned between the reclining diva and the dancing queen is a pink unicorn, which is rearing up on its hind legs, as if mimicking the dancer or the boy/toy soldier who is similarly "rearing" slightly above and to the right—floating across the midsection of the ad.

Anchoring the right side of the ad, and contributing to the formal balance of the layout, is longtime LaChapelle muse Amanda Lepore, donning fairy wings and sitting seductively on a purple unicorn. Slightly to the left a pink-and-purple-clad male breakdancer holds a one-arm handstand. The bottom of the ad is anchored by a three-tier anniversary cake, decorated with a pink sparkly "30" sign. A set of male figurines and a set of female figurines are positioned as same-sex couples on top. A female "fairy godmother" character, complete with magic wand and tiara, lies to the left beneath the cake, peacocks, and cutout flowers. A male "Prince Charming" character lies in similar fashion on the right. Rounding out the fantastic images are pink, yellow, and light-blue cutouts of stars and rays that are strewn on the beach and suspended in the air. Beneath the "action" of the ad runs the following copy:

> ABSOLUT OUTRAGEOUS
> Cocktails Perfected
> CELEBRATING 30 YEARS OF GOING OUT AND COMING OUT

## PULLING THE THREAD—DECONSTRUCTING THE CLOSET

Deconstruction, developed by Jacques Derrida, is an approach to reading texts that assumes there is no center or fixed meaning inherent in the work, but rather that meaning is unstable, "in play," and full of possibilities. By pulling on loose threads that appear in the text, deconstruction reveals how conceptual opposites are more like nested opposites—where concepts can at once exhibit difference/distinction *and* dependence/similarity (Balkin 1995). The position of the viewer at the metaphorical "head of the table" illustrates how the images of gayness included in the ad can be doubly read according to Derrida's hymen (the either/or between an either/or)—as (n)either flowing from the Absolut bottle/closet, (n)or flowing from the viewer (Powell 1997). The possibility of this dual reading renders all images, and thus the overall message(s) of the ad, "in play." It exposes the instability of key binaries—male/female; in/out; presence/absence—and reveals possibilities for meanings that are deemphasized, overlooked, or suppressed (Balkin 1995).

### Male/Female

The Absolut bottle standing at the dominant center of the ad, along with the hot dog, campy drag queens, and frolicking boys, create a very male dominated image of gayness. Feminine "characters" appear to be something less/more than female—fairies, the sun, drag queens—putting the question of gender into play. In *Gender Advertisements*, Erving Goffman (1979) suggested that advertising constructs the female as submissive to the dominant male, imbuing her with childlike innocence and characteristics. This point is further developed by Jean Kilbourne in her thought provoking visual work, *Killing Us Softly 4* (Jhally 2010). In the current example, whether male, female, or other, the corresponding "gender" is presented as the same—childlike and surreal—and thus, non-gender.

The Absolut ad erases gender; both men and women are dehumanized, objectified like dolls or action figures for our viewing pleasure. In the freedom of coming out of the closet, the ad has been constructed as a sort of Liliput, where the people live in miniature in a world created and manipulated by a higher power. This surreality or dehumanization serves two functions. It minimizes the threat the LGBT community poses to the hetero power structure. How can one fear the political power of a group that dons sequined dresses, lounges on life-sized hotdogs, and rides oversized roller skates as if they were cars? It also creates an empty space where the soul of gayness should reside. Instead, we are offered product and services to purchase, which will fill the void. Futhermore, in detaching gays from gender, the ad constructs gays as something not of this world: less than men, and less than women. We are distanced from the rituals that bind together societies and communities, thus pushed further into the closet, and made completely unrecognizable to ourselves and others. The only thing available to bring us back from this abyss of non-gender/non-existence is consumption. And we are, of course, encouraged to "come out" and "go out," as if the two were inextricably linked.

## In/Out

The Absolut bottle, which is presented as a closet (empty, save a lone hanger), appears to liberate gays and lesbians. The tagline "Absolut Outrageous" along with "Celebrating 30 years of coming out and going out" seems to support this thesis. Decentering our gaze, however, the difference between "in" and "out" seems to slip, and we can begin to see how the one (in *or* out) is dependent on the other. Thus, "out" loses its privileged status, leaving the residue of "in" to be detected in, and communicated through, the ad. The image of the closet holds out the hope or promise that one can "come out" once and for all and lead a life of complete transparency. But "being 'out' always depends to some extent on being 'in;' it gains its meaning only within that polarity" (Butler 1990, 123). Butler (1990) goes on to remind us that "being 'out' must produce the closet again and again in order to maintain itself as 'out'" (123). Coming out, in the style Absolut suggests—by "going out"—therefore merely "shifts the opacity" of LGBT identification and results in a further pushing "in" of LGBT folk.

Similarly, the visual likeness of a closet allows the bottle to operate as a form of totem. The bottle/closet becomes the "mark" that signals inclusion to or membership in the clan of LGBT. Members of the clan experience the "alreadyness" that Williamson (1982) claims calls out to us as subjects of the ad. LGBT folk *already were* outrageous; we had these icons/symbols of gay life already within us—and whether emanating from ourselves as the metaphorical head of the table/source of the ad, or the bottle/closet that is made to represent us (see, "Presence/Absence" section below)—the campaign is designed for us and through us. Thus, to express our "gayness" we must consume the Absolut product; we must go out to come out. A powerful political statement is reduced to a display of conspicuous consumption, all to the benefit of brands who (ad)vocate for the LGBT market.

From out of one closet, LGBT America finds itself pushed into another, that of consumption, exposing another Derridian loose thread, which when pulled reveals the positive denoted "out" to be nothing more than a (re)iteration of its opposite, "closeted." Similarly, the Absolut bottle, in addition to the other images that are intended to set us free from the shackles of the closet, can be read, instead, as literally squashing gay pride and visibility. The characters that anchor the bottom of the ad, seemingly basking in the joy of the fantastic world of gay culture created by Absolut, can also be seen as being crushed under the weight of this representation. "Real" people are marginalized while fantastic images— the unreal of the fairies, toy soldiers, and unicorns—are left to represent us.

## Presence/Absence

Given the interplay of fantasy/reality, the LGBT individual is both present in *and* absent from, the ad. Even if visibly present, LGBT individuals can still remain absent, or empty, and must look for themselves in the "transformational spaces between the units of the ad," where signifier becomes signified (Williamson 1982). Williamson (1982) informs us that "there are ads where people become identified with objects" (13). At the denotative level, the object with which LGBT folk should identify is located at the optical center of the ad—the Absolut bottle—which is held out as the vehicle through which our outness is achieved and through which we are connected to the fantastic images of gay life.

The phallic shape of the bottle, holding a dominant position around which the action of the ad takes life, suggests, however, an alternative reading of the image. In this case, what is absent—overt physical sexual representation—is what lies behind the present fantastic images of faeries, unicorns, and super-sized roller skates. The bottle/closet is conspicuously empty, calling to be filled, in the manifest sense with Absolut vodka, but in the latent sense with seminal fluid that can (n)either give life to the fantastic images, (n)or the absent spectator.

Impregnated by the ad, the absent spectator is made present—a surrogate parent to the images seemingly spawned by the bottle/closet. The fantastic images, ones which may or may not be identified at first glance as *natural* to the observer—are now presented as co-productions, flowing from the product and the consumer at once. If the things in the ad are meant to signify us (Williamson 1982), then uncovering the absent meaning of the bottle/closet as phallogocentric illustrates how LGBT folk generally, and gay men specifically, are held hostage, or, in effect closeted, by their sex as being the only mode of identification.

## CONCLUSION

Through gay-specific ads, LGBT individuals are, at once, brought into the spotlight and pushed back into the invisibility of the closet. Marginalized in the gay media, and set apart from the mainstream, the LGBT community, a powerful political force, is reduced to the LGBT *market*, with consumerism becoming the unifier that brings us back into the fold of mainstream society. Conspicuous consumption creates the outward image of progress and equality, while true legal rights for LGBT folk lag woefully behind those of their hetero counterparts.

In this particular case study, the imagery of the Absolut ad has a two-fold closeting effect. First, in its manifest content, it places a rigid structure of identification on LGBT observers. Sedgwick (1990) recognizes the "problematical" in gay identity and discusses "how intensely it is resisted and how far authority over its definition has been distanced from the gay subject her- or himself" (79). Given that we desire to see ourselves in advertisements and to identify with the people represented (Tsai 2011), but we have no authority to define these representations, little room is left for our contribution in making meaning through the ad. If LGBT folks—the intended targets of the ad—cannot see themselves in text, the ad fails to perform its economic function for the brand. If LGBT folks cannot see *themselves* in the text, then the possibility for mainstream viewers to see them—in any real or substantial way—is similarly negated, and the ad fails to deliver its moral and ethical imperatives.

The latent content provides the second closeting effect. As the phallic center of the ad, the Absolut bottle/closet silences the absent signifier of the penis as a key point of identification for LGBT generally and gay men specifically. The practice of being "out," we are reminded, is not a boon for free expression but rather a highly regimented performance which, rather than disclosing the "true and full content" of people, produces "a certain radical *concealment*" of their very natures (Butler 1990). In many ways, one is encouraged to be "out," but not "too out"; or, to be "out" in *this* way, but not in *that* way. The fantastic images of the ad seem "way out" there, yet deeper consideration reveals how they obscure or divert attention from other out performances (such as sexual contact or political activism) that may be more alarming to the hetero-majority.

Even though the ad is an overt display of homosexuality, it still operates within the confines of the closet. By choosing one set of images—fantastic ones like fairies, unicorns, and the like—all other sets of images are negated. These images, specifically, construct members of the LGBT community as "other worldly," real, yet unreal; "characters" that no one, straight or gay can relate to on any substantial level. This suggests that LGBT advertising is insufficient, both as an economic tool for encouraging brand consumption among LGBT consumers, and as a social tool that provides normalizing judgment about the LGBT community to both itself and the world at large.

## REFERENCES

Angelini, J. R., and S. D. Bradley. 2010. "Homosexual imagery in print advertisements: Attended, remembered, but disliked." *Journal of Homosexuality* 57: 485–502.

Balkin, J. M. 1995. "Deconstruction." http://www.yale.edu/lawweb/jbalkin/articles/deconessay.pdf.

Butler, J. 1990. "Imitation and gender subordination." In *The Judith Butler Reader*, edited by S. Salih, 119–37. Malden, MA: Blackwell Publishers.

D'Emilio, J. 2000. "Cycles of change, questions of strategy: The gay and lesbian movement after fifty years." In *The Politics of Gay Rights*, edited by C. A. Rimmerman, K. D. Wald, and C. Wilcox, 31–53. Chicago: The University of Chicago Press.

*Echelon Magazine*. 2011, November 3. "Absolut vodka celebrates 30 outrageous years." http://www.echelonmagazine.com/index.php?id=2421andamp;title=ABSOLUT_VODKA_CELBRATES_30_OUTRAGEOUS_YEARS.

Elliott, S. 2011, October 27. "Absolut celebrates its 30 years of marketing to gay consumers." *The New York Times*, 3.

Gates, G. 2006. "Same-sex couples and the gay, lesbian, and bisexual population: New estimates from the American community survey." http://escholarship.org/uc/item/8h08t0zf.

Goffman, E. 1979. *Gender Advertisements*. Cambridge, MA: Harvard University Press.

Jhally, S. 1990. *The Codes of Advertising: Fetishism and the Political Economy of Meaning in the Consumer Society*. New York: Routledge.

———. (Director). 2010. *Killing Us Softly 4: Advertising's Image of Women* [Videorecording]. USA: Media Education Foundation.

Lameck, F., and B. Witteck. 2011, January. "The growing gay market." *PR Tactics*, 6.

Leff, L. 2011, April 7. "Gay population in U.S. estimated at 4 million, Gary Gates says." *Huffington Post*. http://www.huffingtonpost.com/2011/04/07/gay-population-us-estimate_n_846348.html.

Oakenfull, G. K., and T. B. Greenlee. 2005. "Queer eye for a gay guy: Using market-specific symbols in advertising to attract gay consumers without alienating the mainstream." *Psychology and Marketing* 22 (5): 421–39.

Powell, J. 1997. *Derrida for Beginners*. New York: Writers and Readers Publishing.

*Prime Access and Rivendell Media* (2010). *2009 Gay Press Report*. http://rivendellmedia.com/documents/gaypressreport2009.pdf.

Puntoni, S., J. Vanhamme, and R. Visscher. 2011. "Two birds and one stone: Purposeful polysemy in minority targeting and advertising evaluations." *Journal of Advertising* 40 (1): 25–41.

Sedgwick, E. K. 1990. *Epistemology of the Closet*. Berkeley: University of California Press.

Shullman, B., and K. Kraus. 2011, September 14. "The unique profile of LGBT affluents; And why this population is attractive to marketers." *Advertising Age*. http://adage.com/article/adagestat/unique-profile-lgbt-affluents/229777.

Tsai, W-H. S. 2011. "How minority consumers use targeted advertising as pathways to self-empowerment." *Journal of Advertising*, 40 (3): 85–97.

Tuten, T. L. 2005. "The effect of gay-friendly and non-gay friendly cues on brand attitudes: A comparison of heterosexual and gay/lesbian reactions." *Journal of Marketing Management* 21: 441–61.

Williamson, J. 1982. *Decoding Advertisements: Ideology and Meaning in Advertising,* fourth edition. New York: Marion Boyars Publisher.

Witeck, R., and W. Combs. 2006. *Business Inside Out.* Chicago: Kaplan Publishing.

# FOURTEEN

## Should We Stop Believin'?

### Glee *and the Cultivation of Essentialist Identity Discourse*

### John Wolf and Valarie Schweisberger

The musical dramedy *Glee* premiered on Fox in the spring of 2009 and was an instant hit with critics and fans alike. Critics praised the show for its novelty and quirky spirit, and it made an appearance on numerous "must-see" and year-end "best-of" lists (for example, Poniewozik 2009; Tucker 2009; Respers France 2009). Similarly, *Glee* also resonated with fans, many of whom seemed to identify with the show's focus on a band of social misfits at the fictional McKinley High School, including a stuttering nerd, a wheelchair-bound paraplegic, numerous racial and religious minorities, and, of course, a non-gender-conforming closeted gay teenager. So much did fans identify with these characters that the popular press affectionately dubbed them "Gleeks," a portmanteau of the terms *Glee* and "geek," during the show's first season.

The fan reception of *Glee* is important for thinking about how the show relies on identity to construct narrative. Because the narrative is predicated upon the fact that the lead characters are social misfits, the nonconforming aspects of their identities are continually highlighted throughout the course of the show, even as some of the characters gain social acceptance from their peers. In this way, *Glee* risks making broad and sweeping statements about social identities, the implications of which are complex, although they are often lauded as a celebration of minority representation in the mainstream media. In order to investigate the ways in which popular culture texts like *Glee* promote essentialist identities and, furthermore, in order to explore the potential for television as a medium of audiovisual signs and cues to interrupt the cultivation of these types of messages about identity, this study is driven by the following research questions:

RQ1: Through which textual and narrative mechanisms does *Glee* reinforce essentialist identity discourse?

RQ2: What is the potential for televisual texts to complicate the essentialist discourse?

## ESSENTIALISM AND THE TELEVISUAL TEXT

Essentialism construes identity as "resident within the individual, a quality or trait describing one's personality, cognitive process, moral judgment, and so on" (Bohan 1993, 5). Thus, essentialist views regard identity traits as "fundamental attributes that are conceived as internal, persistent, and generally separate from the on-going experience and interaction with the daily sociopolitical contexts of one's life" (Bohan 1993, 6). In cultural theory, essentialism is often polemically opposed with constructivism, which holds that identity is the product of a mutual "recognition of some common origin or shared characteristics with another person or group, or with an ideal, and with the natural closure of solidarity and allegiance established on this foundation" (Hall 1996, 2). Thus, we can situate identity traits derived from essentialism as coming from within the individual and those derived from constructivism as the product of some mutually agreed upon social interaction (Bohan 1993).

Television is a medium of audio messages and visual signs, the meaning of which is dependent upon viewers to decode. Though televisual messages can be interpreted in a theoretically infinite number of ways, the meaning of televisual signs is generally fixed within certain degrees of interpretation (for example, Hall 2006). Televisual messages, thus, are prone to rely on socially agreed upon conventions to convey meaning. It is in this manner, then, that essentialist understandings of identity can be reinforced by the medium. Conventions related to identity categories become especially problematic where minority representations are concerned. For instance, a dearth of representations of a minority social group (for example, queer people) can lead to mischaracterization and defamation of individuals who may identify with the group but not necessarily with the group's televisual depictions. Therefore, representations of minorities, particularly when they compose a relatively small percentage of the television landscape, can contribute to the endorsement of social stereotypes. Furthermore, failure to identify with televisual representations can result in feelings of isolation and segregation, which is especially germane when thinking about the intersectional nature of individual identities. For instance, the relationship between race, gender, and sexual identity has been the subject of much scrutiny, at the center of which is the argument that experiences related to sexual identity are fundamentally different based on race and gender.

## SOCIAL IDENTITY THEORY

As previously mentioned, *Glee* is an exercise in social categorization. Since its first episode, *Glee* has relied heavily on the principles of both self-identification and social group identification. From the show's pilot through its most current episodes, *Glee* is concerned with clearly demarcating the lines between different social groups ("Cheerios," glee club members, jocks, nerds, and so on) and then consciously blurring them to illustrate the importance of overcoming social differences. Though the show is best known for its musical numbers and zinging one-liners, *Glee* has garnered much attention for being steeped in identity politics.

Any analysis of identity and/or identity politics would be incomplete without reference to social identity theory (SIT). Developed by Tajfel (1981) in the 1970s, SIT refers to "a social psychological analysis of the role of self-conception in group membership, group processes, and intergroup relations" (Hogg 2006, 111). As humans, we are inclined to group ourselves according to familiar schema (Hamilton and Trolier 1986), and adolescents are no exception. After all, research indicates that adolescent involvement in various social groups and activities can do wonders for self-esteem and social adjustment (Payne and Fogarty 2007). SIT is concerned with, among myriad other things, the prejudice and discrimination that can result from that very social involvement and categorization.

A complex and interdisciplinary theoretical construct, SIT relies mainly on psychological theories of categorization and self-conceptualization. Sociological principles of grouping based on demographic characteristics and theoretical work on large-scale social phenomena also play a role in SIT. Put plainly, a researcher employing the SIT framework might be tasked with observing and identifying the social groups in question (for the purposes of SIT, groups exist when "three or more people construe and evaluate themselves in terms of shared attributes that distinguish them collectively from other people"; Hogg 2006, 111), and would also delve into the psychological principles of individual identification with social groups.

Identification with social groups (or social membership as it is more commonly known) is governed first and foremost by identifying one's ingroups and outgroups. In short, ingroups refer to any group with whom an individual identifies; an outgroup, then, is any group for which the same individual does not claim membership (Gorham 2010). Research in the area of SIT states that people are concerned with the maintenance and good standing of their own ingroups, and as a result will interpret actions and behaviors in ways that favor their ingroups (Petti-grew, 1979). In *Glee*'s case, this tendency to preserve oneself and one's ingroup at the expense of an outgroup can be observed in nearly every character's social interactions.

## *GLEE* AND THE REAL ME

Though *Glee*'s creators may never have realized just how complex issues of social membership and identification can be, social identity theorists have much to work with in analyzing the show's character interactions. An overreliance on an essentialist identity discourse serves to maintain traditional ingroup/outgroup dynamics that may be considered discrimi-natory or otherwise hazardous. This idea is put in motion from the show's inception. When Will Schuester, a Spanish teacher who decides to make the struggling glee cub his pet project, goes on the hunt for new club members in the show's pilot, he overhears Finn Hudson singing in the men's locker room following football practice, and he observes, "I suddenly realized why I had wanted to do this in the first place: It was seeing a gift in a kid they didn't even know they had." Thus, Schuester sets the foundation for the essentialist undertone that reverberates throughout the series and reinforces the notion that there is something innate, fixed, and, above all, essential about those traits that, taken to-gether, compose social identities.

Mercedes Jones, the token Black member of the glee club, later sus-tains this idea in "Acafellas" when she learns that fellow glee club mem-ber Kurt Hummel is gay, noting that "the whole point of the [glee] club is about expressing what's really inside of you." Again, the manner in which essentialism is used to construct identity is significant. Namely, Mercedes expresses her belief that glee club is a celebration of self-expres-sion as it is related to and derived from those traits and characteristics that are inherent to one's sense of self. In the case of Kurt, she is referring to his sexual identity.

The notion of the true self (for example, Rogers 1951), rooted in psychology, is useful for thinking about the ways in which *Glee* employs essentialism as it relates to identity throughout the series. The true self is characterized by "identity-important and phenomenally real aspects of [the] self not often or easily expressed to others" (Bargh, McKenna, and Fitzsimmons 2002, 34). In psychology, the idea of the true self relates authenticity to self-actualization, with the former begetting the latter. Yet notions of authenticity are not confined to an individual's sense of self; rather, the idea of a true self also holds that other people possess funda-mental and essential qualities reflective of an authentic nature. This find-ing extends to media as well. For instance, Hill (2002) found that audi-ences enjoy watching reality television, at least in part, because they anticipate and enjoy the moments when "real people are 'really' themselves in an unreal environment" (323; quotes in the original).

*Glee* explores the true self particularly as it relates to the social categories of gender and sexuality. In doing so, the show offers a host of contradictory messages about gender and sexuality as essentialist identity categories and, consequently, what it means to claim or be assigned membership in a given social group. As this analysis reveals, the identity work that *Glee* performs regarding gender and sexuality promotes essentialism as a platform for sensemaking and self-understanding. Though *Glee* has been celebrated for the visibility it has afforded gays, lesbians, and straight allies on television, the merits of such minority representations must be assessed alongside their potential hazards.

## YOU EITHER ARE OR YOU AREN'T: SEXUAL IDENTITY ON *GLEE*

*Glee*'s investment in sexual identity is apparent in its lesbian and gay characters as well as the numerous storylines that focus on contemporary social issues relating to sexual identity. These issues include coming out to friends and family, bullying, promiscuity, and first sexual encounters. Furthermore, Ryan Murphy, one of the show's creators, has been outspoken about incorporating elements from his experiences as a gay man into the character of Kurt Hummel (Fernandez 2009). The show, thus, becomes a gay artifact not only in the stories it tells, but also in its association with a successful, out Hollywood director and producer.

*Glee*'s storylines related to sexual identity are actualized primarily through two characters: Kurt Hummel and Santana Lopez. Each character deals with coming out, self- acceptance, and same-gender adolescent romantic endeavors. By means of these processes, *Glee* essentializes sexual identity as a trait that is fixed and resident within the individual. *Glee*'s investment in sexual identity, thus, is heavily rooted in contemporary identity politics. For Kurt, this identity is reaffirmed by his interactions with other characters, his coming out to his father, and—since *Glee* is, after all, a show about song and performance—the songs he chooses to perform in glee club.

When Kurt finally discloses his sexual identity to his father in "Preggers," his father is unfazed, stating, "I know. I've known since you were three. All you wanted for your birthday was a pair of sensible heels." Kurt's father's reaction serves to link Kurt's gender non-conformity with his sexual identity. In this moment, then, it is made apparent that on account of his predispositions, the only person who struggled to understand Kurt's sexuality was the character himself. For other characters in the diegesis, Kurt's gayness is implied, symbolically inscribed onto his body every time he enters a room. On account of this, Kurt's acceptance of his own same-gender attractions comes in the form of claiming an identity label that purports to account for other aspects of his social identity in addition to his sexual feelings. This act, then, lends credibility to the idea that sexuality in the form of a term or a label is unidimensionally identifiable and resident within the individual.

The songs that Kurt sings throughout *Glee* are not an accident; rather they work to reveal his character's identity and, by extension, reinforce his gayness as an essential part of his nature. Most of the songs that Kurt sings were made famous by female recording artists. When Kurt transgresses this boundary, both his performance and his identity are policed. For instance, in "Laryngitis," Kurt covers Mellencamp's "Pink Houses" in an effort to masculinize his image. While the vocals are satisfactory, the overall performance is met with a lukewarm reception, summarized best by Will Schuester, who states, "That song didn't really sound like you. This group needs you to be you. You can literally do things that no one else can. Don't lose track of who you are just because it might be easier to be someone else." In his critique of the song, Schuester polices identity, linking Kurt's performance of aberrant masculinity with his departure from his usual (that is, feminine) song choice. Kurt later redeems himself in the episode by performing "Rose's Turn," the showstopping finale from *Gypsy* originally made famous by leading ladies Ethel Merman and Rosalind Russell.

Santana Lopez's journey towards realizing a sexual identity is not nearly as clean-cut as Kurt's, though, ultimately, the results are similar. At the beginning of the series, Santana is a popular cheerleader who uses sex as a means of obtaining what she wants. While her sexual identity is not directly stated at the beginning of the series, her sexual relationship with fellow Cheerio Brittany is referenced throughout the first season in addition to her numerous sexual encounters with male classmates. Thus, at least in the first season, the viewer can at best assume that Santana is bisexual. Resolving this ambiguity, however, quickly becomes a several-episode story arc in the second season.

In "Sexy," at Brittany's urging, the two decide to consult Holly Holiday (Gwyneth Paltrow), a decidedly hip and in-touch substitute teacher, for advice about their feelings for one another. When asked if she is a lesbian, Santana replies that she's unsure but that she's not interested in any labels. Uncertain of their feelings for one another and unable to adequately express their relationship in words, the two choose to represent their feelings through song at glee club, after which Santana looks at her fellow glee club members and declares, "Just because I sang a song with Brittany doesn't mean that you can put a label on me. Is that clear?" In this way, the ambiguity around Santana's sexual identity is sustained, though it consistently leads to conflict throughout the series until it is ultimately resolved in the third season.

Finn Hudson calls Santana a lesbian in "Mash Off," effectively resulting in her public outing (her sexual identity and status as head cheerleader is used in a smear campaign against cheerleading coach Sue Sylvester, who is running for public office). Santana ultimately accepts the use of the label to identify her sexuality, though, notably, she doesn't employ the term herself when disclosing her same-gender attractions to her family. The glee club's reaction toward Santana's tacit acceptance of the label is best summed up by Finn, who says, "Glee's about learning how to accept yourself for who you are no matter what other people think. . . . Everyone in this room knows about you and Brittany, and we don't judge you for it. We celebrate it." In acknowledging their support for her relationship with Brittany through her sexual identity, the members of the glee club members symbolically force a label onto Santana's body to which she ultimately acquiesces. While it is clear that the members of the glee club believe they are doing her a service, Santana's continued discomfort with the label (most notably in her hesitation to use the term to describe herself) is unsettling.

## DUDE LOOKS LIKE A LADY: GENDER CONSTRUCTIONS ON *GLEE*

Coach Shannon Beiste (not coincidentally pronounced "beast") was a second-season addition to *Glee*. Introduced after the previous football coach suffered a nervous breakdown, Beiste is positioned as a gender anomaly almost immediately. As the female coach of a football team in Lima, Ohio, Beiste occupies a role almost exclusively filled by men both in reality and in media. Coach Beiste is physically imposing and gruff, with a deep voice, a short haircut, and a lumbering gait. She identifies as heterosexual and engages in flirtations with men, but she is positioned in the show as anything but a woman. One character on the show goes so far as to point out in Beiste's introductory scene that "female coaches, like male nurses, are a crime against nature," thus indicating to the audience exactly how Beiste is perceived within the diegesis.

From the very beginning of her story, it is clear that Beiste struggles with the discursive limitations of gender. She refers to herself in the third person, but not as Beiste. She says things like "don't get up in the panther's business," suggesting a self-conceptualization that manifests itself not as an image of a human man or woman, but as a presumably genderless animal. This might be interpreted as the character's psychological discomfort with or dysmorphia about her own gender. Later during the same episode, one of the student characters refers to Beiste as "dude," infuriating her to the point of kicking him off the football team. Though she has chosen a traditionally male vocation and seems to relish her tough persona, it is clear that Beiste does not appreciate the implication that she is a man. What these instances say about Beiste is at once simple and mind-bendingly complicated. On one hand, it is plainly obvious that Beiste is merely a gender nonconformist. She refuses to perform the role of the traditional female, and she has made a life for herself enacting her idea of personhood rather than pretending to be a feminine, socially acceptable woman. On the other hand, she reacts poorly to suggestions that she might be a man, indicating that she has less an active nonconformist agenda and more a discomfort with the gender roles that have been projected onto her. Gender roles exist (both in fictional television and in reality) because the human need to categorize mandates that we recognize different patterns for different groups of people, thus helping us make sense of the world around us (Gorham 2010). In short, Beiste's problem lies not only in her conceptualization of her own gender, but in everyone else's deep-seated conceptualization of men and women.

Beiste is at once essentialized as a woman and constructed as a man, but never the discursive twain shall meet. Because our verbal expression of self is inextricably bound to the language we speak (or sign, or write), there is little possibility of escaping the reductionism inherent to a common vocabulary. Essentialism is marked by fundamental difference, and those differences are argued to be inherent and fixed. As such, essential characteristics are easy to categorize and reduce to words or phrases. Constructivism, however, is concerned with meaning derived from ongoing social interaction. Constructed characteristics are by definition fluid and ever-changing, all but guaranteeing their transcendence of common language. Beiste's identity is, as all identities are, subject to interpretation as either essential or constructed. In her case (that is, the case of a gender-queer character), an essentialist categorization as "woman" does not accurately describe the complexity of her identity, and as such would be an act of categorical violence. However, she also does not identify as a man, suggesting that a constructivist read of her maleness would also be an oversimplification. In short, both essentialism and constructivism are bound to articulation through reductive, oversimplified language. Any expression of Beiste's identity—indeed, *anyone's* identity—would necessarily be an act of categorical violence.

One of the trans community's most beloved cultural artifacts, *The Rocky Horror Picture Show,* seemed destined to somehow play a role in *Glee.* Indeed, the 1975 film inspired a late-October 2010 episode during which the glee club prepares a production of *Rocky Horror* at McKinley High. The roles are assigned as any regular *Glee* viewer would expect them to be, with one notable exception: Mercedes, a voluptuous black diva-in-training, secures the role of "sweet transvestite" Frank-N-Furter. Originally one of cinema's most notable gender-variant characters, Frank-N-Furter is reduced here to a glorified lounge singer.

Mercedes is awarded the role of Frank-N-Furter after she is inspired by song to chase her dream of landing the lead in a play. This scene, a reaction to another character's less-than-enthusiastic response to having been originally cast as Frank-N-Furter, acknowledges the queer nature of the situation without relying at all on dialogue. When Mercedes first volunteers for the role, the other characters wear confused looks (presumably because the role was originally played by the biologically male Tim Curry) that urge her to explain herself. In her explanation, she announces that her version of Frank-N-Furter will come complete with a "modern interpretation" of the character. Brighter-than-average viewers will pick up on the fact that she's talking about the gender discord, but *Glee*'s writers stop short of making it explicit. Later in the episode, we are treated to Mercedes' version of "Sweet Transvestite." Rather than maintain the several levels of gender performance that would exist simultaneously if she delivered the song the way it was written (that is, for a man), Mercedes performs a version in which the pronouns are switched to accommodate her femaleness, thus completely undermining the concept of the song. In fact, it does nothing but confirm for the audience that the person in the leather bustier is in fact intended to be read as a female. It also confuses the viewer, whose inevitable next question is "What makes this girl a transvestite?"

The curious case of Mercedes' Frank-N-Furter speaks to much more than *Glee*'s willingness to attempt camp. It suggests that contemporary television writers and producers do not have an abundance of faith in the modern American audience. By essentially castrating the male portion of the character, the writers transformed a male transvestite into a cisgender female. One might interpret this as a sign that the show's creators either didn't feel confident enough in their ability to complicate an already-complex gender construction, or that they don't believe American audiences can wrap their minds around a woman playing a man who likes to dress as a woman. In television studies, there is a concept known as "the least objectionable programming." In short, it means that when channel surfing, people will watch not necessarily what they like the most, but what they object to the least. Mercedes' female Frank-N-Furter might be regarded as the least objectionable programming. Because it is plausible that audiences will object less to a *woman* dressed as a woman singing about sex than they might to a *man* dressed as a woman singing about sex, the choice is simple. Audiences may be intrigued by the casting change, but their gender norms remain unchallenged without an actual transvestite to visually confirm the song's title. Without an audience who can interpret and/or deconstruct complicated identity representations, television writers are once again limited to reductive, overly simplified vehicles of expression.

## THE POTENTIAL OF THE TELEVISUAL TEXT

Because communication is strictly bound to certain avenues of expression, and because those avenues are limited further when expression is transmitted through a particular medium (in this case, television), the potential for even the simplest identity expression to be authentic or accurate is at best minimal. At most, television can rely on metaphor and incongruity to augment the limited expression permitted through spoken word and audio cues. For example, Joss Whedon's *Buffy the Vampire Slayer* explores complex queer desires through the metaphor of magic. In his fourth-season director's commentary, Whedon asserts that his magic metaphor is "one of the most powerful and romantic" illustrations of character desire he ever put on film (Whedon 2003). He suggests that the intimation of feeling through metaphor has much more narrative potential than the explicit portrayal of character interaction. Whedon implies, thus, that letting viewers experience media messages through their own lenses is perhaps the more effective way to express complex ideas about identity. Through the metaphor of magic, Whedon may have stumbled upon the most realistic way possible to portray complex same-gender desires and identity traits.

Though *Glee* has a built-in mechanism for harvesting the power of televisual metaphors in the songs the characters perform, this opportunity is never fully recognized. Instead the glee club's members' song choices, though always tuneful, are often times perplexing when they are not altogether lost in a dull void of nonsensical pop vapidity. Instances where *Glee* manages to effectively deploy the use of song as metaphor are occasional, but they are ultimately overshadowed by the numerous befuddling song choices. For instance, when Brittany and Santana choose to express their feelings for one another through song, they sing Fleetwood Mac's "Landslide," which recognizes that Santana is on the precipice of a life-altering situation but ultimately fails to reveal anything substantial about the girls' relationship. When the glee club enters their first competition in "Sectionals," Rachel Berry covers "Don't Rain on My Parade," essentializing her Jewishness and cementing her likeness to Barbra Streisand, but failing to produce anything more than an updated cover of an obvious choice for the character. These examples serve as indicators of song choices throughout the series, where the metaphors are lost in simplistic statements about essentialist identities.

In addition to metaphor, the use of incongruity within the televisual text also serves as a method for disrupting essentialist claims about identity. In the televisual text, incongruity refers to an occurrence of dissonance, contradiction, or inharmoniousness whereby the viewer actively recognizes that at least one element of the audiovisual message is discordant with some pre-existing expectations, standards, or practices. In such instances, the text has the capability to contradict the idea that identity traits are somehow exclusively innate or fixed by eliciting an interpretation in which the cognitive response is humor, confusion, unease, or any combination thereof.

Although instances of incongruity in the televisual text of *Glee* are numerous, they are also more often than not neutralized. In the case of

Sue Sylvester's sexual identity, for example, the text seldom alludes to the character's erotic desires or past romantic relationships. The character's gender nonconforming style and behavior coupled with the paratextual knowledge that Jane Lynch is a self-identified lesbian may encourage viewers to read the character as gay or perhaps merely as a gender nonconformist. Though the viewer can never be certain, the power of the incongruity lies in the character's ability to disrupt popular understandings about what it means to be a woman. Yet this incongruity only retains its effectiveness if the viewer is invited to question Sue's sexual identity (in other words, if she's not labeled as gay or straight). Once Sue is identified with a sexual identity label, her gender nonconformity becomes either acceptable and understood in terms of stereotypes about lesbians or so untenable as a straight woman that there exists the invitation to interpret the character as a cartoon rather than a messy, complicated individual.

As in the case of Santana, *Glee* also refuses to allow sustained ambiguity regarding Sue's sexual identity. In "I Kissed a Girl," while penning an entry in her journal, Sue's voiceover reveals, "Why would someone assume I'm a friend of Ellen just because I'm mannish and highly aggressive and have short hair and I only wear track suits and I coach a girls' sport and I married myself. It just doesn't make sense! The truth is, journal, I'm attracted to men. Sure, I can't stand watching them eat or talking to them, but when it comes to getting sexy, this girl's got a hole in her heart only a fella can fill." This statement resolves the ambiguity surrounding Sylvester's sexuality. Because the show refuses to commit to the development of Sylvester's opposite-gender sexual desires, the incongruity is defused, thereby effectively stripping the device of its potential to deconstruct. Metaphor and incongruity afford the televisual text the power to challenge the cultivation of essentialist identity discourse. While televisual messages often rely on convention to convey meaning about social identities and categorizations, there exists the possibility to disrupt popular notions about identity—and especially minority identity—by giving life to televisual stories that are simultaneously challenging and entertaining. By blurring the lines of social distinctions, the televisual text can invite identification from viewers belonging to multiple social groups—viewers who are undeniably much more complicated than a mere label can approximate and who are no doubt eager to see a part of themselves reflected in the televisual world, an undisputed proxy for a shared national consciousness.

## REFERENCES

Bargh, J. H., K. Y. A. McKenna, and G. H. Fitzsimmons. 2002. "Can you see the real me? Activation and expression of the 'true self' on the Internet." *Journal of Social Issues* 58 (1): 33–48.

Benwell, B., and E. Stokoe. 2006. *Discourse and Identity*. Edinburgh, Scotland: Edinburgh University Press.

Bohan, J. S. 1993. "Regarding gender: Essentialism, constructionism, and feminist psychology." *Psychology of Women Quarterly* 17 (1): 5–21.

Brennan, I. (Writer), and B. Falchuk. (Director). 2010. "Audition." [Television series episode]. In *Glee*, R. Murphy (Producer). Los Angeles: Paramount Studios.

Falchuk, B. (Writer), and Falchuk, B. (Director). (2009). "Preggers." [Television series episode]. In *Glee*, R. Murphy (Producer). Los Angeles: Paramount Studios.

———. (2009). "Sectionals." [Television series episode]. In *Glee*, R. Murphy (Producer). Los Angeles: Paramount Studios.

———. (2011). "Sexy." [Television series episode]. In *Glee*, R. Murphy (Producer). Los Angeles: Paramount Studios.

Fernandez, M. E. 2009, September 8. "Chris Colfer's journey from small town to *Glee*." *Los Angeles Times*. http://latimesblogs.latimes.com/showtracker/2009/09/glee-creator-and-executive-producer-ryan-murphy-discovered-chris-colfer-but-dont-tell-the-young-actor-that-it-makes-him-feel.html.

Gorham, B. W. 2010. "The social psychology of stereotypes: Implications for media audiences." In *Race, Gender, Media: Considering Diversity across Audiences, Content, and Producers*, second edition, edited by R. L. Lind, 16–23. Boston: Allyn and Bacon.

Hall, S. 1996. "Introduction: Who needs 'identity'?" In *Questions of Cultural Identity*, edited by S. Hall and P. du Gay, 1–17. Thousand Oaks, CA: Sage.

———. 2006. "Encoding/decoding." In *Media and Cultural Studies: Keyworks*, revised edition, edited by M. G. Durham and D. M. Kellner, 163–73. Malden, MA: Blackwell Publishing. (Reprinted from *Culture, Media, Language*, edited by S. Hall, D. Hobson, A. Love, and P. Willis, 1980: 128–38. London, UK: Hutchinson.)

Hamilton, D. L., and T. K. Trolier. 1986. "Stereotypes and stereotyping: An overview of the cognitive approach." In *Prejudice, Discrimination, and Racism*, edited by J. Dovidio and S. Gaertner, 127–63. Orlando, FL: Academic Press.

Hill, A. 2002. "*Big Brother*: The real audience." *Television and New Media*, 3(3); 323–40.

Hitchcock, M. (Writer), and E. Stoltz (Director). 2011. "Mash off." [Television series episode]. In *Glee*, R. Murphy (Producer). Los Angeles: Paramount Studios.

Hodgson, M. (Writer), and Donovan, T. (Director). 2011. "I kissed a girl." [Television series episode]. In *Glee*, R. Murphy (Producer). Los Angeles: Paramount Studios.

Hogg, M. A. 2006. "Social identity theory." In *Contemporary Social Psychological Theories*, edited by P. J. Burke, 111–36. Palo Alto: Stanford University Press.

Murphy, R., B. Falchuk, I. Brennan (Writers), and R. Murphy (Director). 2009. "Pilot." [Television series episode]. In *Glee*, R. Murphy (Producer). Los Angeles: Paramount Studios.

Murphy, R. (Writer), and Gomez-Rejon, A. (Director). 2010. "Laryngitis." [Television series episode]. In *Glee*, R. Murphy (Producer). Los Angeles: Paramount Studios.

Murphy, R. (Writer), and Scott, J. (Director). 2009. "Acafellas." [Television series episode]. In *Glee*, R. Murphy (Producer). Los Angeles: Paramount Studios.

Murphy, R. (Writer), and Shankman, A. (Director). 2010. "The Rocky Horror *Glee* Show." [Television series episode]. In *Glee*, R. Murphy (Producer). Los Angeles: Paramount Studios.

Payne, C. and K. Fogarty. 2007. "Importance of youth involvement in sports." *Department of Family, Youth and Community Sciences, Florida Cooperative Extension Service, University of Florida*. http://edis.ifas.ufl.edu/pdffiles/FY/FY100100.pdf.

Pettigrew, T. F. 1979. "The ultimate attribution error: Extending Allport's cognitive analysis of prejudice." *Personality and Social Psychology Bulletin* 5 (4): 461–76.

Poniewozik, J. 2009, December 8. "Top 10 TV series." *Time*. http://www.time.com/time/specials/packages/article/0,28804,1945379_1944142_1944160,00.html.

Respers France, L. 2009, December 23. "Some of the best of 2009's TV." *CNN*. http://articles.cnn.com/2009-12-23/entertainment/best.tv.2009_1_modern-family-risky-business-big-bang-theory?_s=PM:SHOWBIZ.

Rogers, C. 1951. *Client-centered Therapy*. Boston: Houghton-Mifflin.

Tajfel, H. 1981. *Human Groups and Social Categories.* New York: Cambridge University Press.

Tucker, K. 2009, December 28. "10 best TV series of 2009: Ken Tucker's picks." *Entertainment Weekly.* http://www.ew.com/ew/gallery/0,,20326356_20331616,00.html.

Whedon, J. (Writer), and J. Whedon (Director). 2003. "Hush: DVD commentary." [Television series episode]. In *Buffy the Vampire Slayer,* J. Whedon (Producer). Santa Monica: Centinela Studios.

# FIFTEEN

# "The Play's the Thing"

*Representations of Heteronormative Sexuality in a
Popular Children's TV Sitcom*

## Zoe Kenney

In the United States, children and sexuality are separated by social taboos
and institutional regulations. As a result, media products created primarily for children must meet standards of acceptability that preclude overt
sexual content. This chapter illustrates that representations of sexuality
*are* present in children's media, that these portrayals are exclusively normative in nature and function, and that due to pervasive heteronormativity, normative sexuality is assumed to be innocuous and generally goes
unremarked.

In their study of G-rated Disney animated movies, Martin and Kazyak
argue that "heterosexuality is pervasive" in children's media and pro-
ceed to "examine how it makes its way into films that are by definition
devoid of sexuality" (2009, 318). My study shifts the focus to content of
children's live-action TV shows, which, although embellished for entertainment, are constructed within familiar realms (that is, the family,
school, and youth peer groups) and recount experiences common for
young viewers. This chapter examines how sexuality is represented within programming that, according to federal issued TV ratings, must contain "little or no sexual dialogue or situations."

A majority of children's shows on cable channels such as the Disney
Channel and Nickelodeon receive either a TV-Y or TV-G rating, indicating they are acceptable for younger children to view or are "appropriate
for all ages," according to FCC standards. Although the TV-G rating is

not applied exclusively to children's programming, the rating signifies acceptability for child viewers. For a show to receive either rating, its content must be deemed acceptable for children with little or no parental guidance. Society regards sexuality as a topic inappropriate for children to be exposed to, yet maintains heterosexuality's exceptional importance within social dynamics. As a result, observable sexuality in children's TV programming is inconsistently allowed.

Considering the role of media as socializing agent, it is of critical sociological importance to understand the content of media produced for youth audiences. Media messages are intrinsically tied to our everyday lives and are of an inherently social nature. These messages prove to be especially salient social forces for children, who generally lack the critical skills that adults develop. TV remains a media staple to which children are exposed in our increasingly wired (and wireless) world. One study recently found that, on average, children watch over 3 hours of TV daily, with little variance between genders and across family income levels (Roberts et al. 2005).Therefore, it is important for scholars to critique which moral and normative messages are present in TV programming and how socially relevant information is effectively communicated. Youth-geared TV shows can be especially powerful tools for communicating a society's values.

This chapter explores mediated sexual socialization through a content analysis of *The Suite Life on Deck*, the highest-rated program on *The Disney Channel* in Spring 2011. By examining representations of sexuality in this presumably innocuous program, as well as analyzing what identities and behaviors are being promoted or denied both implicitly and explicitly through these portrayals, this chapter deconstructs normative assumptions regarding sexuality in a children's TV show.

## *THE SUITE LIFE ON DECK*: AN OVERVIEW

*The Suite Life on Deck* features sixteen-year-old twin brothers Zack and Cody aboard the SS Tipton, a cruise ship on which they live, work, and go to high school. Their classmates include Bailey, from a farm in Idaho; Woody, Cody's frequently teased roommate; and hotel heiress London Tipton. Aside from cameos, Zack and Cody's divorced parents are largely absent from the show. Mr. Moseby, the cruise director, and Ms. Tutweiller, the children's teacher, are the primary adult characters in the program.

A spin-off of the highly successful Disney Channel Original Program *The Suite Life of Zack and Cody*, which premiered in 2005, *The Suite Life on Deck* (TSLoD) has been on TV since Fall 2008, giving the franchise an overall run of over six years and producing 158 episodes, the most episodes of any Disney Channel Original Program brand to date. During its premiere season, the show was the number-one scripted TV series among six-to-eleven-year-olds and nine-to-fourteen-year-olds (Gorman 2008). New episodes premiere during the prime 8:00 p.m. Friday slot, and Disney reruns episodes throughout the week.

## SOCIAL PSYCHOLOGY AND SOCIALIZATION

Sociologists have long explored media as a socializing force, with many researchers focusing on the relationship between the media and sex-and-gender role socialization (Witt 2000; Galician 2004; Kim et al. 2007; Wright 2009). Analyzing the content of media products for children provides insight into the values and roles they are socialized into understanding, the very values and roles generally assumed to develop naturally from characteristics inherently bound up in sex and essential gender differences.

Children acquire information "from many sources—what they observe directly, what is portrayed in fiction and media, and what they are told" (Huston 1985, 10). Media consumers also are exposed to symbolic social interactions that, combined with lived interactions, socially construct one's reality (Adoni and Mane 1984). Gerbner et al. (1986) have asserted that "the mass ritual" of the daily consumption of TV plays a significant role in the everyday life of many individuals and society as a whole. TV, they argued, remains more homogenous than other media through its "centralized mass production and ritualistic use of a coherent set of images and messages produced for total populations" (1986, 19). The process through which differences in the beliefs and experiences of a heterogeneous people are overcome through TV viewership has been referred to as *mainstreaming* (1986, 31). Mainstreaming limits the diversity of representations and messages, targeting the largest audience and disseminating unified cultural products across demographics. Through mainstreaming, TV products adhere to and reinforce the dominant ideal of what defines appropriate (and profitable) entertainment.

Although alternative TV media have steadily increased in popularity over the past few decades (Boddy 1990; Jones 2005), relatively norm-challenging or sociocritical programs, such as those on Logo, the MTV network's LGBT-oriented offshoot, or Current TV, an innovative and collaborative multiplatform network, are accessible only through costlier deliberate cable or satellite TV subscription. Basic cable and network TV remain significantly more accessible to a much wider base of consumers and, as a result, are more strictly regulated. The Federal Communications Commission (FCC), a U.S. federal agency comprising presidential appointees, rates all TV programs (excluding news, commercials, sports, and unedited movies on premium cable) to reflect the presence or absence of "obscenity, indecency, and profanity" (FCC 2011). FCC regulations prohibit "obscene" content; "profane" or "indecent" content are restricted at times when there is a reasonable risk that children may be in the audience, 6 a.m.-10 p.m.

Most media produced for children is mainstreamed and, therefore, exclusively normative. If exclusively normative representations are permitted in children's media, then a significant range of identities is excluded entirely. Exclusive representations of sexual identities rely on the assumptions of compulsory heterosexuality.

## SEXUALITY AND DIFFERENCE

Adrienne Rich (1982) challenged "the ideology that *demands* heterosexuality" [emphasis is the author's] (228), the belief that heterosexuality is a natural, normal preference. Rich argued that this presumption of heterosexual identity limits and oppresses lesbians and heterosexual women alike. In society, heterosexuality is *compulsory*, seeming to require no explicit sexual identification but assumed of all people and strongly (and often exclusively) reinforced in social institutions such as the media. Johnson (2005) argued that heterosexuality remains unquestioned and goes unremarked. Heterosexuality functions as society's "default," is assumed unless otherwise signified, and, due to its normative nature, stands apart from other categorical sexualities as natural and correct.

Not only does heteronormativity function on a highly privileged and unchallenged level, but it also effectively "makes it difficult for people to imagine other ways of life" (Martin and Kazyak 2007, 316). This reality is especially pertinent to those who are presented with no alternative—in this case, children. Although children may be exposed to non-heterosexual possibilities, mainstream television media produced for them exclusively includes heterosexuality (Dubow et al. 2007). This singular representation of sexual identity eradicates the true spectrum of sexual difference and conflicts with the reality of the world into which children are growing up.

## CHILDREN'S MEDIA AND SEXUALITY

In their analysis of high-grossing children's G-rated films from 1990 to 2005, Martin and Kazyak (2009) examined the presence of heterosexuality in such media, particularly examples of hetero-romanticism and heterosexiness and how these contribute to the construction of heteronormativity. Although the authors acknowledged that children certainly incorporate media messages into the attitudes and behaviors that structure their daily lives and interactions, their focus—as with my study—is on the content, rather than the consumption of, children's media. The authors found that in all but two of the twenty films analyzed, there was a decidedly hetero-romantic storyline. In eight of these, hetero-romantic love was the primary narrative focus and was portrayed as a life-changing and spectacular experience. The transformative power of love between characters on either side of the gender binary could be observed through plotlines that involve characters "defying their parents, their culture, or their very selves to embrace hetero-romantic love that is transformative, powerful, and (literally) magical" (2007, 10). Heterosexuality in children's G-rated films was portrayed as a special, privileged, and highly desired identity that rewarded those who engaged in the lifestyle it provided.

The absence of non-heterosexual content in the most basic children's media is worth noting. Despite increases in non-heterosexual content on TV (although predominantly on networks included in premium cable packages), children's shows stand apart as a genre in which no non-heterosexual content or behavior was present (Fisher et al. 2007). TV content to which most children were exposed was found to be exclusively heterosexual.

This absence of non-heterosexual representations in children's media is alarming to certain media scholars. In a reflection of Michel Foucault's claim that silence "is less the absolute limit of discourse . . . than an element that functions alongside the things said, with them and in relation to them" (1990, 27), Kielwasser and Wolf (1992) found that the "significant silence" that permeates mainstream TV in regard to non-normative sexualities marginalized the experiences of homosexual adolescents and limited their access to positive role models to whom they could relate. Therefore, although the content analysis of the present study analyzed existing content of children's media, it is crucial to note the power of what is absent from it.

## METHODOLOGY

*Sample*: The sample for this study comprised twenty-one episodes from Season 3 of *The Suite Life on Deck*. The only episode that was excluded was a full-length made-for-TV movie possessing a different structure and function from the rest. Season 3 was chosen because of its recency and ratings among children's TV programs. It averaged 3.64 million viewers, primarily within the six-to-fourteen-year-old age range (Gorman 2011).

*Method*: A random sample of episodes from within the general sample was examined, revealing 1) the basic format of the program, including editing and the use of soundtracks (that is, laugh tracks, musical orchestration), 2) the roles of the show's primary characters, and 3) recurring themes relevant to the focus of the study. Rudimentary categories were created based on recurring themes, behaviors, and dialogue. One category, which evolved during data collection into main coding categories, was the prevalence of heterosexuality as a primary focus of a number of episodes' narratives.

The most salient themes were identified, and coding categories were created. All twenty-one episodes were viewed to identify any gaps, overlaps, or inconsistencies that had thus been defined. After initial categories were formed, they were merged, redefined, and modified to most accurately reflect the content. Permanent coding categories were established for a final viewing to thoroughly code the content. For this phase, each episode was viewed in its entirety and coded for instances indicating the social pressure to date and the enactment of heterosexuality (heterosexual roles and scripts). Within each coding category, specific scenes were identified that typify the theme represented.

## DATA AND ANALYSIS

### *Emphasis on romantic heterosexual relationships*

Fourteen of the twenty-one episodes featured primary themes directly pertaining to heterosexual romantic relationships. The manifestation of these themes and their respective emphases on such relationships varied. Eight episodes emphasized the pursuit of or desire to obtain a heterosexual romantic partner; two episodes emphasized the challenges characters faced in a committed heterosexual relationship. Following is a breakdown of a sample of episodes with themes primarily involving the importance of heterosexual relationships in the personal and social lives of the show's primary teenage characters, broken down by the context in which this importance is manifest:

### *Emphasizing the pursuit of or desire to obtain a heterosexual romantic partner*

- *Episode 3.03*, "So You Think You Can Date": Bailey and Cody face pressure to find dates for a dance. Friends tell them they should not go alone following their breakup, as this would make them seem like "losers" who hadn't moved on.
- *Episode 3.04*, "My Oh Maya": Zack falls for Maya, the new girl aboard the ship, and pursues her. He struggles with her indifference as his feelings grow.
- *Episode 3.18*, "Twister, Part 2": Cody flies to Bailey's hometown to win her back. Once in Kettlecorn, he goes to great lengths to convince her (and her family) she should choose him over her ex-boyfriend, also trying to get her back.

These episodes place heterosexual romantic relationships in a position of heightened importance in the personal and social lives of the characters. Each episode centers on complicated efforts toward the ultimate goal of securing a romantic partner, often through achieving certain attractive or desirable characteristics in the process.

*Emphasizing emotional pain from former relationships and/or unrequited love*

- *Episode 3.01*, "Silent Treatment": Emotionally wrecked over his breakup with Bailey, Cody leaves and commits to a silent, ascetic existence at a monastery.
- *Episode 3.16*, "The Play's the Thing": Cody writes a play based on his breakup. Ms. Tutweiller is so impressed that she has the class perform it live, bringing uncomfortable attention to the murky details of the couple's dissolution.
- *Episode 3.07*, "Computer Date": Cody falls for his dream girl, Cali — a robot. However, his interest in Cali diminishes as she becomes too "clingy." When Cody tries to end the relationship, Cali becomes emotional, defiant, and threatening.

These episodes indicate that though relationships are generally desirable, they can bring pain that frames the importance of heterosexual romance and reinforced that, inversely, happiness can be found in cross-sexual romantic relationships.

*Emphasizing the challenges of being in committed heterosexual relationships*

- *Episode 3.09*, "Love and War": Zack is confronted with sacrificing time with, and being taunted by, his male friends now that he is in a relationship with Maya.
- *Episode 3.20*, "Snakes on a Boat": Maya is upset to learn how many girls Zack has dated. Cody fights insecurity when he learns Bailey thinks he is not funny.

These episodes highlight tensions arising from romantic relationships. Trust issues or insecurity arise and are invariably resolved by the end of the episode with one romantic partner reassuring the other that he is happy and intends to stay committed.

Although some episodes with primary themes regarding heterosexual romantic relationships frame cross-sexual interactions positively and others focus on negative aspects of dating (that is, breakups, unrequited emotions), all of the episodes with heterosexuality as the narrative and thematic foundation affirm the heightened attention to romantic relationships in the lives of young people. The ups and downs of the show's star child couples propel the narrative trajectory: the quest for romantic fulfillment.

Aside from episodes featuring heterosexual themes as primary foci, all but one contains significant normative romantic content. Although the remaining seven episodes did not focus on some aspect of heterosexual romantic relationships within the main theme, each episode included significant instances of dialogue or situations addressing heterosexual romantic relationships or interactions. Only one of the twenty-one episodes contained fewer than two scenes (of an average thirteen scenes) centered on heterosexual romantic relationships. The majority of that episode (3.14) took place at an Antarctic research base with only Zack, Cody, Woody, and a male scientist present. In keeping with the show's heteronormative framework, limited romantic behavior or dialogue was expected. In the other twenty episodes, there was ample romantic, heterosexual interaction.

Therefore, twenty of the twenty-one episodes indicated that heterosexuality was pervasive and highly important in the representations of the lives of *The Suite Life on Deck*'s characters.

## NORMATIVE SEXUALITY AND PHYSICAL CONTACT

In addition to the centrality of heterosexual relationships to the lives of the characters, sexuality was reinforced normatively through instances of physical contact. Of the ten instances of significant contact between a female and a male character, nine were portrayed in romantic contexts, whereas only one was marked as humorous, followed with a laugh track. The romantic nature of these interactions was evidenced directly through dialogue and plot and implicitly through editing and audience recordings ("aw" and "ooh" tracks, cheering, and applause). The instances of female-male physical contact often occurred during the climax of an episode, as when Bailey agreed to go out with Cody again after he had followed her back to her hometown (Episode 3.19). These scenes also involved resolution of a previous tension or accomplishment of an ongoing goal. For example, after numerous failures over multiple episodes, Zack finally gets Maya to date him, and the couple shares a romantic embrace (Episode 3.08).

Within the show's heteronormative context, all instances of significant physical contact between male characters were represented as comical, enforcing the idea that such interactions were markedly non-normative. Many of these situations were accidental, such as Woody falling off of a treadmill and pinning Mr. Mosby awkwardly to the floor (Episode 3.07), and all were followed by laugh tracks, even in relatively serious situations, such as when the boys huddled together for warmth while trapped in Antarctica (Episode 3.14). Making comedy of physical contact between boys or men reinforced that same-sex physical contact was not to be taken seriously, but to be viewed as folly or an incidental last resort. Although numerous instances of male-male contact occurred, there were no comparable instances between females. This absence reflected the gender differentiation in same-sex interactions. Male-male physical interactions were easily framed as comical, whereas female-female physical contact might be perceived as either too normal to be amusing (reflecting the assumption that girls are generally more affectionate with one another than are boys) or too overtly sexualized (significant contact might risk being too explicit, reflecting the fetishization and sexualization of lesbianism).

## DISCUSSION: WORKING TOWARD DIVERSITY AND ACCEPTANCE IN CHILDREN'S MEDIA

The data indicated a significant amount of sexuality present in *The Suite Life on Deck*, but due to heterosexuality's privileged and deeply embedded position in society, it was valued and promoted not as one representation of sexual identity, but as *the* representation of appropriate sexual identity.

Since socialization into what are deemed appropriate sex roles is shown to be a normative function of children's media, the depiction of a male-female relationship goes unquestioned, whereas a same-sex relationship would likely be considered inappropriate in terms of explicit and offensive sexuality. If two same-sex characters were to engage in any sexual behavior or dialogue, even no more explicit than that between heterosexual couples on *The Suite Life on Deck*, the TV-G or TV-Y ratings could never be granted. However, comparable behavior and dialogue within a heterosexual dynamic are neither questioned nor rejected. Through its unquestioned and normative inclusion in a children's TV program, heterosexuality was represented as the primary and sole normative possibility for romantic and/or physical relationships and therefore receives a highly valued (and, for the most part, exclusive) status in the production of children's media.

Therefore, when considering the content of children's media, we must consider not only what is present, but also what is absent. The absence of non-normative sexuality in children's mainstream media alongside the continual reification of heterosexuality as the only acceptable way of structuring the social world does not reflect the true range of identities and practices that compose the social world. The universal promotion of heterosexuality alongside the stigmatization of non-heterosexual identities and behaviors is not only inaccurate but also can prove damaging to children who struggle to make sense of a world that does not appear to accept others or, potentially, themselves.

Undoubtedly, if any mainstream children's TV program were to include any non-heterosexual content, the backlash would be enormous (that is, if such a program would get to air at all). In the late 1990s, a costumed creature from the popular 1990s preschoolers program *Teletubbies* was rumored to be gay because he was purple and carried a purselike bag. This rumor gained media traction ranging from an internet article discussing the phenomenon (Millman 1998) to admonition from religious-right figure Jerry Falwell ("Gay Tinky Winky" 1999). More recently, a comment published on the Sesame Street Twitter page hinted at the fictional character Bert's homosexuality. Although discussing the sexual identity of a puppet seems ridiculous, the controversial tweet gained a fair amount of visibility, even prompting a major newspaper's article about Sesame Street's "gay-friendly vibe" (Maerz 2010). In a reactionary society, how can the overwhelming presence of normative representations of sexuality be challenged?

## CONCLUSION

Although assigned ratings indicate that children's TV programming should not possess significant sexual content, this systemized approach to accounting for media content takes for granted that heterosexuality is an identity actively constructed and reinforced through the content of these shows. Heterosexuality per se is not taboo but rather is understood to be socially valuable since it functions as an integral part in the normative structure of the family. Therefore, heterosexual content, as long as it is not graphic in dialogue or gesture, escapes being identified as sexual and is not only allowed in children's media but also privileged within its content. In children's media, as well as through other mechanisms of socialization, heterosexuality is normatively presented to children as *the sole possible* sexuality, rather than *a possible* sexuality.

This was evident in the content of *The Suite Life on Deck*. The characters and plotlines of this show reinforced the notion that romantic heterosexual relationships are a primary source of social and personal fulfillment, and that to pursue such interactions is a natural and integral part of the everyday lives of young people. At the same time, allusions to non-normative sexual identities or behaviors were represented as comical or shameful, reinforcing the exclusive priority placed on sexual normativity.

Therefore, although physically sexually explicit content is not present in *The Suite Life on Deck*, such shows are not free from sexuality. Instead, due to heteronormativity's pervasiveness, the inclusion of heterosexual identities and behaviors is not interpreted as being inappropriate within the context of children's media; rather, heterosexuality is posited for effortless digestion as an unassuming given, an immutable fact of life. Since socialization into what are deemed appropriate sexual identities can be seen as a normative function of children's media, the depiction of a male-female relationship goes unquestioned, whereas it is likely that inclusion of an otherwise comparable same-sex relationship would be deemed inappropriate, explicit, and, quite possibly, offensive.

The sole inclusion and frequent promotion of heterosexual identities in children's mainstream media is problematic on two levels. First, it indicates that to be a normal, fulfilled young person, one must pursue or be in a heterosexual romantic relationship. Other aspects of the social lives of children and teenagers are pushed aside, and their worlds are structured largely around their significant others (or the pursuit of them). This denies the importance of other relationships (that is, friendships, family relationships), and emphasizes a strict matrix of gendered qualities that one must adhere to in order to be perceived as desirable to the opposite sex. Second, exclusively heteronormative representations of sexual identity in children's TV marginalize the experiences of those who might not identify with the images and messages being circulated in the media that are readily available to them. These representations inaccurately portray the diversity that exists in the world, limiting the information provided to young viewers as they formulate worldviews and make sense of their identities, in part, through the media they consume.

A major factor in the production of media that provide alternatives to mainstream narratives and representations has to do with the medium itself. Children's literature, for example, has a far wider range of representations than one might find flipping through channels on television. This is, in part, because FCC ratings filter what makes it on to the small screens in people's homes. The publication of literature, however, is far more liberal; one decides intentionally to borrow or purchase a particular book, rather than purchase an all-inclusive cable TV package.

What can be learned from the progress toward inclusiveness and acceptance in children's literature? Since a sociocultural revolution is not likely overnight, and we should not expect to see open-minded, inclusive children's media on basic cable any time soon, alternative sources are crucial. The internet is a valuable source in providing visibility and access to alternative media that might otherwise be unable to sustain production. An added bonus to viewing conscientious media online lies in avoiding the highly gender differentiated advertisements riddling children's programming on cable networks such as Nickelodeon, the Disney Channel, and Cartoon Network.

A move toward pluralistic media is essential to ensuring that processes of socialization and identity formation are healthy and truly inclusive. Children need media sources that represent honestly the range of sexual and gender identities that compose our society. Rather than learn to mock those who are different or do not meet the criteria for "normal," young consumers of media should learn to expect and accept difference.

# REFERENCES

Adoni, H., and S. Mane. 1984. "Media and the social construction of reality: Toward an integration of theory and research." *Communication Research* 11: 323–40.

"Annotated bibliography of children's books with gay and lesbian characters resources for early childhood educators and parents." (1999). *GLSEN: Gay, Lesbian and Straight Education Network: Home.* http://www.glsen.org/cgi-bin/iowa/educator/library/record/27.html.

Aslinger, Ben. "Creating a Network for Queer Audiences at Logo TV." *Popular Communication: The International Journal of Media and Culture* 7.2 (2009): 107–21.

Boddy, W. 1990. "Alternative television in the United States." *Screen*, 31 (1): 91–101.

Fisher, D., et al. 2007. "Gay, lesbian, and bisexual content on television: A quantitative analysis across two seasons." *Journal of Homosexuality* 52: 167–88.

Foucault, M. 1990. *The History of Sexuality*, translated by Robert Hurley. New York: Vintage.

Galician, Mary-Lou. 2004. "The Influence of the Mass Media." *Sex, Love, and Romance in the Mass Media.* N.p.: Taylor and Francis. 81–98. Print.

"Gay Tinky Winky bad for children." 1999. *BBC News—Home.* http://news.bbc.co.uk/2/hi/276677.stm.

Gerbner, G., L. Gross, M. Morgan, and N. Signorielli. 1986. "Living with television: The dynamics of the cultivation process." In *Perspectives on Media Effects*, edited by J. Bryant and D. Zillman, 17–40. Hillsdale, NJ: Lawrence Erlbaum Associates.

Gorman, B. 2008. "Disney Channel weekly ratings highlights (Week of 9/29)." *TV Ratings, TV Nielsen Ratings, Television Show Ratings. TVbytheNumbers.co m.* http://tvbythenumbers.zap2it.com/2008/10/07/disney-channel-weekly-ratings-highlights-wk-of-929/5853.

———. (2011). "Disney Channel's *Good Luck Charlie* and *The Suite Life on Deck* hit series highs." *TV Ratings, TV Nielsen Ratings, Television Show Ratings. TVbytheNumbers.com.* http://tvbythenumbers.zap2it.com/2011/01/19/disney-channels-good-luck-charlie-and-the-suite-life-on-deck-hit-series-highs/79350.

Huston, A. 1985. "The development of sex typing: Themes from recent research." *Developmental Review* 5: 1–17.

Johnson, P. 2005. *Love, Heterosexuality, and Society.* London: Routledge.

Kielwasser, A. P., and M. A. Wolf. 1992. "Mainstream television, adolescent homosexuality, and the significant silence." *Critical Studies in Mass Communication* 9: 350–73.

Kim, J. L., C. L. Sorsoll, K. Collins, and B. A. Zylbergold. 2007. "From sex to sexuality: Exposing the heterosexual script on primetime network television." *Journal of Sex Research* 44: 145.

Maerz, M. 2010. "Sesame Street Twitter—Some 'Sesame Street' viewers sense a gay-friendly vibe—Los Angeles Times." *Featured Articles From The Los Angeles Times.* http://articles.latimes.com/2010/oct/24/entertainment/la-ca-sesame-street-20101024

Martens, L., D. Southerton, and S. Scott. 2004. "Bringing children (and parents) into the sociology of consumption." *Journal of Consumer Culture* 4 (2): 155–82.

Martin, K. A., and Emily Kazyak. 2009. "Hetero-romantic love and heterosexiness in children's G-rated films." *Gender and Society* 23 (3): 315–36.

Millman, J. 1998. "Tubbythumping." *Salon.com.* http://www.salon.com/media/1998/04/03media.html.

"Obscenity, indecency and profanity." 2011. *Federal Communications Commission (FCC) Home Page.* http://fcc.gov/eb/oip.

Pecora, N. O. 1998. *The Business of Children's Entertainment.* New York: Guilford.

Rich, A. 1982. "Compulsory heterosexuality and lesbian existence." In *The Lesbian and Gay Studies Reader*, edited by H. Abelove, M. A. Barale, and D. M. Halperin, 227–54. Routledge: New York.

Rich, A. 1986. *Of Woman Born: Motherhood as Experience and Institution.* Norton: New York.

Roberts, D. F., et al. 2005. *Generation M: Media in the Lives of 8- to 18-Year-Olds.* Menlo Park, CA: Henry J. Kaiser Family Foundation.

Schor, J. B. 2004. *Born to Buy: The Commercialized Child and the New Consumer Culture.* New York: Scribner.

Seidman, R. 2009. "Disney Channel orders more *The Suite Life* on Deck." *TV Ratings, TV Nielsen Ratings, Television Show Ratings. TVbytheNumbers.com.* http://tvbythenumbers.zap2it.com/2009/05/11/disney-channel-orders-more-the-suite-life-on-deck/18461/.

Ward, L. 2003. "Understanding the role of entertainment media in the sexual socialization of American youth: A review of empirical research." *Developmental Review* 23 (3): 347–88.

Witt, S. D. 2000. "The influence of television on children's gender role socialization." *Childhood Education* 76: 322–24.

Wright, P. J. 2009. "Sexual socialization messages in mainstream entertainment mass media: A review and synthesis." *Sexuality & Culture* 13 (4): 181–200.

# Selected Bibliography

Avila-saavedra, G. 2009. "Nothing queer about queer television: televised construction of gay masculinities." *Media, Culture & Society* 31 (1): 5–21.

Banerjee, B. 2010. "Identity at the margins: Diasporic film and the exploration of same-sex desire in Deepa Mehta's *Fire*." *Studies in South Asian Film &Media* 2 (1): 19–39.

Barnhurst, K. 2007. *Media Queered*. New York: Peter Lang Publishing.

Beard, D. 2009. "Going both ways: Being queer and academic in film and media studies." *GLQ: A Journal of Lesbian and Gay Studies* 15 (4): 624–25.

Beirne, R. 2007. *Televising Queer Women: A Reader*. New York: Palgrave Macmillan.

Benshoff, H., and S. Griffin. 2005. *Queer Images: A History of Gay and Lesbian Film in America*. Lanham, MD: Rowman and Littlefield.

Blackburn, M. V. 2010. "Queer girls and popular culture: Reading, resisting, and creating media." *Journal of LGBT Youth* 7 (1): 74–79.

Bonds-raacke, J. M., E. T. Cady, R. Schlegel, R. J. Harris, and L. Firebaugh. 2007. "Remembering gay/lesbian media characters: can Ellen and Will improve attitudes towards homosexuals?" *Journal of Homosexuality* 53 (3): 19–34.

Bosch, T. E. 2007. "In the pink: Gay radio in South Africa." *Feminist Media Studies* 7 (3), 225–38.

Chambers, S. A. 2009. *The Queer Politics of Television*. New York: I. B. Tauris.

Chung, S. K. 2007. "Media literacy art education: Deconstructing lesbian and gay stereotypes in the media." *International Journal of Art & Design Education* 26 (1): 98–107.

Clayton, J. L. 2011. "How the media suppress Japan's gay past." *The Gay and Lesbian Review Worldwide* 18 (6): 10.

Cooper, E. 2008. "Framing *Brokeback Mountain*: How the popular press corralled the 'gay cowboy movie.'" *Critical Studies in Mass Communication* 25 (3): 249–73.

Davis, G. and G. Needham. 2009. *Queer TV: Theories, Histories, Politics*. New York: Routledge.

Driver, S. 2007. *Queer Girls and Popular Culture*. New York: Peter Lang Publishing.

Drushel, B. and K. German. 2011. *Ethics of Emerging Media: Information, Social Norms and New Media Technology*. New York: Continuum.

Gomillion, S. C. and T. A. Giuliano. 2011. "The influence of media role models on gay, lesbian, and bisexual identity." *Journal of homosexuality* 58 (3): 330–54.

Gray, M. L. 2009. "Queer nation is dead/long live queer nation: The politics and poetics of social movement and media representation." *Critical Studies in Mass Communication* 26 (3): 212–36.

Gross, L. 2002. *Up from Invisibility: Lesbians, Gay Men, and the Media in America*. New York: Columbia University Press.

Johnson, C. W. and R. Dunlap. 2011. "'They were not drag queens, they were playboy models and bodybuilders': Media, masculinities and gay sexual identity." *Annals of Leisure Research* 14 (2–3): 209–23.

Juhasz, A. 2010. "Queer media loci." *GLQ: A Journal of Lesbian and Gay Studies* 17 (1): 167–69.

Kang, D. B. 2010. "Queer media loci in Bangkok: Paradise lost and found in translation." *GLQ: A Journal of Lesbian and Gay Studies* 17 (1): 169–91.

Keith, M. C. 2001. *Queer Airwaves: The Story of Gay and Lesbian Broadcasting*. New York: M E Sharpe.

185

Landau, J. 2009. "Straightening out (the politics of) same-sex parenting: Representing gay families in US print news stories and photographs." *Critical Studies in Mass Communication* 26 (1): 80–100.

Lewis, T. 2007. "He needs to face his fears with those five queers!: *Queer Eye for the Straight Guy*, makeover tv, and the lifestyle expert." *Television and New Media* 8 (4): 285–311.

Mitra, R. 2010. "Resisting the spectacle of pride: queer Indian bloggers as interpretive communities." *Journal of Broadcasting & Electronic Media* 54 (1): 163–78.

Moscowitz, L. M. 2010. "Gay marriage in television news: Voice and visual representation in the same-sex marriage debate." *Journal of Broadcasting & Electronic Media* 54 (1): 24–39.

Moss, K. 2011. "Queering ethnicity in the first gay films from ex-Yugoslavia." *Feminist Media Studies*: 1–19.

Padva, G. 2008. "Educating *The Simpsons*: Teaching queer representation in contemporary visual media." *Journal of LGBT Youth* 5 (3): 57–73.

———. 2008. "Media and popular culture representations of LGBT bullying." *Journal of Gay & Lesbian Social Services* 19 (3–4): 105–18.

Peele, T. 2007. *Queer Popular Culture: Literature, Media, Film, and Television.* New York: Palgrave Macmillan.

Peters, W. 2011. "Pink dollars, white collars: *Queer as Folk*, valuable viewers, and the price of gay TV." *Critical Studies in Mass Communication* 28 (3): 193–212.

Pullen, C. 2012. *Transnational Identity and the Media.* New York: Palgrave Macmillan.

———. 2009. *Gay Identity, New Storytelling, and the Media.* New York: Palgrave Macmillan.

Pullen, C., and M. Cooper. 2010. *LGBT Identity and Online New Media.* New York: Routledge.

Ross, K., editor. 2011. Front Matter, in *The Handbook of Gender, Sex, and Media.* Oxford, UK: Wiley-Blackwell. doi: 10.1002/9781118114254.fmatter.

Saucier, J. A. and S. L. Caron. 2008. "An investigation of content and media images in gay men's magazines." *Journal of homosexuality* 55 (3): 504–23.

Walters, S. D. 2003. *All the Rage: The Story of Gay Visibility in America.* Illinois: University of Chicago Press.

Wirthlin, K. 2009. "Fad lesbianism: Exposing media's posing." *Journal of Lesbian Studies* 13 (1), 107–14.

# Index

# About the Editors

**Jane Campbell**, professor of English at Purdue University Calumet, received her BA from the University of Arkansas and her MA and PhD from Northern Illinois University. She is author of *Mythic Black Fiction: the Transformation of History* (1986). Her literary criticism has appeared in *Callaloo: A Journal of African and African American Arts and Letters*, *Obsidian*, *Black Women in America*, *The Oxford Companion to Women's Writing in the U. S.*, the *Dictionary of Literary Biography*, the *Heath Anthology of American Literature*, *Belles Lettres*, and *U. S. Media and the Middle East: Image and Perception*. She has coedited, with Theresa Carilli, *Women and the Media: Diverse Perspectives* (2005); a special issue on women and the media for the *Global Media Journal* (2006); and *Challenging Images of Women in the Media: Reinventing Women's Lives* (2012). Having volunteered at animal shelters for more than thirty years, Campbell finds strength in cat rescue and in living with her partner of twenty-three years, Theresa Carilli.

**Theresa Carilli**, PhD, is professor of communication at Purdue University Calumet. Her areas of concentration include media studies and playwriting. She has published three anthologies that delve into media depictions of women and ethnicity: *Challenging Images of Women in the Media* (2012) coedited with Jane Campbell; *Women and the Media: Diverse Perspectives* (2005), coedited with Jane Campbell; and *Cultural Diversity and the U.S. Media* (1998), coedited with Yahya Kamalipour. She coedited, also with Jane Campbell, a special issue of women and the media for the online *Global Media Journal* (2006). As a playwright, Carilli has published two books of plays (*Familial Circles*, 2000; and *Women as Lovers*, 1996). She edited a special theater issue of the journal *Voices in Italian Americana* (1998). Her plays have been produced in San Francisco; San Diego; Victoria, B.C.; Melbourne, Australia; Athens, Greece; and most recently, New York City. In addition to her book *Scripting Identity: Writing Cultural Experience* (2008), which features student scripts, Carilli has published numerous performance articles and creative scripts. Carilli enjoys her garden, her cats, and an engaged life with her longtime partner, Jane Campbell.

# About the Contributors

**Kimiko Akita**, PhD, is associate professor in the School of Communication at the University of Central Florida in Orlando, where she teaches international and intercultural communication and a cultural studies honors seminar in *manga* and *anime*. Her more than two dozen research articles on gender and cross-cultural issues have appeared in books and journals, including *Global Media Journal, Women and the Media: Diverse Perspectives, Women and Language*, and the *Journal of Mass Media Ethics*.

**Richard Besel**, PhD, is associate professor of Communication Studies at CalPoly in San Luis Obispo, California. His areas of expertise include rhetorical theory, history, and criticism; environmental communication; media studies; and political communication. His work has been published in a variety of books and journals including *Communication Theory, Environmental Communication: A Journal of Nature and Culture, Making Connections: Interdisciplinary Approaches to Cultural Diversity*, and the *Southern Communication Journal.*

**Kristin Comeforo**, PhD (Rutgers University) is professor of marketing communications at Berkeley College in New York City. Before teaching, she spent several years working in advertising, direct response, and trade marketing. She tweets and blogs about industry news as BrandDR. Her current research interests include LGBT images in mainstream advertising and how audiences envision the "gay" ad.

**Bruce Drushel** is associate professor in the Department of Communication at Miami University of Ohio. His teaching and research interests are in the areas of media policy and economics, media audiences, media history, and queer representation in electronic media and film. He currently chairs the Gay, Lesbian & Queer Studies interest group for the Popular Culture Association/American Culture Association and in 2012 received its Charles Sokol Award for his service to the organization. He is editor of a forthcoming book on Star Trek fan culture, and was coeditor (with Kathy German) of the books *Queer Identities/Political Realities* and *Ethics of Emerging Media*. His work also has appeared in *Journal of Homosexuality, Journal of Media Economics, European Financial Journal*, and *Fem-Spec*, and in books addressing free speech and social networks, free speech and 9/11, media in the Caribbean, C-SPAN as a pedagogical tool,

LGBT persons and online media, minority sexualities and non-Western cultures, and AIDS and popular culture. He is currently editing a special issue of *Journal of Homosexuality* on AIDS and Culture and shortly will begin coediting (with Joseph Hancock of Drexel University) a special issue of *Journal of American Culture* and (with Michael Johnson, Jr.) a special issue of *Reconstruction: Studies in Contemporary Culture.*

**Jennifer Guthrie** is a doctoral candidate and graduate teaching assistant in the Department of Communication Studies at the University of Kansas. Jennifer has received various teaching recognitions awarded by students, the Department of Communication Studies at KU, and the University of Kansas. She was also named a KU Woman of Distinction (Graduate Students for Social Advocacy, 2011–2012). Her research interests include the dark side of communication, romantic relationships, gender, and social support processes.

**Brittani Hidahl** graduated from California Polytechnic State University in 2009 with a BA in communication studies and a minor in psychology. Her chapter began as her senior project, advised by Dr. Richard Besel. She is currently employed by the University of Oregon as a Program Coordinator in the Academic Extension/Conference Services department.

**K. Nicole Hladky** received her MA in communication studies from the University of Kansas. Her research interests include gender and gender identity issues in communication as well as communication pedagogy.

**Rick Kenney**, PhD, is associate professor in the department of communication and philosophy at Florida Gulf Coast University in Fort Myers, where he teaches news literacy and media law and ethics. His research has been published in books and journals including the *Journal of Mass Media Ethics*, *Queers in American Pop Culture*, and *Doing Ethics in Journalism.*

**Zoe Kenney** is executive assistant to the director of the Institute for Communitarian Policy Studies at The George Washington University. She is a graduate of New College of Florida. She has presented research in gender studies and sociology at state and national conventions.

**Adrianne Kunkel**, PhD, is associate professor in the Department of Communication Studies at the University of Kansas. Adrianne also serves as associate faculty member for the Gerontology/Life Span Institute and as courtesy faculty member for the Women, Gender, & Sexuality Studies Program at the University of Kansas. Adrianne teaches a variety of undergraduate and graduate courses in her primary department and has been recognized with several teaching and mentoring awards over the past few years. Her research interests include studying emotional support/coping processes in personal relationships and support group settings, romantic relationship (re)definition processes, sex/gender similarities and differences, social advocacy processes, and sexual harassment and domestic violence prevention. Along with several book chapters, Adrianne has published across many journals in communication studies, psychology, and grief studies.

**Lori L. Montalbano**, PhD (Southern Illinois University), is division chair of Communication, Visual, and Performing Arts at Governors State University. She taught at Indiana University Northwest for seventeen years, where she was most recently chair of the Department of Performing Arts and Artistic Director of *Theatre Northwest*. She is also professor of Communication and Performing Arts. Montalbano has published articles, book chapters, and a book entitled *Taking Narrative Risk: The Empowerment of Abuse Survivors*. She recently coauthored a textbook, *Public Speaking and Responsibility in a Changing World*, with Dr. Dorothy W. Ige.

**Kristen Norwood**, PhD (University of Iowa), is currently a postdoctoral research fellow of gender and communication at Saint Louis University. Generally, she is interested in the ways identities and relationships are connected to cultural discourses, specifically regarding sex, gender, and sexuality. In other work, she has focused on trans-identities and transitions in the context of family relationships.

**Valarie Schweisberger** is a PhD candidate in mass communications at the S. I. Newhouse School of Public Communications at Syracuse University. Her research interests focus on the intersection of queer communities and emerging digital technologies.

**Rachel E. Silverman**, PhD (University of South Florida), is assistant professor of communication in the Department of Humanities and Social Science at Embry Riddle Aeronautical University. Her research focuses on the intersection of Jewish and queer identities in popular culture, women's health, and social justice pedagogy. She has published journal articles and scholarly book chapters about televised representations of Jewish-gay dyads, memory and memorialization, and communication strategies to improve women's health exams. Some of her work can be found in *GeoJournal*, *Sexuality and Culture*, *Women and Language*, and *The Journal of Jewish Identities*.

**Shannon Weber** is a PhD candidate in Feminist Studies at the University of California, Santa Barbara, as well as a 2012–2013 Visiting Scholar in the Women's, Gender, & Sexuality Studies Program at Northeastern University. She is the author of "What's Wrong With Be[com]ing Queer? Biological Determinism as Discursive Queer Hegemony," published in the international journal *Sexualities*. Her research interests include LGBTQ studies; marginalized and abjected bodies; popular culture, representation, and new media; feminist theory; critical disability studies; and fat studies. She is currently at work on her dissertation about the experiences of LGBTQ students at two Massachusetts women's colleges and is also completing a project about same-sex marriage activism after the passage of Proposition 8 in California.

**John Wolf**, PhD (S. I. Newhouse School of Public Communications at Syracuse University), focuses his research on popular culture and social deviance. His work has been published in such journals as *Communication, Culture, and Critique* and *Newspaper Research Journal*. He currently teaches in the Science, Technology, and Society Program at the New Jersey Institute of Technology in Newark.

**Jason Zingsheim**, PhD (Arizona State University), is assistant professor of communication studies in the College of Arts & Sciences at Governors State University. His work has been published in *Text & Performance Quarterly*; *Cultural Studies Critical Methodologies*; *Howard Journal of Communications*; *Review of Education, Pedagogy, and Cultural Studies*; and *Liminalities*. He coedited *Communicating Identity: Critical Approaches* (with Dustin Bradley Goltz, 2013).